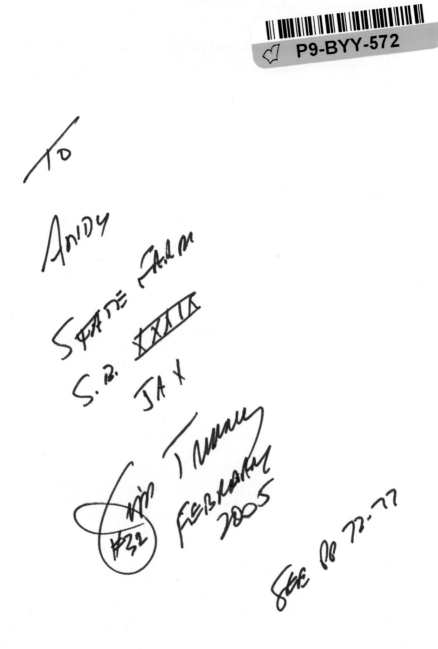

To

Andy

State Farm
S.B. XXXXX
JAX

Jim Tummy #32 February 2005

SEE PB 72-77

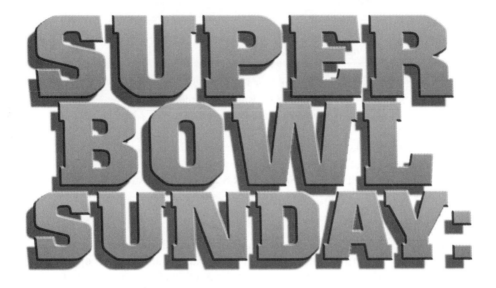

SUPER BOWL SUNDAY:
THE DAY AMERICA STOPS

Presented by ●**CBS** _SPORTS_
Edited by Matt Fulks
Foreword by Phil Simms
Introduction by Sean McManus

ADDAX
PUBLISHING
GROUP

Published by Addax Publishing Group, Inc.
Copyright © 2000 by Matt Fulks
Edited by Joe Lofaro
Designed by Randy Breeden
Cover Designed by Laura Bolter

Back Cover Photo: © Michael Burr/NFL Photos

Super Bowl and Super Bowl Sunday are registered
trademarks of the NFL and NFLP.

ISBN: 1-58497-007-3

Printed in the USA

1 3 5 7 9 10 8 6 4 2

ATTENTION: SCHOOLS AND BUSINESSES
Addax Publishing Group, Inc. books are available at quantity discounts with bulk
purchase for education, business, or sales promotional use. For information, please
write to: Special Sales Department, Addax Publishing Group, 8643 Hauser Drive,
Suite 235, Lenexa, Kansas 66215

Library of Congress Cataloging-in-Publication Data

Super Bowl Sunday: the day America stops/presented by CBS Sports;
edited by Matt Fulks; foreword by Phil Simms; introduction by Sean McManus.
        p. cm.
ISBN 1-58497-007-3
1. Super Bowl—History. I. Fulks,Matt. II.CBS Sports.
GV956.2.S8 S933 2000
796.332'648—dc21
                00—52180

Dedication

To Joshua David Fulks...
Here's proof that dreams
do come true.

Table of Contents

Acknowledgments

As usual with a book such as this, there are a ton of people who need to be thanked for their involvement. As always, too many people. Since my brain feels like Jan Stenerud just booted it for a 48-yard field goal, you may not be mentioned by name. Don't take it personally ... I'm sure I was thinking of you. Thanks to the following, who offered game ideas, contact help, and/or support: Pat Bennett, Jim Fitzgerald, Bil Ryckman and Ken Samelson. A special thank you to Keith Zimmerman, who might have the coolest Rolodex of anyone I know.

To some of the NFL teams' Public Relations Directors and their staffs, plus various Administrative Assistants, for providing media guides, contacts, various stories for the book, and contact with a few extra people. All of you are probably tired of me. The most helpful were (in no particular order): Lee Remmel, Rich Dalrymple, Aaron Salkin, Pat Hanlon, Jim Saccomano, Ron Wahl, David Lockett, Neal Gulkis, Jane Walsh, Patricia Gilda, Cindy Rasco, Linda Bell, Edie Walker, Mary Albright, Roz Cole, Mary Knox, Hurvin McCormak, Shawn Craig.

In addition to various newspaper articles and media guides, a forest-full of books was used as research material for this book, and to clutter my desk. The main ones have been: *The Super Bowl* by Austin Murphy; *75 Seasons: The Complete Story of the National Football League; Super Bowl: The Game of Their Lives* edited by Danny Peary; *Sidelines* edited by Richard Kucner.

To each of the athletes, coaches and broadcasters, who contributed stories. Your stories are extraordinary ... hopefully as good in print as in person. Obviously this project is not possible without you.

To Brian Hakan, Tom Tilden and the rest of the staff at Hakan & Associates, CBS Sports' Exclusive Licensing Agency. To Joe Browne and his staff at the NFL. To Paul Spinelli and Polly Swann at NFL Photos, for helping select some great art. Speaking of art, thanks to Sam Wyche and J.D. Crowe for providing various comic strips throughout the book from their "No Huddle" collection, including one drawn specifically for this project. To Laura Bolter and Randy Breeden, each of whom did a wonderful job in their designs.

Thank you to Phil Simms for your willingness to write a great foreword. To my main editor, Joe Lofaro, who again realized why he got out of the newspaper editing business. To Keith Ritter, LeslieAnne Wade, Robin Brendle, and Terry Ewert and his staff at CBS Sports, each of whom is ready for this book to be released, if, for no other reason, so I'll stop calling for a few months. To Bob and Sharon Snodgrass, Lois Heathman and Michelle Washington at Addax Publishing, for keeping me on a straight course and helping this become "our" project. The deadline was not met without your help.

To my core support, guidance and mountain of encouragement: Barry Landes; Don McLaughlin; John and Alicia Wood; MoJo and Jelaine; Gig; Tom Lawrence; Ronnie and Sharon Carnahan; Jim and Amy Wissel; Kevin and Sarah Oats; my in-laws, Todd and Pat Burwell; my parents, Fred and Sharon; my brother, Josh; my daughter, Helen, who has forgotten what I look like (that's why my picture's on the jacket); and my best friend, Libby, who puts up with my writing and Elvis habits ... you've got your husband again.

Preface

"The Super Bowl has always been a Mardi Gras, no matter what city it's in," says Lesley Visser of CBS Sports. She may have summed it up best. Super Bowl Sunday. Saying those three words provokes an enthusiasm from football, and non-football, fans around the world. For most of us, Super Bowl Sunday is almost the final winter holiday. One last chance to gather with friends or family, pig-out all day, watch a ton of new commercials ... oh yeah, and catch a football game between two of the top teams in the NFL.

During the writing of Super Bowl Sunday, however, I realized that for the men who have played or coached in THE GAME, Super Bowl Sunday provokes a much different feeling. For the men involved, there is a certain amount of reverence; a reverence for the Super Bowl and a reverence for the men who have played in the game. They realize that making it to THE GAME takes an overwhelming amount of hard work. Not to mention, having enough energy as a team to still be standing at the end of the season, teams need to be somewhat fortuitous.

When the idea of *Super Bowl Sunday: The Day America Stops* was first presented to me, it seemed like a great project. One thing we wanted to accomplish with this book was to hear stories from both sides, winning and losing, and see if one appreciates the game more than the other. The answer is no. Even for the guys who have been to more than one Super Bowl and still don't have that championship ring, there still is an understanding of what it took to reach that level. There's an appreciation that some of the greatest players in the game have never played in a Super Bowl. Some of the most storied franchises in history have not made it to the Super Bowl.

The National Football League and CBS Sports have a long history together. CBS was, after all, the first network to sign a deal with the NFL. In late 1961, early 1962, the two reached an agreement and a two-year deal worth $9.3-million. (My, how times have changed.) CBS was the first network to offer its viewers a pregame show. Thus, it seemed a natural fit for CBS Sports to be involved in *Super Bowl Sunday*.

Like its predecessor, *CBS Sports Presents: Stories from the Final Four*, *Super Bowl Sunday* offers first-hand accounts from the people involved in these games. Each Super Bowl story through the first 34 presents at least one person talking about his experience in the game, whether it be a player, a coach, an administrator, a referee or a team owner. There also are sidebars throughout the book from members of the CBS Sports team who, while they have not played in a Super Bowl, still offer a unique perspective.

As you're reading through the following pages, you will notice there are five people – Bart Starr, Matt Bahr, Tom Flores, Bill Walsh and Bob Harlan – who contributed two main stories. Each has a distinctive reason. Starr, for instance, was the first two-time Super Bowl Most Valuable Player. Bahr, as a rookie, put the first points on the board in Super Bowl XIV with the Pittsburgh Steelers and then at the end of his career, kicked what turned out to be the game-winning field goal in Super Bowl XXV for the New York Giants. Flores was the first person to win a Super Bowl as a player, an assistant coach and a head coach (the only other to do that is Mike Ditka). Walsh, the long-time head coach of the San Francisco 49ers, was not only a part of one of the few true dynasties in the National Football League, but he was considered one of the few offensive masterminds in the history of the game. Harlan, the President and CEO of the Green Bay Packers, saw his team go to back-to-back Super Bowls, winning the first and losing the next one.

Another thing you'll notice as you read through the book is that there are various comic strips. What? Comic strips in a Super Bowl book? These aren't ordinary comic strips. These strips were contributed by Sam Wyche with J.D. Crowe. Wyche is one of four people (along with Flores, Ditka and Dan Reeves) to reach the Super Bowl as a player, an assistant coach and a head coach. The strip in Wyche's story (Super Bowl XXIII) is an original, drawn and written specifically for *Super Bowl Sunday*.

For a journalist to pontificate on the Super Bowl and how that game has changed someone's life would be unfair. So, sit back, relax (grab your chips and dip, or whatever you would normally eat on Super Bowl Sunday) and reminisce with some of the greats of the NFL ... the people who have turned one day into a national celebration ... a world-wide holiday ... Super Bowl Sunday. The day America stops.

M.W.F.

Introduction

There is no bigger event in television and there is no bigger event suited for bringing both the media and fans from across the globe together than the Super Bowl. Super Bowl Sunday is truly The Day America Stops. In fact, all the world focuses on this single field of play where heroes are made and a single World Champion is determined.

CBS is proud to be a part of bringing the NFL into the homes of football fans everywhere. We are also proud to present *Super Bowl Sunday: The Day America Stops*. This book will give you a special appreciation for the emotions, efforts and, at times, the frustrations of the players, coaches, officials and executives that have made it to THE GAME. As you will read in the stories that follow, the Super Bowl has literally changed the lives of its participants. You will relive the highs and the lows, the successes and the disappointments, as recalled by the participants of what many call the greatest day in sports. We have also added a collection of up-close stories from members of the CBS Sports family who have shared in the excitement that is the Super Bowl.

I hope you enjoy the pages ahead. From everyone here at CBS Sports, thank you for allowing us into your homes each week in the fall and for making THE NFL ON CBS a success.

SEAN McMANUS
President
CBS Sports

*W*atching quarterback Phil Simms during the New York Giants' first drive of Super Bowl XXI, you would never get the impression that he was nervous. *Well, actually, he wasn't. Through a combination of advice he had received from other players who had played in previous Super Bowls, to the thorough preparation the Giants did before the game, to wanting to soak in the experience of what was happening around him, Simms was relaxed. In fact, he confesses that during that first drive, while other players were experiencing typical early Super Bowl jitters, he was relaxed and enjoying what was happening around him.*

Simms' cool demeanor showed through his performance, as he put on a passing clinic in Super Bowl XXI. By the end of the game, in which he led his team to a 39-20 win, Simms was 22-25 for 268 yards and three touchdowns. During a stretch in the second half, the New York quarterback completed 10-straight passes.

Simms attributes his success in the broadcast booth to the success he enjoyed on the field in Super Bowl XXI. He is widely considered one of the top NFL game analysts on television.

Foreword

Phil Simms

The Super Bowl is every young boy's dream.

I am extremely biased, but I believe in the Super Bowl. In my opinion the Super Bowl is the biggest spectacle in sports. As it should be. Of course, I'm very prejudiced about the game of football. I think all ex-players are very protective of the Super Bowl. I don't like to hear people say bad things about it. I don't see it the same way others probably do.

When you think about all the great players who have played in the league over the years, who didn't have a chance to play in the Super Bowl, it is amazing. If a player were to play 15 years in the league, he's fortunate if he plays on four or five teams that stand a chance, a real legitimate chance of getting there. When you start doing all of the math and figuring the odds, it's almost impossible to reach the Super Bowl.

There are a lot of factors that intertwine to help teams reach a Super Bowl. You have to be fortunate. I feel fortunate simply that I got to play. The Giants were fortunate that they didn't fire Bill Parcells after 1983. Thank goodness the New Orleans Saints didn't draft Lawrence Taylor (they took George Rogers instead). Think how that would have changed the course of history in football! There's a little luck there.

When I think about the past Super Bowls, besides Super Bowl XXI, one that sticks out to me is Super Bowl XIII, the 35-31 game between the Pittsburgh Steelers and the Dallas Cowboys. I was in college at the time. That might have been one of the most exciting games I've ever watched in my life, let alone possibly the most exciting Super Bowl from start to finish of any of them. The game was just incredible. Super Bowl XXXIV with the St. Louis Rams and the Tennessee Titans had a great finish, but it wasn't an exciting game. Super Bowl XIII was incredible for all four quarters. Part of what made it special was that back then, if you named 20 stars of the NFL, 15 of them played for the Steelers and the Cowboys.

The other moment that comes to mind is Joe Montana's drive to beat the Cincinnati Bengals in Super Bowl XXIII in Miami. That had been a tough game all the way through, and the Bengals kicked a field goal to take a three-point lead late in the fourth quarter. I will always remember the situation and that last drive. One of Montana's passes during that drive was a sure interception by Lewis Billups, but he dropped it. Think how that would have changed things. That's how close games are sometimes. You've got to be a little fortunate to win. The 49ers went on and completed a couple more passes to score and win the game. If the interception is made, the game is over, and the Bengals win. Sam Wyche would have been a Super Bowl winning coach. Boomer Esiason would have been a Super Bowl winning quarterback. Joe Montana would have actually lost one. You can look back to one or two plays in close games and see how it changes the whole complexion of things.

The New York Giants earned the right to play in Super Bowl XXI against the Denver Broncos. Not only did I get to play in that Super Bowl, I also got to play the Super Bowl in the best stadium of all, the Rose Bowl. There were more than 100,000 people, which is the biggest crowd I ever played in front of. It was not that hard for me to block out the Rose Bowl crowd that day. They were close to 50-50 in terms of their allegiance. The day and the atmosphere couldn't have been better. It was a beautiful, sunny California day. I see some of the games now in the domes and think, oh my gosh, it's terrible. It's a shame that the game can't be played at the Rose Bowl more often.

Growing up, I watched the Super Bowl on TV. Early in my pro career, I talked to enough people that had played in it, that before we left New York for California, I told myself that I was going to go out there and enjoy the experience and the atmosphere of the game. I never really got caught up in winning and losing, thinking, "What would it be like if we lost?" I just didn't think about that stuff a lot.

Terry Bradshaw said on CBS' "The NFL Today" pregame show, "Looking at the Giants and Phil Simms, I get the sense they're not afraid to lose. That makes them dangerous." When he said that, I thought, "He's right. I'm not afraid of losing. I'm just going to play." We weren't going to get consumed with the outcome. Terry captured my feelings and the feelings of our team in that one little statement.

While preparing for the Broncos, we had a growing sense of confidence. We weren't cocky, but we were pretty confident and pretty sure of what the Broncos would try to do against us. One thing that helped was that we had two weeks to prepare. That was great. I can't imagine playing it any other way. I think the players need that time so they can practice a few days in their home stadium, and then get down to business.

In most games, we didn't know our first play until we were running out onto the field. The coach would say, "O.K., let's do this." It's common now for teams to know the first 15 offensive plays of a game. Normally, we didn't plan any of those things. For Super Bowl XXI we planned a little differently. We knew what we were going to do on the first two plays, and in certain situations. We hadn't really done that before but I think it eased a lot of tension.

We practiced those plays quite a bit during Super Bowl week. I practiced the first play of that game about every day in practice the week leading up to the game. We knew we were going to throw this play-action pass and we were convinced what coverage the Broncos would be in. It worked exactly like we practiced it. That helped our team and me greatly.

About halfway through our opening drive, I just stood in the huddle, looked around and thought, "Wow!" Everybody on my team was almost hyperventilating.

They had to gasp for air. The nerves were cracking, they were moving. And the great thing was walking up to the line of scrimmage and every Denver player had red faces, everybody was breathing deep for air. There are a lot of nerves that first drive of the Super Bowl.

I don't think athletes always realize when they're supposed to be under pressure. They're just out there performing. We scored on that drive on a pass to Zeke Mowatt, but no special thoughts went through my head. I didn't feel any sense of pressure. I just went to the sidelines, sat on the bench and waited for our next series. The rest of the first half went fast as both teams held the ball for a long time.

I remember going into the locker room at halftime and lying down. I still wasn't consumed with winning or losing. It was a pretty quiet locker room, pretty normal. The thing I remember most is that it was a little longer halftime than usual. With Bill Parcells as head coach there was not a lot of talk. Everybody went in, got a drink and hung out. Coach said, "O.K. guys, you've got 30 more minutes. Let's get it done." At that point, the talking phase of halftime was over. It was a low-key, quiet halftime. We had a lot of good things happen in the first half and we figured we'd see what would transpire in the second half.

Our opening drive in the second half was a big key for us in the ballgame. We were faced with a fourth-and-1 and we went for it, which was pretty gutsy. We got the first down and scored shortly thereafter. All of a sudden a 10-9 game at halftime became 16-10. It really never stopped from there. After kicking a field goal to go up 19-10, we got the ball back late in the third quarter. We were moving it again and called a flea flicker. I threw the ball to Phil McConkey who was tackled at the 1-yard line. When he got tackled, the only thing in my mind was, "Oh my God, we're going to win the game." I thought we just won the game. There was no way they could come back. That was a great experience.

On the very next play, Joe Morris ran to the right side, untouched, for the touchdown. We had a couple of unbelievable blocks in that play. The play worked exactly how it was drawn.

There is one moment in the game that will always stand out for me. I threw a long pass downfield where I thought there should have been pass interference called. In disgust, I threw my helmet down because there was no call. Referee Jerry Markbreit walked up behind me and said, "Phil, you dropped your helmet, right?" I gave him a quizzical look, like, "What are you talking about?"

He said, "If you threw your helmet that would be a 15 yard penalty." The he asked again, "You dropped your helmet, right?"

As he said that we both looked at each other and smiled. It was a light moment during a very intense game. Jerry was one of the great referees in the league.

Super Bowl XXI has changed my life, there's no question. I wouldn't be in TV now if I wasn't the MVP or in the Super Bowl. It changed everything. I laugh about it all the time. A lot of how you're looked upon as a player, and after your career, has to do with that one game. Right or wrong, I know that's the way it is with me. There are not many days that go by when someone doesn't say something to me about Super Bowl XXI. I can be in an airport and someone tells me how I had one of the greatest games ever. I look at them and get embarrassed. What can I say besides, thank you?

Every once in awhile I'll open my drawer and see those two Super Bowl rings sitting there, and I think that's pretty cool. I think about how I can't wait to some-day give them to my kids. It's been a long time since I watched Super Bowl XXI, but I've watched the tape a few times. It's pretty funny to go back and look at it now and think how great the experience was and how everything worked for us that day.

When it all comes down to it, the Super Bowl still means the same to the play-ers. It still is the ultimate dream for all the football players.

It Became Super at Age III

The Kansas City Chiefs beat the Buffalo Bills on January 1, 1967, for the American Football League Championship. Lamar Hunt (left, with glasses), owner of the Chiefs, and Chiefs' head coach Hank Stram (right) sit at a Buffalo motel watching the National Football League Championship game between Green Bay and Dallas. Next to Hunt is his daughter Sharron, who, with her brothers Lamar, Jr. and Clark, planted the idea in Hunt's mind of naming the AFL-NFL World Championship Game, the Super Bowl. The children were constantly playing with Super Balls in the Hunt household. The name and the liveliness of Super Balls fascinated Hunt. The Super Bowl tag became official at game III.

Super Bowl I

© James F. Flores/NFL Photos

*W*hen he started his professional career with the Green Bay Packers, few people could have imagined that quarterback Bart Starr would turn into (pardon the expression) ... a star. The 17th-round pick waited patiently for his opportunity. When Vince Lombardi became the head coach at Green Bay in 1959, things started to turn around.

At the end of the 1966 season, the Packers, representing the NFL, met the Kansas City Chiefs, representing the AFL, for what is now known as Super Bowl I. Many observers saw the AFL as a "Mickey Mouse" league. The Chiefs hoped to disprove that idea, and show they deserved to be on the same field with the Packers.

Kansas City kept things close in the first half, trailing 14-10 at the intermission, but couldn't slow down the offense of Green Bay. As Starr and Chiefs' head coach Hank Stram point out, experience was the key in the Packers' win. Starr (above) finished the day 16-23 with 250 yards and two touchdowns. He was selected as the game's Most Valuable Player. Did you say 17th-round draft pick?

Bart Starr

We were honored and grateful for the opportunity to represent the National Football League in the First World Championship Game between the AFL and the NFL. Our head coach, Vince Lombardi, expressed similar feelings to us. He was very poignant in his comments, saying how we had an opportunity of representing the tradition and history of the National Football League.

There may have been some people in the NFL who were, perhaps, looking forward to the new championship series at the end of the season, but weren't paying attention to the teams in the American Football League. Believe me, the players and coaches knew about all the talent on the other side. We could see that they were very talented and extremely fast, big and strong. We had a lot of respect for them. There never was a feeling from the Packers that the Kansas City Chiefs were inferior. We had a great deal of respect for the Chiefs.

As representatives of the National Football League and the Green Bay Packers, there was a certain amount of pressure on us going into that first Super Bowl to maintain a posture and a state of preparation leading up to that game to make sure that nothing negative happened. There was a lot of pressure on us because everyone on the NFL side was looking to us to carry the tradition and history of the league. Similarly, the Chiefs were looked at from their fellow AFL players and fans to show the people of the NFL that their league deserved to be playing in the championship.

The tone of the game against the Chiefs was set early for us. On a pass play in the first quarter, Buck Buchanan of the Chiefs hit me just as I was releasing the ball. Obviously that took most of the momentum off the pass. Max McGee, who replaced an injured Boyd Dowler, made a great one-handed catch and managed to elude a couple of defensive backs on his way to scoring a touchdown on the 37-yard play.

Max played extremely well during that game, which was typical of him. Max, who was a "character" with a fun personality, was very committed on the practice field. In games he was astute and extremely aware of the situation. He constantly analyzed what was happening on the field. Based on those things he saw or experienced during the course of a game, over the years he gave me numerous suggestions and tips when he'd come back to the huddle after a play.

Simply put, Max was a clutch performer. He and Paul Hornung – who missed Super Bowl I because of an injury – were two of the greatest clutch performers ever to play the game. Max was typically representing that aspect of himself when he stepped in that day against the Chiefs. His performance proves one advantage we had over the Chiefs in Super Bowl I, team experience. The ability of Max shows a classic example of that because when our normal receiver, Dowler, was injured during our first offensive series of the game, Max stepped in and had a marvelous game. By the end of the day, he had caught seven passes for 138 yards and two touchdowns.

The experience of our team was a great advantage for us against the Chiefs. Even though we were leading at halftime by only 14-10, we didn't make any major adjustments for the second half. All we needed to do in the second half was execute better. We felt, as I'm sure the Chiefs did, that the first half was more of a feeling out

Hank Stram

Going into Super Bowl I, we knew the Green Bay Packers were obviously going to be a tough team. At the same time, we had a lot of pride because we were representing the American Football League. All of the AFL was seen as the underdog and the Mickey Mouse league, but we took an awful lot of pride in the fact that we had some outstanding teams. Teams in the American Football League took a lot of pride in what they did and how they did it. The emotional feeling involved in our locker room before the first championship game was simply incredible. But it was a typical illustration of attitude of the teams in the American Football League.

Even though most people didn't view our league on the same level with the NFL, our players had a tremendous amount of pride. In fact, before the game with the Packers, I asked our equipment manager to go to the five-and-dime store and get some Mickey Mouse ears and the Mickey Mouse theme song. When the players walked into the locker room, the equipment guys were wearing the Mickey Mouse ears, while the theme song played in the background. We had the music playing again when they walked out of the locker room. I thought, "What the hell; we'll have a little fun with this and maybe get them relaxed to play like they're supposed to."

The excitement and pride carried over to the field for us against the Packers. In fact, Mike Mercer hit a 31-yard field goal attempt right before the end of the first half to cut Green Bay's lead to 14-10 at halftime. We did a lot of good things, yet not enough good things to dominate the game. Early in the third quarter, Willie Wood intercepted a Lenny Dawson pass and the Packers scored a couple plays later to go up 21-10. After that we had a hard time running the football and we had to throw the ball a lot. Our main problem was on the defensive side. Green Bay scored two more touchdowns to win the game 35-10. We played as well as we could play, but we were not good enough defensively. That was the difference in the game.

Even though the Packers were favored going into that game, we never felt like we were an underdog. That was just a matter of opinion. The writers are going to write what they want to write and calling us underdogs was a natural reaction, I'm sure. But our league was surviving. Other leagues tried to survive, but we were the only one that really did. It was a great run and a fun ride.

process because this was a new experience. We had not played each other before.

We felt that if we continued to execute our game plan, we would win. If it were a close game, we knew our experience would work to our advantage. As a team, we were very close, and we knew we could count on each other to come through in the clutch. That bond has been a special one through the years. Even today, when we see each other we don't shake hands, we hug. We're like brothers. It's hard to describe those relationships. That bond is not easy to appreciate unless you've been there, seen it and experienced it. I was fortunate enough to be a part of it.

As we felt at halftime, we were able to get going offensively in the second half. Ironically, it was our defense that helped our offense get a jump-start early in the third quarter. On Kansas City's first possession, Willie Wood intercepted a Len Dawson pass and returned it 50 yards, all the way to the 5-yard line. Elijah Pitts ran in for the first of his two touchdowns. That put us up 21-10. Near the end of that same quarter, I hit McGee for a 13-yard touchdown play to extend our lead to 18 points.

The Chiefs were beginning to have trouble stopping our offense. Our team experience was taking over. The team concept was the foundation of our success for the years in which we played for Coach Lombardi. From the day he took over as coach and general manager of the Packers, he emphasized that to us. He continuously stressed that team concept through his unique way of emphasizing and re-emphasizing how you win as a team. Obviously individual talent is very, very important, but it's meaningless if the entire team is not at the same level of consistency, roughly the same intensity. If the drive, the commitment, and all of the appropriate adjectives and descriptions are not there, you're not going to consistently win.

Coach Lombardi always talked about the strength of the team, and that's what won for us. We may have played against teams that had more talent than we did, or that had individuals who were more talented than the person in that position on our team, but collectively there were few people who could play with us. That's why we won five championships in seven years.

It's stunning to sit back and realize the Super Bowl has become the event it is today, and that we were a part of the first championship game. All of us are thrilled to have been a part of the experience. We had won NFL championships before the First World Championship Game, yet the experience was something special because we have never seen such a meaningful championship as there was with that first one. Playing in that game was a very humbling experience.

Super Bowl I

Date: January 15, 1967
Place: Los Angeles Memorial Coliseum
Attendance: 61,946

AFL: Kansas City Chiefs
Head Coach: Hank Stram

NFL: Green Bay Packers
Head Coach: Vince Lombardi

Kansas City	0	10	0	0	**10**
Green Bay	7	7	14	7	**35**

Most Valuable Player: Bart Starr (QB, Green Bay)

Super Bowl II

© Tony Tomsic /NFL Photos

When the Oakland Raiders and Green Bay Packers met for Super Bowl II, both teams were ready to play. If the game had been played a few days earlier, that may not have been the case. Remember the "Ice Bowl"? The Packers sure do. The Dallas Cowboys and the Packers met in Green Bay for the NFL Championship. The game was the typically hard-fought battle one would expect between the two teams. To add to the exhausting game was the fact that they were playing outside with a temperature of 13-degrees below zero, and a wind chill of minus-46-degrees. (Some have said it was minus-50-degrees ... when it gets that cold, is there a difference?) The Packers won, but they had a difficult time preparing for the Raiders.

Even with the tough week the Packers had, the Raiders really proved to be no match for the three-time NFL champions. The Packers won the 33-14. It was the last game for Vince Lombardi (being carried off in celebration) as the head coach at Green Bay.

Bart Starr

One mark of our teams at Green Bay that will always stick out to me was the closeness of our teammates. That turned out to be a key for us during the 1967 season. We had a number of injuries, plus other teams definitely wanted a little extra piece of us because we were pursuing three consecutive NFL championships, thus we had to bear the challenge and that pressure. It was a tough year for us and it took all the courage and mental toughness we possessed to get through it. If not for the closeness of the team, we would have been unable to tackle those challenges.

A game that really forced us to play well together as a team was the NFL championship game against Dallas, the game known as the "Ice Bowl." Winters in Green Bay are rarely mild, but this day was particularly brutal because the temperature was 13-degrees below zero, with a wind chill of minus-46-degrees. In the final five minutes of the game, we trailed 17-14 despite leading 14-0 in the first half. We had moved down the field and were at the goal line with less than a minute to play. The ground was very hard and the footing made it difficult for the backs to get to the line of scrimmage on our first two scoring attempts. We seemed to be stuck at the goal line.

Our lead play for short yardage was called the wedge play. There was nothing wrong with the wedge play at that point in the game, except the field was frozen, so it was difficult for the running backs to explode. With 16-seconds remaining, we called our final timeout and I asked the linemen if they could get their footing for one more wedge play. They said yes. So I ran to the sidelines and said to Coach Lombardi, "Coach, the frozen ground is preventing the backs from getting to the line of scrimmage. I can sneak it in with the wedge play." So help me, all he said was, "Then run it, and let's get the hell out of here."

As I was running back to the huddle on that miserably cold day, I was chuckling at what Coach Lombardi said. If anyone had noticed my laughing, they would have thought I was crazy. It was unbelievable. That comment took some of the pressure off me for the play, but at the same time it wasn't a completely unexpected reaction. That's simply how direct the man was. Here we were in a brutally cold situation and that was his response. To this day I still laugh about it.

I am grateful for the relationship that Coach Lombardi and I enjoyed. It was one that obviously developed over time. Our relationship ties in with the greatest lesson I learned from my father, that trust and respect are to be earned. I've always remembered my father telling me that as a youngster. Not having succeeded much at Green Bay prior to Coach Lombardi's arrival, I had to earn his trust and respect, which took some time.

It was very easy to get along with him. I didn't have a great deal of responsibility at first in terms of the game plan, but once we worked together and that relationship evolved, we exchanged suggestions and input. We had to be very close in order for our team's game plan to work the way that it did. The experience of creating and developing that relationship is simply indescribable. I've never enjoyed anything more -from a working standpoint- than that relationship.

Coach Lombardi's quest for excellence was unmatched. He noted when he first met with us that we were going to chase perfection, and although we would never be perfect, if we relentlessly chased it, we would achieve excellence. He was not remotely interested in being just good. I will always remember that initial meeting he had with us, and the comments he made that day about excellence.

Several years ago, one of the greatest cars to come down the pike, Lexus, started to use as their tag line ...the relentless pursuit of perfection. That was Coach Lombardi and that quest is what drove that man each day. Every time I walk into the office in the morning and begin my day, I think about that. I want to be better than just good. I'm not remotely interested in the people who work with us to settle for just being good. I want them to seek to excel. The only way you're going to do that is to chase the heck out of perfection.

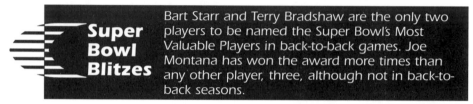

Super Bowl Blitzes

Bart Starr and Terry Bradshaw are the only two players to be named the Super Bowl's Most Valuable Players in back-to-back games. Joe Montana has won the award more times than any other player, three, although not in back-to-back seasons.

My responsibility was to make sure I gave Coach Lombardi everything that he expected of me. Once we had a relationship, it was a tremendous help to my daily performance. I think you needed to have been there and done that – as they say today – to appreciate what that type of relationship means. It can best be described by saying that I knew what he was expecting of me and I knew what I was capable of giving him because I knew his expectations. I can't begin to express how excited and yet comfortable I was in working with Coach Lombardi and his system.

Needless to say, that final play against Dallas worked and we won the game, 21-17, for a trip to Super Bowl II against the Oakland Raiders. As intense as that Dallas game was, it didn't take away any of the meaning from the Super Bowl for us. However, the Dallas game drained us emotionally to the point where we were two-thirds into the week of preparing for the Raiders before we really began to come together as a team and reach the level we needed to be in order to not only compete, but to win. After the trials of the season and the "Ice Bowl," we were unable to completely focus on the Raiders until Thursday. We were just emotionally drained.

Although we were depleted, energy-wise, we had to prepare for what we knew was going to be a difficult Oakland team in the biggest game of the year. We had a great deal of respect for the Raiders because obviously they were a very good football team. Luckily there were two weeks between games. Still, that was a difficult period of preparation.

To add to the fact that we were drained, rumors started to circulate about the possibility of Coach Lombardi leaving the Packers. The rumors were tough on us,

---

◉CBS SPORTS Presents

In the Trenches with Dan Dierdorf

As a player I was fortunate enough to make the Pro Football Hall of Fame and to be recognized and singled out for my accomplishments. So in that respect I can't look back at anything as a player and say I feel like I've been robbed or cheated. Far from it. Then, to turn around and have a second career in broadcasting and to have it be as successful as it has been – to do Monday Night Football for 12 years, sandwiched in between two different stints at CBS Sports – I've been blessed. I have seen the best of two different businesses.

---

too. He made subtle comments about the possibility of retiring. Depending how his comments were interpreted, there could be a difference in opinion as to when we knew Coach was going to resign. In a team meeting prior to the game, he was very emotional which added some speculation. To us, it was just speculation. Regardless, the story helped create an interesting atmosphere leading up to the game with Oakland.

A positive for us was the fact that this wasn't our first Super Bowl. The lessons we learned playing against the Chiefs in Super Bowl I were invaluable in our preparation for -and the actual game against- Oakland. After playing the Chiefs the previous year, we had immense respect for the other league, which we had obviously not seen that much of. Coaches and players know better than anyone else, and can recognize, the talent on the other team. We knew the Raiders were extremely talented.

The Chiefs and the Raiders each won Super Bowls just a few years later, so they were already on their way. It was just a matter of time for them. That shows, though, our biggest advantage in each of those games ... team experience. Just having that championship game experience was a huge plus and a big key for us against the Raiders. Since we hadn't played them before, we didn't know what to expect, so every advantage helped.

The first thing that pops into my mind when I think about the actual game with the Raiders is Herb Adderley's interception early in the fourth quarter. We were leading 26-7 when Adderley picked off that Daryle Lamonica pass and returned it 60 yards for a touchdown. Our confidence was building throughout the game, so once Herb scored to give us a 33-7 lead, we knew we were going to win. As it turned out, the Raiders scored on their next drive, but that was all. Neither team scored again.

Adderley was a cornerback who had that commitment, intensity and unselfish attitude about being a contributor as well as a great player. Herb was a very fast defensive back and a great cover man. He was a vicious tackler and a smart player. Herb picking off that pass against the Raiders and running it in for a score, is my fondest memory of Super Bowl II.

Another aspect that many people forget from Super Bowl II is the play of our kicker, Don Chandler, who had four field goals -39, 20, 43 and 31 yards- in addition to three extra-points. Don was one of the strengths of our team. He was an exceptional person, a super gentleman and a clutch performer. There are many accolades about him. Chandler came to us from the New York Giants and it was great to have him on our side. I always admired him.

Stu Voigt

The 1960s were an incredible time to be growing up in Madison, Wisconsin. We had the Milwaukee Braves winning the World Series with the likes of Warren Spahn and Henry Aaron; and the Green Bay Packers winning their NFL championships. In those days in Wisconsin, Packers' football was a religion. I can still name the Packers' starting line-up. In fact, I'm 52 years old, played next to some of football's best players with the Minnesota Vikings, but I still get a kick out of seeing Bart Starr. During the season, I sat through church hoping the pastor wouldn't speak too long. I bet every TV set in the state was tuned to the Packers on Sunday afternoons. More often than not they didn't disappoint. Even today, there still is no bigger legend in football than Vince Lombardi.

Therefore, my most memorable Super Bowl in which I wasn't playing was Super Bowl I between the Packers and the Kansas City Chiefs. That game really was super. The Chiefs weren't ready to be on the same field with the Packers. That certainly was an exciting time in my life that I'll never forget.

Overall in Super Bowl II, I was impressed with the way our defense handled the Raiders' offense. Oakland had a big strong group of guys on the offensive side, able to dominate throughout their season. Additionally, the fact that we had smart receivers who were alert, helped us make a couple of good adjustments on pass routes. From my perspective, obviously, that was a huge assistance that had a major impact on the game. Ultimately, Oakland's dominance against their opponents landed them in the Super Bowl, yet because of the great team effort we had, we were able to offset the Raiders' strengths and win the championship, 33-14.

Winning those first two Super Bowls is something I will always remember. I will never forget that we were fortunate enough to be a part of history. Prior to beating the Chiefs in the first NFL-AFL championship, Coach Lombardi made the statement of how we were starting a new chapter in the National Football League and in professional football.

At the same time, I don't know that I can appropriately describe what it means to have been named the Most Valuable Player in those first two championship games. What an honor. I think the reality of the MVP is that it's a mixture of recognizing your performance and the others around you who made it possible. You can't win a championship or an award like the MVP without the total team structure. A perfect example of that is John Elway, the former quarterback of the Denver Broncos, who was an exceptional talent. However, the Broncos weren't able to win a Super Bowl solely on John's ability. When they finally had a solid running game and the right people surrounding him, the Broncos won back-to-back Super Bowls and John was the MVP in Super Bowl XXXII. That's the classic example of the team concept.

I was blessed with a great organization, an exceptional coach and staff, outstanding talent and superb people. The total strength in that was the key to our Super Bowl championships and gave me a tremendous ultimate experience. The fact that I was a 17th-round draft pick out of college helps make that experience with the Packers even more special. I have been richly, richly blessed. I can't begin to tell you how much that means.

Super Bowl II

Date: January 14, 1968
Place: Orange Bowl, Miami, Florida
Attendance: 75,546

AFL: Oakland Raiders
Head Coach: John Rauch

NFL: Green Bay Packers
Head Coach: Vince Lombardi

Green Bay	3	13	10	7	33
Oakland	0	7	0	7	14

Most Valuable Player: Bart Starr (QB, Green Bay)

Super Bowl III

*B*y Super Bowl III, the assumption was made that the NFL was better. After
Baltimore won the NFL title, most people picked the Colts to win the Super
Bowl. To most, it didn't matter who the Colts were playing from the AFL ... the
game was a foregone conclusion. Most people didn't realize what they were about
to witness.

New York Jets' quarterback Joe Namath (No.12), from the University of
Alabama, blended perfectly with the Big Apple. If he wasn't a household name
before Super Bowl III, he certainly became one after the game.

One of the men responsible for Namath's success was offensive lineman Dave
Herman (No.67). When Herman was drafted out of Michigan State, he had a choice
of two New York teams ... the NFL's Giants or the AFL's Jets. Herman didn't have a
strong desire to go to New York, and admits that if any NFL team other than the
Giants had selected him, he would have gone. Luckily for Jets' fans, the Giants did
select him. Herman probably feels the same way.

Dave Herman

The Super Bowl is a bigger game today than it was when the Jets played it. The feeling when the New York Jets got ready to play in Super Bowl III was very simply that it was just an additional championship game. At the time, the American Football League was perceived to be in the shadow of the National Football League by most fans across the country. Our main focus and commitment was to finish the 1968 season beating Al Davis and the Oakland Raiders for the AFL championship. That was a much bigger game for us at the time. After we won, we got ready to play in the Super Bowl and it was just another championship game. As a matter of fact the Super Bowl was probably, in my viewpoint, a lesser game because we weren't on a perceived comparable basis with the NFL back then. However, our guys viewed the Super Bowl as another opportunity to play together. We liked each other, so we had fun getting ready for it.

In spite of the fact our American Football League was in the shadow of the NFL, three days before the Super Bowl, quarterback Joe Namath predicted that we would beat the Baltimore Colts. Even though the Colts were double-digit favorites, that prediction was more prophetic than crazy. In fact, Joe was not the first from our team to have those thoughts. When we looked at films of the Baltimore Colts on a position by position basis, Pete Lammons, our tight end, stood up at one point and told head coach Weeb Ewbank to shut off the film because, "were going to get over-confident watching this." The Jets being a 19-point underdog was not an analysis of our team against the Colts as much as it was the National Football League against the American Football League.

Our confidence was looking at it objectively across the offensive line of scrimmage with the Jets versus the Baltimore Colts. At left tackle we had Winston Hill, 275 pounds, a great athlete, against Ordell Braase, their defensive end, who was 6 feet 4 inches, 230 pounds. After viewing the Colts game films we said, "Winston, don't hurt him." At left guard we had Bob Talamini, playing against Fred Miller. If Miller was unfortunate enough to get hit by one of those pops that Talamini would put on a defensive football player, he probably wasn't going to get up. And then at right guard was Randy Rasmussen, a rookie, who moved from left to right guard when I moved to tackle for the championship game against the Raiders and the Super Bowl against the Colts. Randy, at 265 pounds and 22 years old, was playing against Billy Ray Smith, 6 feet 2 inches, 240 pounds and about 35 years old.

Then at offensive tackle on the right side was me, an offensive guard, at 6 feet 1 inch and 255 pounds, against a 6-foot-8-inch, 320-pound man, Bubba Smith. Do you want to know where the huge 19 point-spread came from? One spot. Right there. The challenge I had was to nullify the athletic prowess that Bubba Smith possessed. He was a 1999 football player back in 1969. He was like the kids today with all the weights and conditioning. That was Bubba Smith, a big guy.

Sure, we looked at the point-spread. Joe Namath looked at it. Pete Lammons looked at it. Everybody looked at it and we said there's no way it should be that big. If any of the "experts" had analyzed that game on a player by player basis, position by position, we would not be the underdogs at 19 points. The worst it should have been was one or two points, if not an even spread. From a public standpoint we were inferior, but in no way did my Jet teammates and I think we were inferior from a team standpoint.

The key in showing that we weren't a legitimate 19-point underdog team was preparation. In fact, preparation is the one thing that sticks out to me from that whole experience. We knew what we had to do. We had to nullify and control Baltimore's linebackers and beat their defensive backs. Then with Earl Morrall as their quarterback -and he had great success in 1968- we had to control their offense with our aggressive, well prepared defense.

We put the game plan together. That was the challenge. Since I can't say exactly what other people thought, I can say that when we got on the field, the anxiety I had was great. Here I was playing against a guy like Bubba Smith in a championship game that important, knowing full well that if I couldn't accomplish my goal, the team wouldn't accomplish their goal. Joe Namath has said several times over the years that football is the ultimate team game. It's not like baseball where one guy is standing up there batting by himself or basketball where he's shooting the ball by himself. In football for a play to be effective, 11 guys have to do 11 things exactly right. So I knew that my performance had to come for us to have an opportunity to win. That was the build up for me.

The key for me to be able to stop Bubba was to attack him. And I'll say very simply that I certainly attacked him. My plan was to go after him when he was moving his back foot forward from the three-point defensive stance, and get into him before he got that foot into the ground to move forward. Guess what? It worked. It not only worked once or twice, it worked for 60 minutes. I blocked and attacked him on every play. I wanted to and did nullify his height advantage and keep him as far removed from Joe as possible.

Bubba was the biggest guy I faced in my whole career. I played against Joe Greene, who was about 285-290 pounds, Merlin Olsen, and other big guys like that. But in terms of pure size of height and weight, Bubba was the biggest. He was obviously a challenge during the entire game to the extent that I never felt relaxed or comfortable out there.

At the same time, I never did feel like we had a safe -or comfortable- lead in the game, especially when Johnny Unitas replaced Morrall at quarterback. When he came in as the Colts quarterback, my heart stopped for about four plays because I'd seen him bring teams back many times before. Regardless though of who was playing quarterback for them, every time I came off the field from offense, I'd make sure that I did all I could in terms of yelling and encouraging our defense to make sure the Colts could not get back in the game.

My concern with the Colt offense probably shouldn't have been a major concern considering we had "Joe Cool" on our sidelines. Namath was a terrific teammate. We played together for nine years. People say to me, "You played with Joe?" I say, "No, Joe played with me." (Because I was there first.) Never have I played with one guy who was more of a team player than he was. In fact, everybody on our team was supportive of each other in accomplishing our main goal. And that's what Joe was like. In all the years I played with him, not once do I ever remember him coming up to me and saying, "I wish you would have done a better job at this." He was always full of compliments. He was the ultimate team player. He was fun to be with, and still is. We see each other quite often. We're so lucky that we were on a team that liked each other.

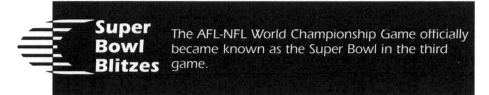

Super Bowl Blitzes The AFL-NFL World Championship Game officially became known as the Super Bowl in the third game.

There was a lot of hype around Joe when he came out of college. The attention he received was not a distraction to me at all. But that's just the way I'm built. It definitely wasn't a distraction that had an impact on anybody's performance, although it was a source of irritation for some guys, which is understandable. It's human nature to be a little jealous in that situation. Joe didn't ask for that hype, but he did have an awesome ability to attract that kind of media attention.

A perfect example of his magnetism happened about 10 years ago. A lot of past and present NFL owners and players were in the Waldorf Astoria in New York for a big dinner. We looked up and saw a huge line of people waiting to get to this one guy at this one table. They were fans trying to get Joe's autograph. Here we were though, other players and owners, just sitting around talking like anybody else. We didn't have long lines of people wanting our autographs; they all wanted Joe's. That's the kind of attraction he has had since he got to New York more than 30 years ago. So, sure, there were some guys who would choose to look at the attention Joe received as an affront to them. But that's not the way Joe wanted it interpreted, because, again, he's a team player.

As once predicted, Joe helped lead us to a Super Bowl for the Jets and the first win in the Super Bowl championship game for the AFL. Joe completed 17 passes for 206 yards, while Matt Snell ran for 121 yards. It was a great overall team performance as the Jets won 16-7.

As the years pass by, having played in a Super Bowl becomes more special to me because there are so many lessons that I can teach kids from my experiences. I'm currently working with my two younger sons' high school team. I often present this example to them from our Super Bowl III team. "When a game is over, you've got two football teams walking off the field. One of them is smiling and one of them is not. Now tell me who's smiling."

And they say, "How can you be so dumb, the winner is smiling."

I say, "You're right, the winner's smiling. Now tell me this. Is he smiling because he won or did he win because he's smiling?"

"What do you mean?"

And I go on to explain to them, "The winners win because they're smiling. They win because they're happy. They win because they're confident. They win because they're well prepared."

When young kids are playing on a team, whether it's Pop Warner football or little league soccer, or some other sport, we need to help them gain confidence, let them have some fun, then let them see that the wins and losses will take care of themselves. It works all the time with these kids. Getting them to want to play the game for what the game is worth, versus going in there and playing only to win. That is true for everything they do in life.

That describes our teams with the Jets. We weren't necessarily a close team socially, but on the field we were tight. That closeness on the field helped us communicate effectively and enjoy each other. We had that closeness with Weeb, too. There are a thousand guys out there that know the Xs and Os of football, but not all of them can communicate with their players. If that individual can communicate what he knows about those Xs and Os to the players as they are today, it's effective. When you have a quarterback like "Broadway" Joe Namath, and a wide receiver like "Barnyard" Don Maynard, who came from Texas and fit in Manhattan like an elephant did, and you're a head coach who can communicate effectively with both, you've won half the battle. Weeb could do that. He was a lot like a Bill Parcells, and a lot of other guys out there coaching in the National Football League, who can communicate with the players as they are today. That's what was effective about Weeb.

Weeb was also my dad away from home. He was very special to me, largely because I came from a farm in a small town of about 415 people in the northwestern corner of Ohio, called Edon. The New York Giants and the New York Jets drafted me out of Michigan State (remember, it was two leagues back then). If an NFL team other than the Giants had drafted me, I probably would have gone there instead of with the Jets. I didn't really have the ambition to go to New York City, the largest market in the country, from the town of Edon, Ohio. When you come from a small town like that and you go to the big city, there can be some culture shock.

When I got to New York, guess what? Here was coach Ewbank, who'd won all those games and the NFL championship in Baltimore, now coaching the New York Jets. However, Weeb was from Richmond, Indiana, so I had that identification with him because he came from close to the same area in the country where I grew up. He was a great help to me. If I had any concerns whatsoever, whether it dealt with football, getting around in New York, or whatever else, he was somebody I could always talk to. Again, he was my dad away from home. He helped our team instill a pride in our ability. The pride of what we accomplished as a team in being the first AFL team to be the Super Bowl champions is in my heart today.

I was in the Pro Bowl right after Super Bowl III. As I walked into the locker room for the first time, the Kansas City Chiefs and Oakland Raiders players who were also in the Pro Bowl came running up to me and saying, "Man, you did it. We did it." We referred to the American Football League beating the National Football

League. That was bigger for all of us than having the Jets beat the Colts.

Winning that Super Bowl and playing with the different guys we had on the team is something I never will forget. There are different occasions to remember the game, from different people's perspectives. I was at a broadcast convention 10-15 years after we played in Super Bowl III, and Bubba Smith happened to be there. My business partners said, "Geez, there's Bubba walking down there on the floor. Why don't you go say 'hi' to him; you have never seen him since you played Super Bowl III." And I said, "No, I never have." So I decided I was going to say something to Bubba. I passed him walking up the aisle, stuck out my hand and said, "Bubba, I just wanted to say hi to you. My name is..."

I didn't even get the rest out before he said, "I know who the hell you are." Then he turned and walked away. I haven't seen him since.

Was the experience of the Super Bowl fun? It absolutely was fun. That experience with Bubba happened to be such an occasion to remind of just how much fun we had in winning Super Bowl III.

Super Bowl III

Date: January 12, 1969
Place: Orange Bowl, Miami, FL
Attendance: 75,389

AFL: New York Jets
Head Coach: Weeb Ewbank

NFL: Baltimore Colts
Head Coach: Don Shula

New York	0	7	6	3	16
Baltimore	0	0	0	7	7

Most Valuable Player: Joe Namath (QB, New York)

Super Bowl IV

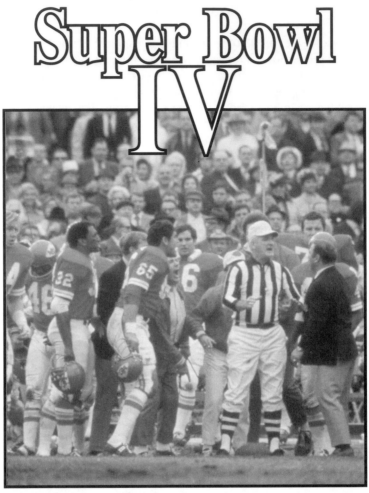

© Darryl Norenberg/NFL Photos

When the Kansas City Chiefs lost to the Green Bay Packers in Super Bowl I, Chiefs' head coach Hank Stram (in coat, talking to the official) evaluated the situation and decided that his team was not good enough defensively to compete with some of the teams in the NFL. So he added the likes of Curley Culp and Willie Lanier.

With their front defensive four known as the "Purple People Eaters," the Minnesota Vikings looked like a team poised to win several NFL titles. Little did anyone know that Super Bowl IV marked the beginning of the Minnesota Vikings being known as the "team that couldn't win the big one." They were on the verge of four Super Bowl losses in less than 10 years.

For Stram and the Kansas City Chiefs, it was fitting that they were in Super Bowl IV, which marked the end of the AFL facing the NFL. After all, it was Chiefs' owner Lamar Hunt who helped start the AFL. With that in mind, some would say it was fitting that the Chiefs defeated the Vikings to win their first Super Bowl championship.

Hank Stram

One thing about playing in a Super Bowl game is that if you have any shortcomings, they're going to be exposed. When we played in Super Bowl I against the Green Bay Packers, we were a very good football team at that particular time offensively, but we knew going into the game that we were not where we wanted to be from a defensive standpoint. That was our shortcoming. After we lost that Super Bowl game, we immediately went out and got great defensive players. Emmitt Thomas became our right cornerback and Jim Kearney became our safety. Our top draft pick was Jimmy Marsalis, who started every game for us that season in the defensive backfield. We also picked up Jimmy Lynch and Willie Lanier. All of those guys helped us tremendously from a defensive standpoint in our win against the Minnesota Vikings in Super Bowl IV.

Before the game, we had the seal of the American Football League put on the sleeves of the players' jerseys. I can still see Jerry Mays and all the other guys when they came in and put their jerseys on, or just saw those jerseys for the first time. They were yelling and screaming like kids with their first little league uniforms. It was amazing just how great they felt and how proud they were of wearing that badge on their sleeve. That was a typical illustration of the type of players we had in the American Football League.

We went into the game against the Vikings with a great feeling of confidence. We knew Minnesota was a very good football team because we played them in a preseason game that year. The Vikings' head coach, Bud Grant, was one of the great coaches in the business. But, overall, we felt the match-ups in the Super Bowl were in our favor because we had a very large football team, especially on the offensive and defensive line.

Minnesota was used to playing against a four-man line with a middle linebacker and nobody on the nose of their center, Mick Tingelhoff. We went into the game thinking we would have a big size advantage over Tingelhoff with Buck Buchanan and Curley Culp. We used a lot of the triple-stack, which Minnesota hadn't seen very much. The triple stack has an odd spacing with somebody on the nose of the center instead of having a middle linebacker off the line of scrimmage. That scheme was more difficult for the center to execute his blocks. So, our defense was really the essence of the game.

Offensively, our line did a great job of protecting quarterback Lenny Dawson against Minnesota's tough defense. Lenny certainly deserved to be the game's Most Valuable Player, which he was. The players called him "Lenny the Cool" and "The Governor" because he was always under control. Nothing bothered him. The bigger the game, the better he played. The worse the weather, the better he threw. It was amazing. That's just his personality. He never wavered about anything.

We had a tough couple of weeks with Lenny leading up to the Super Bowl. In fact, it all started before the AFL championship game against the Oakland Raiders. When we got off the plane in Oakland, Mark Duncan, who worked for the league

35

Tom Flores

As a head coach, Hank Stram was organized and professional; everything was structured well, and we followed his scheme and his plan. He always portrayed a public image. The team always dressed the same in public, which helped give us self-discipline. He was a good coach because he prepared everyone well.

The fact we only had a week to prepare for Minnesota was in our favor. The Vikings didn't know what to expect and they didn't realize how good the Chiefs were that year. The credit for our preparation mainly goes to Coach Stram.

I started out the 1969 season at Buffalo and then got cut. I ended up in Kansas City only because Lenny Dawson was hurt and he was going to be out for several weeks. In my Kansas City career, I threw one pass, which turned out to be a completion and a touchdown. (It doesn't get much better than that.) I also held for kicker Jan Stenerud. Still, it was such a thrill to win the Super Bowl that season; I was kind of numb. That was only the fourth Super Bowl, and the second time the AFL had won convincingly. Even at that point we realized that there is no guarantee we'd be back to the championship game. My career was winding down as a player, and at that point I had no intention of coaching.

Before Super Bowl IV, we beat the Raiders in Oakland for the AFL championship. We went back to Kansas City after the game, and then left for New Orleans the next day. At that time, everyday was media day at the Super Bowl. They didn't have press tents with players reporting on Wednesday and Thursdays like today. The press got your room number if they wanted to talk to you, so we stayed in our rooms and they walked through the halls and stuck their nose in the doorway. We just tried to lead a normal life within the insanity of the whole thing.

In those days the insanity of the event wasn't that great. The Super Bowl is so big now that it's almost beyond wild. I don't think there is anything like the Super Bowl anywhere in professional sports.

office, stopped me as I walked off the bus and said, "Coach, you've got to ride with me because I've got something very, very important to talk to you about."

I said, "No, I'm not going ride back with you because I'm going to ride back with the team on the bus."

"No, you have to come with me because this is very, very important."

I knew Mark well enough to know that I should go ahead and ride with him. On our way to the hotel, he said, "This is a terrible thing to have to tell you the day before the championship game. There was a betting scandal in Detroit with a guy by the name of Donald Dawson [no relation to Lenny]. They got his notebook and say that Len Dawson's name was in the book with regard to betting."

I said, "I don't think that's true. I know Lenny well enough to know that he's not involved in anything like."

Mark said, "Well, but that's what's going to come out in the papers, so we've got to do everything we possibly can to squelch the story." Later, Mark called me back and said, "Don't worry about it, Coach, we've got the thing resolved. Just play the game, beat the Oakland Raiders and good luck."

That's what happened; we won the game, 17-7, and earned a trip to the Super Bowl in New Orleans. We thought the scandal was over. However, when we got off the bus in New Orleans, we heard the same thing again about Lenny and this betting nonsense. Only this time it was all over the papers. The story was absolutely absurd! We wanted to have a press conference so Lenny could tell the media exactly what the dope was, that he wasn't involved in the scandal.

Pete Rozelle, who was a great commissioner and a great friend, said, "Well if you have the press conference, make sure that there are no questions at all about the betting scandal; just talk about the Super Bowl game." Pete was a terrific person. The great thing about him at that time was that even though he was with the National Football League, he was still very kind to us in the AFL, and in this situation he didn't look at us like we had done something wrong. He was mainly concerned about having a good Super Bowl. I was, too, but I didn't agree with his thoughts on Lenny's press conference.

I told Pete, "I can't do that. If Lenny talks to the media and talks about just the game and evades the gambling thing, the media will assume that he's guilty." Some of the writers that I knew very well, and had great confidence in, told me they thought that plan was a smart thing to do. We had a press conference that night at 11:00. Lenny talked about the whole thing and everybody was satisfied. Of course he handled everything with typical class and style and grace and dignity; and did a fantastic job, as everybody knows.

Obviously I was hoping that this story wouldn't be a distraction to the team going into our game with the Vikings. I didn't think it would be, but I didn't know for sure. The morning after the press conference, our team ate breakfast together. I told them what we did the night before. Then I asked, "Does anybody have any questions?" E.J. Holub, our center, said, "Yeah, I've got a question coach. When are we going to eat? And when are we going to get the tickets for the game?" That's how distracted they were. It was amazing how they responded to the situation and rallied around Lenny. The whole team just did a fantastic job of not letting the story affect them, which was obvious in the game.

Everybody played great. Jan Stenerud had a fantastic day kicking, as did punter Jerrel Wilson. He did a super job keeping the Vikings deep in their own territory. And of course Otis Taylor had a great day with six catches for 81 yards, including a 46-yard touchdown reception from Lenny. Overall it was just a very well played game on our part, against a very good football team in the Minnesota Vikings. If you win two of the three areas -offense, defense or special teams- in a game, you're going to win most of the time. We won in all three categories, which is something that rarely hap-

Tom Flores

I started out the 1969 season at Buffalo and then got cut. I ended up in Kansas City only because Lenny Dawson was hurt and he was going to be out for several weeks. In my Kansas City career, I threw one pass, which turned out to be a completion and a touchdown. (It doesn't get much better than that.) I also held for kicker Jan Stenerud. Still, it was such a thrill to win the Super Bowl that season; I was kind of numb. That was only the fourth Super Bowl, and the second time the AFL had won convincingly. Even at that point we realized that there is no guarantee we'd be back to the championship game. My career was winding down as a player, and at that point I had no intention of coaching.

Before Super Bowl IV, we beat the Raiders in Oakland for the AFL championship. We went back to Kansas City after the game, and then left for New Orleans the next day. At that time, everyday was media day at the Super Bowl. They didn't have press tents with players reporting on Wednesday and Thursdays like today. The press got your room number if they wanted to talk to you, so we stayed in our rooms and they walked through the halls and stuck their nose in the doorway. We just tried to lead a normal life within the insanity of the whole thing.

In those days the insanity of the event wasn't that great. The Super Bowl is so big now that it's almost beyond wild. I don't think there is anything like the Super Bowl anywhere in professional sports.

pens. It's a great tribute to our team and the way they dominated in all areas.

Stenerud helped us get things started on the right foot in the first quarter. On our opening possession, I sent Jan out for a 48-yard field goal attempt, which at the time was a Super Bowl record. I had no reservations whatsoever about doing that. We wanted to get on the board first. The Minnesota Vikings were laughing on the sidelines. They were poking each other, thinking we were nuts for the attempt. They thought it was a joke. But when Stenerud kicked the ball, it looked like it had helium in it. The thing never did come down. I think it's still hanging up above New Orleans someplace.

Once we took that 3-0 lead, we never trailed in the game. In fact, Stenerud hit two more field goals in the first half. When we went to the locker room for halftime, we led 16-0. We were playing so well; there wasn't much to talk to the guys about, really. We just wanted to make sure we maintained the same level of enthusiasm in the second half and continued to play like we were playing. We dominated a very good Viking defense in the first two quarters.

Minnesota's offense didn't concern me in the first half because they didn't have much of a running game going. Joe Kapp, their quarterback, was more dangerous out of the pocket than he was in the pocket, but our defense did a fantastic job of putting a lot of pressure on him. As a result, we felt our game plan was working beautifully.

Super Bowl IV

Offensively we felt like we needed to go on quick counts because their defense was very quick with guys like Jim Marshall and Carl Eller. We wanted to make sure that we kept them at home and kept them off balance. David Hill, our right tackle, did a great job of blocking Eller. Frank Pitts, one of our regular wide receivers, was very instrumental in giving us a big lift the way he ran the ball on the reverse from our tight-I formation.

Sometimes the game plan that you expect to work is not very effective. And sometimes you send in a play that you think is going to work but it doesn't work. In this particular game, everything that we thought we could do, we did, which is a great compliment to the way our players played. The team earned the Super Bowl title with a 23-7 win. Lenny was 12-for-17 with 142 yards passing and 11 yards rushing.

When I arrived at our postgame party, some guys carried me around the room on their shoulders. That was very special. I think anytime you have an opportunity to become world champions, and are able to execute the plan and win the game like we did, it's a very gratifying experience. It was great not only for myself, but also for my coaches and the entire organization.

Lamar Hunt, the team's owner, was the one that started the American Football League, so we felt good that we were the team representing the American Football League, or the "foolish club" as some people called the teams in the AFL, in the Super Bowl game. It was poetic justice that we were the first team to play and represent the American Football League in Super Bowl I. So, it also seemed appropriate that we were the team to win Super Bowl IV, the last championship game before the two leagues officially merged. There was a lot of satisfaction in that. Then, of course, anytime you win that kind of a game, it's very emotional and very exciting.

That was an event and a time that will always linger in my mind in my book of happy memories. And the amazing thing is that the memories are so vivid, it seems impossible that it happened 30 years ago.

Super Bowl IV

Date: January 11, 1970
Place: Tulane Stadium, New Orleans, LA
Attendance: 80,562

AFL: Kansas City Chiefs
Head Coach: Hank Stram

NFL: Minnesota Vikings
Head Coach: Bud Grant

Kansas City	3	13	7	0	23
Minnesota	0	0	7	0	7

Most Valuable Player: Len Dawson (QB, Kansas City)

Super Bowl V

*A*fter the American Football League and the National Football League merged, some of the former NFL teams were asked to move to the new American Football Conference. The Baltimore Colts, a team that represented the NFL in Super Bowl III, was one of those teams that changed leagues.

Throughout his 15-year NFL career, linebacker Ted Hendricks never missed a game. In 1994, he was selected for the NFL's 75th Anniversary team, an honor Hendricks ranks with being named to the Pro Football Hall of Fame. With only one NFL season under his belt, Super Bowl V was the first of four Super Bowls for Hendricks.

Another young player on that Colts' team was rookie kicker Jim O'Brien. In the final few seconds of the game, O'Brien kicked the Colts to a 16-13 victory over the Dallas Cowboys with a 32-yard field goal. Understandably, O'Brien (No. 80) was ecstatic. Chuck Howley of the Cowboys became the first (and still only) player from the losing team to be named the MVP.

Ted Hendricks

I had been in the league with the Baltimore Colts for two years when we went to Super Bowl V to face the Dallas Cowboys. That experience made quite an impression on me. It was such a memorable moment, that even though I was on three other Super Bowl teams in the next 13 years of my career, that first one ranks at the top.

The game was being played in Miami's Orange Bowl. That added to the thrill of the championship game because I was from Miami and played collegiately at the University of Miami. It was almost like a home game for me because the Orange Bowl is where we played our collegiate games and sometimes high school games. Tickets for the game were $15 a piece for the game. That's pretty easy to remember because since I'm from Miami, I had a lot of people that wanted to come and see it. I bought 1,000 tickets. In case you're trying to add that up, it's 15 grand. My Super Bowl paycheck.

That also was the first Super Bowl played on artificial turf. When I played for Miami, the Orange Bowl was still a grass-covered field. Artificial turf was different for me because it usually makes the backs coming out of the backfield a lot quicker. Not only that, but they can change directions a lot faster. Artificial turf speeds up the game a little bit.

We didn't know what type of game to expect from the Dallas Cowboys going into Super Bowl V. To try and confuse them; we put Bubba Smith over the center, Dave Manders. There never was anybody on the top of the center before. All the NFL teams were playing four-man fronts with the center not facing anyone. Dallas tackle Ralph Neely was calling the offensive signals for the Cowboys and he had never seen that type of defense before, so he called out a "bastard" defense. Meanwhile, our tackle, Billy Ray Smith, started screaming back at Neely about Dallas' new offense. It took all I had to keep a straight face, listening to those two guys talk back and forth throughout the game.

As the game progressed, it seemed like it was going to be a close one. We were on pins and needles throughout the whole game. Usually, games are decided by the end of the third quarter, or you can at least get some grasp on who's got the upper hand. We were playing each other pretty evenly. Quarterback Johnny Unitas got hurt in the game, and Earl Morrall came in and replaced him.

The Colts were the only NFL team that had its games televised in the Miami area, so I had watched these guys while I was growing up. Unitas was a folklore or hero down in that area. It was quite an honor just to be on the sidelines with the all-pros that I had watched on TV.

We weren't nervous at all about Morrall being in there. Our defense was pretty good that year and we thought that the game would rely heavily on us. We just had to do our job defensively. We knew if we stopped Dallas from scoring, we would win because Morrall would protect the ball.

It's interesting to look back at the game and try to figure out how certain situations affected the game. On one play, Craig Morton set up a screen to Duane Thomas. I went in and rushed Morton instead of taking Thomas man-to-man, like I was supposed to do. I blocked the pass and the ball went up in the air, and if Morton hadn't grabbed me, I would have gone 95 yards the other way for the touchdown. If that had happened, who knows how the game would have turned out?

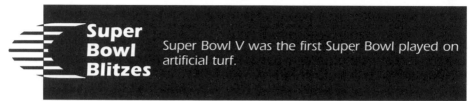

Super Bowl Blitzes

Super Bowl V was the first Super Bowl played on artificial turf.

Early in the second half, with us trailing 13-6, Dallas' Duane Thomas fumbled at our 2-yard line. Our tackle, Billy Ray Smith was at the bottom of the pile yelling that he had the ball. "I got it! I got it!" he screamed. The referees signaled that we had the ball, although I really don't know if we did or not. I think they ruled it, mainly because he claimed it. To this day, I don't know who came out of there with it.

The other big moment in the game was in the fourth quarter, the scored tied at 13-13, with less than two minutes to play, and Mike Curtis intercepted a Craig Morton pass. Curtis returned the ball to the Dallas 28, putting us in field goal position. A couple plays later, with less than 30 seconds to play, Rookie Jim O'Brien was going to come out for the 32-yard attempt.

Jim and I were kind of close that year because it was his rookie season and my second year. We were the youngsters of the team. On the contrary, he was loose and things didn't bother him. It was a big kick and there was a lot of pressure on him. I guess there would be pressure on anybody that was in that position ... 16 seconds left to go and the game, the Super Bowl championship, depending on it.

I couldn't watch. I waited for the fans to react. We were all huddled in a circle on the sideline, holding hands, looking at the ground, praying that everything would go OK. It went better than OK. He hit the field goal with time expiring to give us the championship. I ran on to the field to greet Jim, and started bouncing up and down like I was on a pogo stick.

Super Bowl Blitzes

"The Super Bowl changed tremendously between my first and fourth ones. Tickets for Super Bowl V barely sold out. Ticket-scalping definitely wasn't an issue. People didn't care about the game like they do now. Everybody seemed content watching it on TV. Now the game is seen all over the world. The ticket prices have gone up 100-fold."
– Ted Hendricks, who played in four Super Bowls, one with Baltimore and three with the Oakland/Los Angeles Raiders.

It was such a relief to reach the Super Bowl after we played so tough all year. The team drafted me after it lost Super Bowl III. The guys thought they should have beaten the New York Jets in that game, but didn't. It was great to be there and experience the team's first Super Bowl title. Here I was, my second year in the league, and already I had a Super Bowl championship. A lot of players, all-pros and people that played in the NFL for long periods of time, never even reach a Super Bowl. I had proven myself for only one year, and here I was with a Super Bowl ring.

I'll never forget any of the four Super Bowls I played in because each of them still means so much to me. But Super Bowl V will always stick out because it was such an intense, hard-fought game. Every play seemed like it counted toward the outcome of the game. Especially with the speed being picked up by the artificial turf, it was a real hard-hitting game. The impacts were a lot more collision-like. It felt like we were constantly running at 110 percent. There weren't any periods that you could take a break during the game. It was the hardest fought game out of the four Super Bowls I played in. Super Bowl V made an impression on me because I'd never experienced anything like that before.

Super Bowl V

Date: January 17, 1971
Place: Orange Bowl, Miami, Florida
Attendance: 79,204

AFC: Baltimore Colts
Head Coach: Don McCafferty

NFC: Dallas Cowboys
Head Coach: Tom Landry

Baltimore	0	6	0	10	16
Dallas	3	10	0	0	13

Most Valuable Player: Chuck Howley (LB, Dallas)

Super Bowl VI

© Photo /NFL Photos

*T*he Miami Dolphins had a well-balanced offense with quarterback Bob Griese, wide receivers Paul Warfield and Howard Twilley, and running backs Larry Csonka and Jim Kiick. The Dolphins defeated the Kansas City Chiefs in the playoffs in what many consider one of the best-ever football games, a 27-24 double-over-time classic. They went on to blank the defending Super Bowl champion Baltimore Colts in the AFC championship game, 21-0.

After losing to the Green Bay Packers in the 1966 and 1967 NFL championship games, and being downed by the Baltimore Colts in Super Bowl V, the Dallas Cowboys had developed the reputation as the team that "couldn't win the big one." They were able to shake that stigma with a 24-3 win over the Dolphins. Quarterback Roger Staubach (No. 12), who didn't mind scrambling when needed, threw for 119 yards and two touchdowns before being named the game's MVP.

Roger Staubach

My first exposure to the Super Bowl as a player was in Super Bowl V against the Baltimore Colts. We lost and I didn't see any game action, but I gained a ton of experience in learning about the distraction of the championship game. Even though I didn't play in the game, I was nervous sitting on the bench. Through that experience, I learned to get everything taken care of before you get to the Super Bowl site – friends and tickets and all of the extra things that go along with the Super Bowl.

During the 1970 season, starting quarterback Craig Morton -a great guy and a great quarterback- was having trouble at the end of the year with his arm. It was really bothering him. But our defense played so well and our running game was doing well enough, that I didn't get called on to play in Super Bowl V.

On the plane going back to Dallas after the game, I said to coach Tom Landry, "Coach, I'd really like to be traded. If I feel I can't play when there's an injured quarterback, when am I going to play?" He told me, "Roger, I really believe it takes X amount of time for a quarterback to get his chance." That isn't the general mentality today, but that was Coach's feeling back then. He continued, "You will get your opportunity next year."

So in training camp in 1971, Craig came back healthy, and we both had a great camp. The team really needed a leader and it's hard to have two quarterbacks, it divides the team. But Craig and I both were ready to play. We split time as starters during the first half of the season. The team was 4-3 in the middle of the year and I was confident that Coach Landry was going to select one of us to start regularly. He chose me. When he did that, my life changed. If he would have selected Craig, I obviously would have been disappointed and that probably would have been my last year with the Dallas Cowboys. Needless to say, that year was a very emotional one.

After Coach Landry designated a regular starter, our team started on a nice winning streak that I really feel Craig could have conducted, too. It was simply that the team got behind one quarterback and I think it would have gotten behind either of us. That was a big year for me. We continued our winning streak by beating San Francisco, 14-3, in the NFC championship to earn a trip to Super Bowl VI.

Coach Landry had our game plan pretty much in place by the time we got down to New Orleans to face Miami. When we got there, we worked on improving the existing game plan. With the extra week, and knowing about the distractions, Coach made sure we were prepared when we got there. We just worked on making it better. In the evenings I went and watched game films. The only night I went out was early in the week to watch the movie, Dirty Harry.

I think we were more ready for that Super Bowl than any other game in which I played. We learned a lot from Super Bowl V, especially making sure that we handled the distractions and the hoopla that goes along with the Super Bowl.

Our game plan on offense was to block Miami linebacker Nick Buoniconti. They also had a guy, Bob Matheson, number 53, that I had to see. Wherever he was, we audibilized off him and then we blocked Nick. We had to do that to have an effective passing game. We went into the game with a strong running philosophy and our passes were used in tight or important situations. But our running game really set up the offense. Blocking Buoniconti was a key to the running game, plus audibilizing off Matheson because he would line up on both sides. We had a lot of audibles that game.

Defensively, the key for us was stopping Miami's outstanding wide receiver, Paul Warfield. We set up a game plan to make sure that he wasn't going to beat us. We also had to watch out for their powerful running back, Larry Csonka. As a matter of fact, he fumbled, which was a big play because he hadn't done it all season. Our defense was able force the Dolphins to make mistakes in the Super Bowl. On the other side, it was a pretty error-free game for us.

Before the game we felt confident and well prepared, but we were nervous because we had already been that far in the season without winning. This was my first chance to really help the team overcome that stigma of not being able to "win the big one." We went out extremely determined. On our first drive we moved the ball very well, which only reinforced our confidence.

On that first drive, we had a third down on the 4-yard line. We called a play-action pass. My first look was to Mike Ditka running to the corner of the end zone. If he was covered, I would dump the ball off to Duane Thomas out of the backfield. On this particular third-down play, I spun around, faked to Walt Garrison, and threw the ball to Thomas who went out to the flat. I didn't even look at Ditka. As a result, we didn't get the first down. That was my fault because Ditka was wide open. Needless to say, he wasn't too happy with me as we were coming off the field. Boy, he was mad.

Later in the game, Ditka dropped a pass. Sarcastically I said, "Nice catch, Mike." We had fun with that. He did catch a touchdown pass late in the game. On another series, we ran a reverse and he got knocked out of bounds around the 1-inch line. So, he nearly scored three touchdowns in that game. To this day, Ditka blames me for his not winning the Most Valuable Player award. He probably would have been MVP if I would have thrown him the first one and if he had scored on that last run. Instead, he scored only once. We've always joked back and forth about that.

Even though we had scored only three points, we continued to move the ball well. Lance Alworth caught some key passes. In the second quarter, he caught a ball over the middle on a third-and-12 situation. With a 3-0 lead, we connected on a 7-yard touchdown score. I felt at that point that we knew we could move the ball on offense. And our defense really played great. Whereas we weren't able to move the ball on offense in Super Bowl V, in the Miami game, we felt that if something bad happened, we had the ability to overcome it.

Winning the Most Valuable Player award was icing on the cake for me. I had an effective game and did some things right. Really, though, it was a very team-driven football game. The running game was powerful that day. Thomas, our main running back, wouldn't talk to the press because of a couple issues he was having. Otherwise, he probably would have been the MVP. If Ditka had scored three times, he probably would have earned the award. Being named the MVP surprised me, but

⊙CBS SPORTS Presents

In the Trenches with Mike Ditka

One play that sticks out to me from Super Bowl VI is when Roger Staubach threw me a pass and I dropped it. I was wide open. That was probably the most embarrassing moment of my whole football career, because it wasn't against Detroit or Green Bay during the season, it was in the Super Bowl. Everybody in the world was watching. That season was a great time of my life. I watched what happened to our football team. You see, for a long time the Cowboys featured a lot of great individuals. But that was the year when we finally became a team. Yes, becoming a team, that was the part that made it fun.

it was a nice award that no one can take away from me.

The Super Bowl has gotten bigger and bigger each year. It's an event. The year we won the Super Bowl, I was getting $35,000. That's not complaining, that's just life. Today, player bonuses alone for the Super Bowl, are more than that amount. The Super Bowl has become a major advertising vehicle. You've got the highest ratings, so you've got corporate sponsors that buy the advertising and, therefore, get the seats at the game. It's become a big two-week party; however, the game itself is still a big deal. The players are still nervous. They still want to win the game with a passion, because being second is not fun.

Television has really been very good for football. The game shows well on TV and people are into it. If you're at home, you're planning your Sunday around that Super Bowl. It's a big deal. With all those people watching it, fans know who the players are. They now know who Kurt Warner is. We played on Thanksgiving and I've always believed people know the Cowboys from that TV exposure. Obviously we won and that's why we were on TV, but it certainly helped our popularity.

There are so many people watching the Super Bowl, and such a relatively small number of players who have played in the game, that it's a great accomplishment for a player to have a Super Bowl victory.

I've never been as excited in my professional life as I was after we won Super Bowl VI. Even Coach Landry was smiling. I once asked Walt Garrison if he ever saw Coach Landry smile. He said, "No, but I was only there nine years."

Winning that Super Bowl just validated Coach Landry's philosophy, part of which was consistency. In fact, the first thing that comes to my mind about Coach Landry is consistency. He was consistent in his behavior as a coach and as a person. Sure, he'd get upset on the field, but he'd go on to the next play, the next game, the next season. Off the field, he was even better than what people knew of him through the press. He was consistent in his behavior as a husband and a father.

Even for players who didn't know him as well, if they had a problem and needed

Dan Reeves

Super Bowl VI was special because we had knocked on the door for so many years in Dallas. We had been known as "next year's champions." We lost to Green Bay in the championship game for the right to go to Super Bowls I and II. Then we lost to Cleveland in the playoffs the next two years. To finally get to the Super Bowl in 1970 was great, but then to win it the next year was just an unbelievable thrill.

I think about that first world championship for Dallas all the time. One thing that really brings a team together is the tough times. Our Dallas teams through the 1960s and 1970s had been close to winning a title, but couldn't get over the hump. Then to finally win it was unbelievable. We were so happy for Coach Tom Landry. I can still see the smile on his face as he was being carried off the field in New Orleans.

I took a lot of things for granted playing for Coach Landry. For me it was almost like growing up at home. When you're raised at home, you really don't understand your parents until you become a parent yourself. You don't understand the great job they did. We tend to teach our children in the same fashion that our parents taught us. I was influenced a great deal by Coach Landry in that way. Later I learned to appreciate what he was and how tremendously successful he was because of certain things that he did. I thought that was the way everybody did things. I didn't realize until I went out on my own that there was so much insecurity and different ways of doing things. At Dallas, we had done things for so many years the same way and had been successful, I just thought, "Gosh, as long as you do these things you're always going to be successful."

The discipline, organization, preparation, being a stickler for details and worrying about the little things, is the difference between winning and losing. All of those are things I learned from Coach Landry. Coaches have to have a philosophy on how to go about things and I accepted his because I believed in it and because we had success. I knew when my team played against his, that we were playing a team that wasn't going to beat themselves. Today, I try to have a football team that isn't going to beat themselves. That's the toughest team to beat.

Winning Super Bowl VI was truly a great accomplishment. We had come so close so many times. I have a tremendous feel for my teammates. We know that we can handle adversity. The friends that I had on that team - are some of the greatest friends I have today. They are lifetime friends. You don't ever lose relationships like those as you keep up with the guys and their families. That's something that lasts a lifetime.

him, he would be there. He wasn't one of the guys, but he had a decency about him that is really as good as it gets in a person. I think that consistency in his behavior as a coach and as a person – you could say concentration and competitiveness –

was what set him apart from other people. His consistency as a leader of a football team allowed us to win for so many years.

Coach Landry's strength was always preparation. Offensively, we were well prepared to play in each of our Super Bowl games. Preparation is the key to being able to go into a game and, percentage-wise, understand what the other team is doing. Football is a game of percentages. It's making the right decisions, then executing and having talent that can do it. Coach Landry had us prepared, no question about it. I think Coach did learn though, that you still had to have a formula on the field that executed that plan. Between his understanding of Xs and Os, and the Cowboys getting the right formula of players on the field, we always were in the thick of postseason. I'm just sorry we didn't win more Super Bowls, which I think we could have done but didn't. All of us were as thrilled for Coach Landry as we were for ourselves that we were able to win Super Bowl VI.

It felt good beating Denver in Super Bowl XII, and beating Army in the Army-Navy game, but the most satisfied I ever felt as a football player was in the locker room after winning Super Bowl VI. That win meant a ton to a team that had come close so many times, but couldn't win the big one. It was really a great feeling. Winning the Super Bowl took a lot of pressure off the Cowboys because we had been seen as a team that could not win the big game. That was an ugly tag to wear.

Looking back, each Super Bowl is special, regardless of the outcome; although, obviously, the wins are much more special than the losses. When you lose a Super Bowl, you almost wish you weren't in it. But then you look back, and still there is a history in being part of a team's Super Bowl era. It shows you won your conference. Dallas has been in eight Super Bowls out of 34, more than any other organization. People can say all they want about eras of football teams, but Dallas is the most consistent winning football team in the history of the National Football League in the modern era. That's something to be proud of. It's a pretty neat history, and I'm lucky to be a part of it.

Super Bowl VI

Date: January 16, 1972
Place: Tulane Stadium, New Orleans
Attendance: 81,023

AFC: Miami Dolphins
Head Coach: Don Shula

NFC: Dallas Cowboys
Head Coach: Tom Landry

Dallas	3	7	7	7	24
Miami	0	3	0	0	3

Most Valuable Player: Roger Staubach (QB, Dallas)

Super Bowl VII

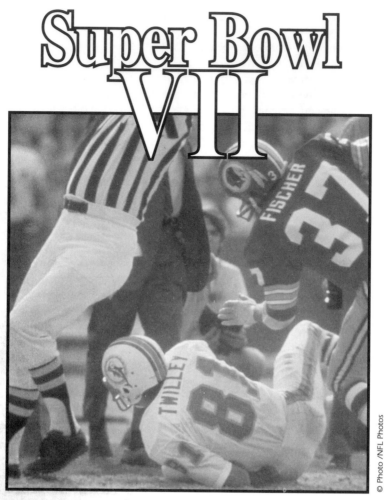

© Photo /NFL Photos

*J*ust say, "1972 Miami Dolphins," and most football fans know exactly which team is being discussed. That version of the Dolphins did the nearly impossible by going through the entire season as the National Football League's first (and still only) undefeated and untied team.

Howard Twilley was one of the wide receivers on that Dolphins' team. Twilley, who finished second in the Heisman Trophy voting in 1965 behind Mike Garrett, was an original member of the Miami Dolphins' franchise. Late in the first quarter of Super Bowl VII, quarterback Bob Griese found Twilley, who made run before landing in the end zone (above, in photo) for the Dolphins' first touchdown of the day.

Howard Twilley

The Miami Dolphins never set out to go undefeated in 1972. In fact, not until we won our fourteenth game, the last of the regular season, did we feel any pressure to go undefeated. The only reason we felt pressure at that time was because our goal was to win the Super Bowl. Obviously we couldn't lose in the playoffs. We also wanted to get rid of that sick feeling we carried around in our stomachs the whole season after being defeated in Super Bowl VI.

The one thing we tried to remember in Super Bowl VII was that we were playing a football game. We forgot that when we played the Cowboys. We thought it was a vacation. It was a fun circus, but it caused us to lose focus. It's very hard as a football player to regain focus in the middle of the game, because you start trying harder, start pressing, and then you start stressing. It impedes your performance. Being focused, relaxed and ready to play is something that needs to happen before the game starts. Although not impossible, it is hard to change focus once the game is under way.

Our head coach, Don Shula, did a wonderful job of creating motivation. He came into the locker room after we lost Super Bowl VI to Dallas and said, "Listen, the people on defense can say it is the offensive team's fault we lost because we only scored three points; and they'd be right. The people on offense can say this was the defense's fault. You can be divided if you want to, but you really need to remember we are in this together. And you need to remember the sick, ugly feeling you have right now and make sure it doesn't happen next year."

The only way to do get rid of the bad taste was to get back to the Super Bowl and win it. After we won the regular season and went undefeated in 1972, we didn't celebrate. We didn't even get excited about it because we hadn't finished our job and accomplished our goal to win the Super Bowl. The media asked us why we weren't celebrating. They thought something was wrong because we went through the season undefeated and nobody celebrated. We won our first playoff game. Nobody celebrated.

Quarterback Bob Griese had broken his leg in the fifth game of the season. Our back-up quarterback, Earl Morrall, played the rest of the season and the first half of the AFC championship game. He had a great year. This would be unheard of today, but Shula benched Morrall after the first half of the AFC championship game in Pittsburgh. It wasn't that Earl was having a bad game, but we needed a kick-start. Bob was ready. He came in the game in the third quarter and sparked us to a victory. If that happened today, the player being replaced would throw a temper tantrum. But Earl isn't that kind of guy. Most of our guys weren't so interested in their own personal success as they were in the team's success. We were unbeaten at 15-0 but we had to play the AFC Championship game in Pittsburgh. Great home field advantage after going undefeated.

We knew our Super Bowl opponent, the Washington Redskins, was a good football team. However, we knew we could be successful against the Redskins if we executed our game plan. The cornerback who was going to be covering me was Pat Fischer. Pat, who was a great defensive back, is probably the only guy that we ever played against who was smaller than I am. Bob Griese and I were good friends, and we were roommates during the Super Bowl. While we were preparing for the Redskins, I said to him one night, "Bob, Pat Fischer is a great defensive back, but he's the type of guy that's going to look and study our tendencies. Our tendencies over the season, inside the 20-yard line, where we are throwing the football, is either a quick post slant or a quick post corner."

A post move is when you normally plant your foot, take three steps inside, then either continue if it's a slant, or go over to the corner. We went through this situation where instead of taking three steps, I took five steps. We thought that Fischer would have to believe we were going to the post because I was taking those two extra steps before changing direction. We ran that pattern probably 80 or 90 times the two weeks before the game.

Bob said, "Howard, here's the situation when we want to do this. When they are in man-to-man they are going to double-cover Paul Warfield and leave you with single coverage." The third time we got the football, I didn't even have to go to the huddle; I knew what the play was going to be. As Bob predicted, on third-and-6 the Redskins double-covered Warfield and single-covered me. I ran the route and Bob threw the ball perfectly. I caught it on the 5-yard line and Fischer caught me at about the 2-yard line. Determined, I bowled over him into the end zone. It's funny when you think of something and then the situation works exactly the way you planned.

One of the referees in the Super Bowl was a guy who I knew in Miami, Tom Kelleher, a sporting goods dealer. After I scored the touchdown, I was concerned they were going to call me out of bounds because my whole body was out, but the football was inside the flag. When they called it a touchdown, I went up and patted Tom on the back. He said, "Howard, you can't do that on national TV." I was pretty excited about scoring.

There were a lot of key plays in the game. One of the things that sticks out in my mind is just how well the team played together and hung together. Griese played a fabulous football game, even though we didn't throw the football much. Larry Csonka played a great game. We had a play called P-10 Express where we pulled one of the guards and hoped the tackle would go with him. We didn't block the defensive tackle; we just read their keys. On one particular play, Csonka came back against the flow and had a long run. Fischer tried to tackle Csonka; big mistake. Using his forearm, Csonka knocked Fischer down like a rag doll. Another big play came at the end of the first half when Jim Mandich, our tight end, made a diving catch to set up a first-and-goal at about the 4-yard line. We ultimately scored and were ahead 14-0 at halftime.

Another play that almost turned out to be a key was the infamous Garo Yepremian pass. That's the only reason the game was close. With less than three minutes left to play, we lined up to kick a field goal. The kick was blocked, but Garo, our kicker, picked up the ball and tried to pass it. That attempt was intercepted by Mike Bass, who ran it back 49 yards for a touchdown. That made the score 14-7. Had Garo made the kick, we would have probably won 17-0 (how ironic would it have been had we finished our 17-0 undefeated season with a 17-0 score?).

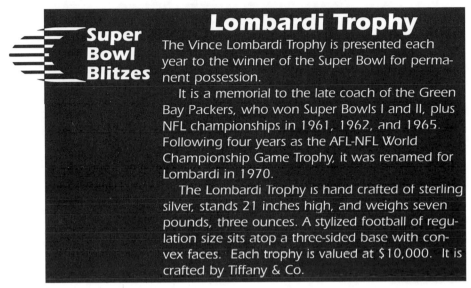

Super Bowl Blitzes

Lombardi Trophy

The Vince Lombardi Trophy is presented each year to the winner of the Super Bowl for permanent possession.

It is a memorial to the late coach of the Green Bay Packers, who won Super Bowls I and II, plus NFL championships in 1961, 1962, and 1965. Following four years as the AFL-NFL World Championship Game Trophy, it was renamed for Lombardi in 1970.

The Lombardi Trophy is hand crafted of sterling silver, stands 21 inches high, and weighs seven pounds, three ounces. A stylized football of regulation size sits atop a three-sided base with convex faces. Each trophy is valued at $10,000. It is crafted by Tiffany & Co.

Garo has since made light of the play, but it wasn't funny at the time. He was not a popular guy for a few minutes. I thought Don Shula was going to kill him. If we hadn't won the game, Garo probably would have been cut. I'm totally convinced of that. Even though Garo was a good kicker and a nice guy, Shula really wanted to win that football game. It's easy to see why Coach Shula and the rest of us were so ticked at Garo, because all of a sudden the Redskins had a chance to win despite having been dominated.

The game wasn't very close. We dominated the entire time, we just didn't score many points. The Redskins crossed into our territory only once or twice in the whole football game. Our defense just crushed them. The closest they came to scoring (before Garo's infamous pass) was earlier in the fourth quarter when Jake Scott intercepted a Bill Kilmer pass in the end zone and returned the ball 55 yards. Largely because of that play, Jake was named the game's most valuable player. He also ran back punts and intercepted two passes in the football game. He just played great. Everybody played great.

There was such a sense of unity and a sense of purpose because we had been beaten in the Super Bowl the year before and we wanted to get that monkey off our back, and off Coach Shula's back. Shula hadn't won a Super Bowl up to that point. He lost in Super Bowl III to the New York Jets when he was at Baltimore. Then we got crushed by the Cowboys in Super Bowl VI, 24-3. We didn't even compete. We were really disappointed because we were a better football team than what we showed.

⊙ CBS SPORTS Presents

In the Trenches with Mike Ditka, Dallas Cowboys' assistant coach in Super Bowl XII

Coach Tom Landry was the ultimate football teacher. He also was meticulous as far as preparation was concerned. I don't think I ever got as close in that aspect in my coaching, as I would like to have gotten. I do know that everything I learned about the game of football was from him. He taught me how to present our goals and philosophy to the players, including why and how we were going to accomplish our goals. I learned one more thing from him ... the best teacher is good results. You can tell anybody anything. You can show them anything. But, if they don't get good results from applying what you are teaching, they're not going to buy into it. Once they get some good results, that, to me, is the greatest formula in the world for success. Tom did it that way better than anybody I have ever been around.

There are a lot of players such as Paul Warfield, Bob Griese and Larry Csonka who were Hall of Fame players. People like me will never be in the Hall of Fame, but all the players on that team have their own kind of hall of fame because they're still members of the only undefeated, untied NFL team. We've had that honor for more than 25 years. There will always be teams like the 2000 St. Louis Rams that look like they could go undefeated. We'll just have to wait and see. I worry about that sometimes. But then again, I worry each year until every team finally gets beat.

I don't have many claims to fame, but one I do have is that I was an original member of the Dolphins. That is a special feeling, considering I was on the undefeated team, although I don't want to overstate that. In the scheme of really important human events, our undefeated season doesn't make the list. In football history, our football team is near the top of the list. A lot of people are going to win the Super Bowl, but not many will go undefeated. It was great winning the Super Bowl and getting the ring, but being a part of football history is something that not everyone gets to do. It was a real fun time to play professional football. Particularly for a little guy. Me.

Super Bowl VII

Date: January 14, 1973
Place: Memorial Coliseum, Los Angeles, CA
Attendance: 90,182

AFC: Miami Dolphins
Head Coach: Don Shula

NFC: Washington Redskins
Head Coach: George Allen

Miami	7	7	0	0	14
Washington	0	0	0	7	7

Most Valuable Player: Jake Scott (S, Miami)

Super Bowl VIII

© T. Matika/NFL Photos

*D*espite the fact the 1973 Miami Dolphins didn't finish the season in the same undefeated fashion as they did the previous year, most contend the 1973 Dolphins were a better team. Players on that team, as well as their opponents, believe that to be true. The Minnesota Vikings, returning to the Super Bowl for the first time since losing in Super Bowl IV, were hungry. The Vikings felt that even though the Dolphins were the defending Super Bowl champions, they could win. Instead, the Dolphins were able to control the ball and the clock, largely behind the running of Super Bowl MVP Larry Csonka. "Zonk" rushed for 145 yards and two touchdowns, including (above) this first quarter 5-yard run to give the Dolphins the lead in the game.

Stu Voigt, one of Minnesota's tight ends, was an integral part of the Vikings' success through the 1970s. He was on three-of-the-four Minnesota teams that went to Super Bowls during that successful stretch. Currently, Voigt serves as the team's radio color analyst.

Stu Voigt

There has been a lot of discussion through the years about which team has been the best in football. Usually, the 1972-73 Dolphins are in that mix. Having played against them in Super Bowl VIII, I can say they certainly rank up there with some of the best ever. They had great players, there is no question. Were they as strong defensively as they were offensively? Probably not, but they got a lot of mileage on their "no-name" defense. For guys being no names, they certainly remain on the tips of everybody's tongue. The Dolphins would have to rank right there toward the top of all-time.

In addition, I would agree with the thought that the 1973 Dolphins were better than their 1972 undefeated team. Things just rolled properly for the undefeated team. The 1973 Dolphins were quite a bit stronger and better prepared for playoff football. The experience they got the year before was invaluable. Unless you've been through that two-week period leading up to the big game, you just can't comprehend all that happens before the Super Bowl. Being from Wisconsin, growing up as a Green Bay Packers fan, I would rank the Dolphins a notch below the legendary Packer teams of Vince Lombardi. In 1972 and 1973, however, the Miami Dolphins were the clear-cut best team in football.

Looking back, I think Miami was the favorite in Super Bowl VIII because of their undefeated season in 1972, and because we hadn't been to a Super Bowl since 1969. As players, we didn't buy into the hype, though. We certainly gave them their respect but we knew we stacked up pretty well against them.

The Super Bowl that year was held in Houston, Texas. The practice conditions for us weren't very good. Since it was the AFC host city, the Dolphins got the Houston Oilers' facilities while we got some junior high school, or something. We had birds in our locker room, we hung our clothes on nails, and then we were on a little practice field. Did all of that affect the outcome of the game? No, but it certainly wasn't what you'd expect when you hear the words Super Bowl. But, again, that's not why we lost. The Dolphins just had a better game than we did.

We knew going into it that with Miami's running attack of Larry Csonka and Jim Kiick, their passing combination of Bob Griese to Paul Warfield, and their great offensive line, that they were going to score some points and get some yards. Quite frankly, we thought we were going to be able to put some points on the scoreboard against their "no-name" defense, and make it a high-scoring contest.

The way the Dolphins controlled the ball, using misdirection plays, was the big key in the ballgame. Miami tried to take advantage of the fact that our "Purple People Eaters," the guys up front, were so agile and mobile that they would over-pursue the Dolphins. It worked. Larry Csonka had probably his best game as a pro. He was dominant in that game. It's not that he wasn't being hit; he was dragging tacklers as he hung on to the ball. He was a one-dimensional back, running inside the tackles, but he was like a steamroller. I thought they would be containable. Maybe not stopped, but contained. To Csonka's credit, he was a determined guy. He was by far the most valuable player in that game.

With our front four of Carl Eller, Gary Larsen, Alan Page and Jim Marshall, it was surprising that the Dolphins could control the ball like they did. Griese didn't have to throw the ball much, so when he did, he hit some nice passes to Warfield. The Miami Dolphins had some great players that played very well that day. They deserved to win.

There were some things we could have done offensively, but we didn't have the ball enough. Late in the first half, down by 17 points, we had the ball on Miami's 6-yard line, but we lost it on a fumble. Our margin of error in that game was very small, so not to convert there hurt us. Offensively we never really had a lot of momentum. We were playing their game.

As the game progressed, things weren't improving for us. My own reaction is that I didn't see a team in that 1973 season control the ball, move the ball, and just dominate on offense like Miami did. I thought that after some of those misdirections were figured out that things would settle down and we would shut down the Dolphins like we'd done to teams throughout the season. It didn't happen. The Dolphins kept moving the ball, and, to their credit, they didn't make any mistakes. The score was never so bad that we couldn't come back, but in terms of field position and moving downfield, we were kind of swimming up stream. Unfortunately, we never caught up.

I don't lose any sleep over losing 24-7 in that Super Bowl. That was a good effort by the Dolphins. In this day and age with St. Louis running up 50 points and a margin of victory 30 points, 24-7 almost seems like a close game. When you're playing in it, you realize it wasn't that close. But we played as well as we could that day. Head coach Bud Grant wouldn't have it any other way.

Bud was a common sense coach. There was talk after each of our Super Bowl losses that maybe we should have done things differently; installed a different game plan. We put our A-game on the field, defensively and offensively, in every Super Bowl. Using things we hadn't done before was not Bud Grant's credo. We "danced with the girl that we brung," so to speak. We thought it would be enough to bring the game that got us to the Super Bowl.

Bud Grant was a great coach. Obviously, his record speaks for itself. After all, he took four teams to the Super Bowl. I'm glad for Bud Grant that he got his just rewards of being inducted in to the NFL Hall of Fame.

It's a shame that guys like Eller, Marshall and Mick Tingelhoff don't get a place in the Hall of Fame. That's a prime example of to the victor goes the spoils. The Dolphins with that victory in Super Bowl VIII, solidified their place in history. They had a bunch of guys deservingly go into the Hall of Fame, but, few Vikings who had as illustrious careers as some of the other guys, have made it. Super Bowl champions seem to reap the rewards.

Even though we didn't win one of our Super Bowls, it's still special to think that I played in three of them. If people ask me if I would trade in all three losses for one win, my answer would probably depend on what day of the week I'm asked. But, I played alongside some of the best players in the NFL. The thrill of winning the conference championship game on our home field was great. The memories I have are fantastic. I'm a little sensitive that people have forgotten what a dominant team we were in the late 1960s and throughout the 1970s. A day doesn't go by when I don't think about those things.

We played against teams in those Super Bowls that beat us. The Super Bowl is a one-shot deal. It's not the best of seven or anything like that. If the other team has a better game than you do on that one particular Sunday, then you'll probably lose. Some days we'd like to forget those Super Bowls. One championship for the Vikings out of those four tries would have changed the whole way the history looks at those teams.

It's tough to swallow when people refer to us and the Buffalo Bills of the 1990s as teams that "couldn't win the big one," but that's a fact. We have our faithful fans in Minnesota that stuck with us, and none of us can fully express our appreciation for that. A lot of great players don't even have the luxury of going to the playoffs, let alone the Super Bowl. For me to have played all 11 years of my career in one place, on a team that consistently won its division or was in the playoffs every year, and went to three Super Bowls, is pretty humbling.

Super Bowl VIII

Date: January 13, 1974
Place: Rice Stadium, Houston, TX
Attendance: 71,882

AFC: Miami Dolphins
Head Coach: Don Shula

NFC: Minnesota Vikings
Head Coach: Bud Grant

Minnesota	0	0	0	7	7
Miami	14	3	7	0	24

Most Valuable Player: Larry Csonka (RB, Miami)

Super Bowl IX

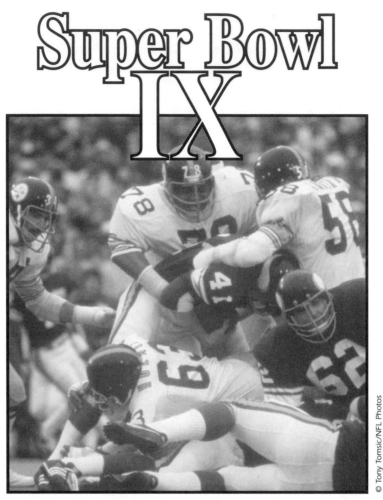

© Tony Tomsic/NFL Photos

*A*fter losing their second Super Bowl, VIII, the Minnesota Vikings were hoping the third time was a charm as they made a return trip to the NFL championship game to face the AFC's Pittsburgh Steelers. Unfortunately for the Vikings, the Steelers were about to embark toward football history. Super Bowl IX was the first-of-four Super Bowl championships for the Steelers in six years.

Considering this was the first Super Bowl for the Steelers, the players didn't want to miss it. One player in particular, Dwight White (No. 78), a member of Pittsburgh's famed "Steel Curtain" defense, was determined to play. White got sick on Sunday, the team's first day in New Orleans. He was taken to the hospital, where he stayed for the majority of the week with a viral infection. He lost nearly 20 pounds during that week in the hospital. Once the game started, White's plight didn't seem to affect him ... it only affected the Vikings. He helped the Steelers get on the board first with a second-quarter sack of quarterback Fran Tarkenton in the end zone for a safety.

Dwight White

The Pittsburgh Steelers had not reached the Super Bowl since the event's beginning. In fact, they hadn't won any championships in 40 years. When we reached the NFL's championship game after a rugged 1974 season, it was special. We knew we had to make the most of the opportunity. The entire team had a tremendous sense of pride. As it turned out, the game nearly didn't happen for me.

We went down to New Orleans for the game on Sunday. That night, Joe Greene, L.C. Greenwood and I went to the French Quarter to eat some seafood. The atmosphere down there was incredible, with Pittsburgh fans everywhere in the Quarter. The people from Minnesota had these skull hats with horns like a Viking. This is no exaggeration, I actually saw Pittsburgh fans take those hats from the Minnesota people.

While we were in the French Quarter, I got sick. Very sick. Joe picked me up, threw me in a cab and took me back to the hotel. I went in the hospital that night with pleurisy and viral pneumonia. I stayed in there until Thursday.

After getting out, I tried to practice but had to go back in the hospital. Things didn't look good for Super Bowl Sunday. I was so weak and had lost about 20 pounds in one week. Talk about sick! But, I couldn't miss the big dance; it was my lifetime dream. Being sick for the Super Bowl is totally unacceptable. I felt bad, but it scared me more because my lungs hurt so badly I couldn't breathe.

They let me out of the hospital the Saturday night before the game. I woke up the next morning, went to pregame meal, went through everything like normal, then got dressed for the game. The doctors were shocked that I made it through warm-ups.

Things actually got to be very annoying, to be honest, because everybody in the huddle kept asking me, "Are you OK?" I said, "I'm fine, just leave me alone."

When I got back to the sidelines, the doctors were over there asking, "Are you OK?"

"I'm fine if you'll just leave me alone and let me catch my breath. You're cutting my air off." I'm proud to say that I played in all but the last series of the game.

My getting out of the hospital and playing can be likened to the adrenaline flow that a mother has when her child is stuck under the car, and she lifts it up to pull the child out. It was that type of thing for me. I don't consider myself any type of hero or anything. As players, we were just so programmed. Football was my job. I had to be there. My job wasn't going to get done right unless I was there. We each felt a huge responsibility that went along with the work ethic that we had. I just sucked it up, went out there and did my job. I felt very good about not missing a day's work.

There was one particular play that stuck out from the Super Bowl. Midway through the second quarter, with the game still scoreless, I sacked Minnesota quarterback Fran Tarkenton for a safety. I didn't actually tackle Tarkenton; all I did was tag him. And then I kept moving. We led 2-0. Despite what a lot of people think, I was the one who sacked him. Most of the photos, however, show Jack Lambert standing over Tarkenton. But if you look at the record books, I'm credited with the safety. If you look at the pictures, it looks like Lambert sacked him because I'm not even in the picture. A miscarriage of justice.

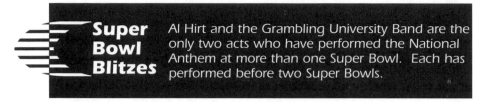

Super Bowl Blitzes Al Hirt and the Grambling University Band are the only two acts who have performed the National Anthem at more than one Super Bowl. Each has performed before two Super Bowls.

Speaking of photos and miscarriages of justice, something that really ticked me off is that after being in the hospital, I missed the Super Bowl team picture. What's worse it that they didn't even think enough to put my name on the damn photo saying I was there. This was the first Pittsburgh team ever to go to the Super Bowl, I had been in the hospital all week and scored the first two points of the game. I was an inspiration and they didn't even think enough to put my name as missing. Life ain't fair. But I got that championship ring.

Following the safety, the rest of the game was simply a matter of us clicking on all eight cylinders. It was a scary thing. We were a runaway roller coaster. It was a ground swell of momentum, positives and convictions. Our win shows what a group of people, focused and determined, can really do. The conviction all the players had on our team is something I'll never forget from that game. It was unique. I've never experienced that type of camaraderie, closeness and focus. Head coach Chuck Noll used to call it a sense of purpose.

Here I am, 30 years later still quoting him. I give Chuck Noll high marks for being a great propaganda guy. We bought into it. He made us believe in ourselves, believe in the game plan. When you've got 50 pit bulls in a room for six months, they can tear each other apart. They can become combative. Chuck kept all of our different personalities on the same page.

You almost need a psychology guy, a heady guy like Chuck, to play the head games with these people. You need some way to get into their heads and then make them focus and channel all that energy in the right direction to win football games. We had some characters, but Chuck was able to find that middle ground to keep everybody content. The talent we had spoke for itself. We'd play every day if you wanted to play every day. We had that type of attitude. As far as motivating people, Chuck didn't have to do that. That was not the issue. Keeping everybody focused was the issue. Chuck kept us all on the same page.

We believed in ourselves. This was our destiny. We lost at home to Miami in the AFC title game on a fake punt in 1972, the year Miami went 17-0. But deep down we won that game. We had every reason to feel confident we could win. That mentality overflowed to the following seasons.

When I came to Pittsburgh, I heard the statement, "Same old Steelers. They always find some way to lose the game. They're always just a cellar team." We had

Please Rise ...

... for the singing of our National Anthem. The singers, musicians, actresses, and others who have performed the National Anthem at the Super Bowl:

I	Al Hirt	XVII	Leslie Easterbrook
II	Grambling University Band	XVIII	Barry Manilow
III	Anita Bryant	XIX	San Francisco Bay
IV	Al Hirt and Doc Severinsen		Area Children's Choir
	with Pat O'Brien	XX	Wynton Marsalis
V	Marvin Gaye	XXI	Neil Diamond
VI	Air Force Academy Chorale	XXII	Herb Alpert
VII	Holy Angels (Chicago)	XXIII	Billy Joel
	School Choir	XXIV	Aaron Neville
VIII	Charlie Pride	XXV	Whitney Houston
IX	Grambling University Band	XXVI	Harry Connick, Jr.
X	Tom Sullivan	XXVII	Garth Brooks
XI	Vicki Carr	XXVIII	Natalie Cole
	("America the Beautiful")	XXIX	Kathie Lee Gifford
XII	Phyllis Kelly	XXX	Vanessa Williams
XIII	Colgate University Band	XXXI	Luther Vandross
XIV	Cheryl Ladd	XXXII	Jewel
XV	Helen O'Connell	XXXIII	Cher
XVI	Diana Ross	XXXIV	Faith Hill

always find some way to lose the game. They're always just a cellar team." We had a unique group of guys who were high strung with strong personalities -cocky, if you will. But that's a good thing in football if you can back it up. It isn't bragging if you can back it up. My daughter has the expression, "Don't talk about it, be about it."

We knew we could back it up, but at the same time there were few games where we felt at ease about winning. That includes Super Bowl IX. That's part of our competing and winning attitude. Win everything. Don't take any prisoners. Losing is unacceptable. Winning is a habit. I tell my daughter that you've got to learn to be a winner. Accept nothing less. That was just the way we generally approached it.

To us, that first Super Bowl was just another game. But winning that game meant that we were the best. It's hard to explain. You work so hard to get to that point, but then you want to hurry up and get it over with. We were high-strung (that's the word I like to use because I think that's really what we were) guys in a positive type of way.

Winning one Super Bowl takes you a long way in learning how to win another one. After we won Super Bowl IX, we were determined to experience that feeling again. That feeling helped drive us in the following years. To win one Super Bowl decade, is spectacular. The way in which we won was the key.

In turn, that also gave us a lot of fans. We'd go anywhere -San Diego, Kansas City, wherever- and have as many fans as the home team did, because we did it with an attitude. We kicked your butt really good. Some of the games were close, but you knew at the end of the day that we had control. We always had control of the game.

When I think back it was a matter of knowing just how good we really were in comparison to all the other great teams. Ranking teams, if we're not at the top -and I'll throw in the San Francisco 49ers- I don't know who is. We feel that we were the best team ever. I definitely don't think there will ever be another dynasty like we enjoyed in Pittsburgh. Today, with free agency, guys have mercenary attitudes. That's not necessarily bad. Owners pay you; you play.

Our Steel Curtain defense was incredible. People still refer to us as the last of the great front fours. There really hasn't been another one since us. Merlin Olsen and the rest of the "Fearsome Foursome," and the "Purple People Eaters" in Minnesota were two great lines before us. Somehow, the Cowboys always force their way into the mix with "Too Tall" Jones, Randy White, Harvey Martin and Jethro Pugh. They get negated though, because guess what? We kicked their butts in two Super Bowls. But I'll throw Dallas in that group if they want to force their way in. Still, I contend that there hasn't been such a dominating front four since us. Not only up front, but there has been no other overall team like ours, where everybody was so focused, had so much pride, and won four championships.

Like a lot of the guys on our team, football for me was a way to improve my life. Of our defensive front four, three of us came from Texas and one from Arkansas. We grew up at a time when a lot was going on around us. We came up through the civil rights movement and Vietnam. There were a lot of issues in the late 1960s when we were in college. Football, at least for the four of us up front, was a great way to be exposed and to have some opportunities put in front of us. Football was more than just a game we played. This was a way of taking a step up to reach the bottom.

I grew up in the projects with wonderful parents and a great family. However, I did not come out of the typical Cleaver household on "Leave It To Beaver." Football for me was a way out. It was an opportunity to be something, to make something out of myself, more so than just playing a game.

After graduating from East Texas State University, I was in Los Angeles with my agent for the NFL draft. I got the call I had been waiting for ... almost: "Dwight, this is Chuck Noll from Pittsburgh. I want to let you know we just drafted you in the fourth round. We think there's a lot of opportunity here in Pittsburgh."

I'm on the other end of the phone saying, "Yes, yes," because this old boy's cash flow just picked up significantly. When I hung up the phone, in all the excitement, I couldn't remember if he said Pittsburgh or Philadelphia. Then I realized, "Pittsburgh, Pittsburgh? I've got to go to Pittsburgh?" Pittsburgh at that point was in the bowels of the NFL. I don't forget that story.

I tell it because you never know what can happen. I was very proud and extremely pleased to have made the Steelers squad and to be a starter during my rookie year in 1971. There was a great amount of pride in that feeling of self-accomplishment. We had a great group of guys with great chemistry. Pride was something synonymous with all of us in a good way, a friendly rivalry way. Everybody had the mentality "I'm tougher than you. I'm just as tough as you are. I'm the best."

I never would have expected the type of career I had with the Steelers. As a result of coming to Pittsburgh, I met my wife, who is from the area. I made a wonderful life here. I thought life was as dark as it could get, being drafted by the Pittsburgh Steelers. But you never know. So take the hand that's dealt to you and play it. Keep hope alive. Oh, and I collected four Super Bowl championship rings. Good things do happen.

After Super Bowl IX, which we won 16-6, I went to the little diner across the street from our hotel. The rest of the team was out partying because we had reached the promise land and ended the Steelers' 40-year championship drought, but I felt like death warmed over. One of the Pittsburgh sportswriters was in the diner with his son. I sat with them, ate a cheeseburger, went back to the room and crashed. I flew back to Pittsburgh the next day and went to the hospital, where I stayed for a week. But I got that championship ring.

Super Bowl IX

Date: January 12, 1975
Place: Tulane Stadium, New Orleans, LA
Attendance: 80,997

AFC: Pittsburgh Steelers
Head Coach: Chuck Noll

NFC: Minnesota Vikings
Head Coach: Bud Grant

Pittsburgh	0	2	7	7	16
Minnesota	0	0	0	6	6

Most Valuable Player: Franco Harris (RB, Pittsburgh)

Super Bowl X

© Tony Tomsic/NFL Photos

*P*ittsburgh cornerback Mel Blount (No. 47, right), one of the mainstays on the
Steelers' "Steel Curtain" defense, enjoyed one of his best seasons in 1975. On his
way to becoming the NFL's defensive player of the year, Blount made 11 interceptions
and earned his first Pro Bowl appearance. Understandably, the Dallas Cowboys did
all they could to avoid the quick and tenacious Blount in Super Bowl X.

On the flip side, Dallas defensive back Cliff Harris was unable to intimidate
Pittsburgh wide receiver Lynn Swann. Throughout the week leading up to the Super
Bowl, Harris publicly suggested that although he wasn't going to hurt anyone intentionally, Swann should avoid the Dallas defender. Swann, en route to becoming the
game's MVP, practically eluded the entire Dallas defense on his way to 161 yards
on four spectacular catches and the game-deciding touchdown reception.

Woody Widenhofer, one of the most entertaining college coaches, currently at
Vanderbilt, was a young linebackers' coach for the Steelers during their four-Super
Bowl championship march.

Woody Widenhofer

Going into Super Bowl X, coming off a NFL championship the previous year, we knew we had a great football team in Pittsburgh, but it was a very young team and coaching staff at that time. We didn't think of repeating as pressure, we thought of it as something we were good enough to do. We just had to make sure we got ourselves prepared properly to get the job done. The only pressure, if any, was self-plight, because we wanted to win, and we felt like we had the best team in the National Football League.

Head coach Chuck Noll made sure we were prepared heading into Super Bowl X to face the Dallas Cowboys. Chuck is the best I've ever been around as a football person and as a private person in terms of family and spiritual ways. He had things in the right perspective. He loved his family. Football meant a lot to him, but it wasn't everything. There was a great spiritual side to him and he was a great teacher. He really took a lot of pride in teaching. I think the number one asset he had, though, was self-control when it came to his emotions. When he lost a game he wasn't emotionally too low and vice versa when he won. There was an even keel about him that everybody looked up to because he was the leader. He was probably tougher on the players and coaches when we won. One great thing about Coach Noll was he really let the coaches coach. He gave you the opportunity to develop as a football coach and gain respect of the players.

Chuck hired me when I was 28 years old. I never played pro football, but I was coaching at the University of Minnesota when I met him. He put me through a six- or seven-hour interview. The first thing he said to me was, "Coach, I'm a football player, teach me the defense of the University of Minnesota. I'm a linebacker, teach it to me." I took him through every fundamental little thing that I knew about it. Then he turned on some game films and said, "I want you to critique the linebackers. I know you're not really sure what we're doing, but just tell me about how they're playing. Don't be afraid to express yourself."

When we finished, about six hours later, we went upstairs to the stadium club for lunch. On our way back down in the elevator he looked at me and he said, "Do you want this job?"

I said, "I sure do, coach."

He stuck out his hand and said, "You got it." It was unbelievable.

I had just walked out of college football and was about to coach the likes of George Webster, Andy Russell, Henry Davis and a young Jack Ham; Jack Lambert wasn't there at that point. When I first got hired there, I coached two or three guys older than me. I actually played behind Russell at Missouri, so I knew him before I got the job. He was a big help because he was a leader and a very experienced guy. He really supported me as a coach when I was there.

In Super Bowl X we were playing against a great Dallas team, but I don't think we felt like we would ever lose to the Cowboys. It was just the type of mentality we had when we played Dallas. The attitude of our team going into the ball game was that we

Roger Staubach

The 1975 season was a memorable one for me. Of course, if we had pulled off the Super Bowl X victory over the Pittsburgh Steelers, it would have been even better. However, the season was very gratifying because we were not picked to do anything that year. To some, it looked like our team was in a rebuilding phase, but we got great players in the draft, we played hard all year, we played as a team and we won. Generally, whenever we lost a game we came right back the next week and won. It was one of the most satisfying seasons that I've ever had because we weren't expected to do very much, but we excelled.

We had some big wins and finished the regular season with a record of 10-4. In the NFC divisional playoff game in Minnesota, we had the 50-yard "Hail Mary!" touchdown pass to Drew Pearson for the 17-14 win to extend our season. Then, going into the Super Bowl as a wild-card team, we came very close to beating Pittsburgh.

Trailing 21-17 in the fourth quarter, we got the ball on our own 39-yard line with 1:22 remaining. We made a couple big plays in that stretch, but we weren't as organized as we needed to be. We didn't use our time very well. I felt that we could have won if we had used our time more wisely. It's funny; we spent more time working on the 2-minute drill during the rest of my career, largely because we didn't use the clock effectively in that Super Bowl. We did have a shot to score. We hit a couple passes and were down to their 30. If we could have gotten out of bounds and changed a couple other decisions, we would have been much more comfortable of having a shot at winning. As it turned out, we only had one desperation pass, and it was intercepted. I still feel that we didn't do our job in that 2-minute period.

Take nothing away from Pittsburgh, though. The famed Steel Curtain defense of the Steelers was fantastic. They totally shut down our running attack in that game, and for the most part, shut down our wide receivers. We had to scramble to make plays. They started controlling our offense in the second half behind the play of linebacker Jack Lambert. He wasn't really somebody that I liked, but I respected him. I still get mad at our players for not reacting when Lambert kicked Preston Pearson on the ground, but he fired up the Steelers. He made it happen. He was the glue in that defense. They had other great players on the defensive side like Mel Blount and Joe Greene, but there still needs to be one guy that can bring it all together. Lambert was magnificent at doing that.

I don't think the National Football League has seen a better defense than Pittsburgh's Steel Curtain. We weren't the type of offense that they liked to play against because we tried to finesse them. They liked it when opponents tried to go head-to-head with them so they could beat the tar out of that team. They were very physical. We tried to trick them and they didn't like that. Unfortunately we didn't trick them enough.

I really felt that we overachieved in that Super Bowl game, even though we had a shot at winning. The Steelers had to make big plays to beat us. I still think about some of the plays that made a difference.

I still think about the last couple of plays in the game. That series doesn't keep me up at night ... well, once in a while it does.

were better than Dallas at that time, and we would win. One thing that sticks out from the game was Lynn Swann making a couple of great catches that kept drives going. He also had a big 64-yard touchdown catch late in the game to put us up 21-10.

Swann, the game's MVP, is a tremendous competitor. I can remember in practice one day, he ran a quick slant and Joe Gilliam threw the ball and hit him on the end of the finger. Swann fractured the finger so bad the bone went through the skin. Doctors stitched it up and put it back in place. They had to put a steel pin in it to keep it in place. When Swann went out and played that following Sunday, you wouldn't think of him being anything but a real tough guy. He was just great elegance. At the same time, he took ballet lessons to improve his coordination and balance. Swann worked at every angle and tried to be the best.

There were a number of big plays throughout the game that kept us a notch above them. Dallas, after scoring to make it a four-point game, got the ball back with 1:22 to play. Normally for quarterback Roger Staubach, that was plenty of time. Still, we didn't have to tell our defense a whole lot. Our guys were a pretty experienced group of defenders and they had a lot of pride. The Steelers knew they had an advantage over everybody because they were so tough. When our guys took the field, they thought they were the best, and the toughest. I think that's why we had so much success against Dallas in those years, even though Dallas had a great football team. I think our players felt Dallas was a finesse football team and not real tough. As time expired in the game, Glen Edwards came up with a big interception

© 1999 Sam Wyche & J.D. Crowe
Dist. by United Feature Syndicate, Inc.

www.comiczone.com

⦿CBS SPORTS Presents

In the Trenches with Terry Ewert

In 1974, shortly after graduating from college, I was working as the sports director for KALB television in Alexandria, La. Sure enough, Super Bowl VIII in January of 1974 was in Houston's Rice Stadium, which is not very far away from Alexandria. I talked my station manager into letting me get a Super Bowl credential, which I viewed as the nirvana of sports credentials. The NFL sent me reporter credentials as well as photographer credentials, allowing me to shoot film from the sidelines. Here I was a local reporter from a very small station, allowed to stand on the sidelines of the biggest professional football game of the year.

From the sidelines I sensed the unbelievable power of Larry Csonka and saw into the eyes of Bob Griese. It was amazing. My hero at the time was Minnesota quarterback Fran Tarkenton and, of course, the Vikings went down in a disappointing performance. It was still very exciting to be there.

My fondest memory of any Super Bowl came after that game when I was standing outside with my camera crew. NFL Commissioner Pete Rozelle walked out and was standing there waiting for his car. I asked him if he would mind being interviewed. He accepted and was extremely polite and answered all my questions (most of which I thought were pretty tough). That moment still ranks up there as my number one Super Bowl memory. I still have the little brown satchel that the NFL gave out as the press gift, which is a great reminder to me of being able to interview Commissioner Rozelle.

to secure our victory, 21-17.

I don't think we actually realized we were with one of the best teams ever until that game was over. The city, which is a blue-collar city, just loved its Steelers. It was an unbelievable feeling to be part of it, especially with those players. They were unselfish and team oriented. I give a lot of credit to Chuck Noll for that. He disciplined them; he didn't care whether it was Terry Bradshaw or Reggie Harrison. It didn't make any difference.

Basically we all grew together. With great ownership, the chief, Art Rooney, and his sons, and of course, Chuck Noll was a just a terrific teacher and a great leader. We had great chemistry and it was fantastic to be part of that.

What really sticks in my mind, when I think back about those glory days, is not individuals. This team cared so much about each other and wanted to win. It had so much confidence, and each player had a love affair for one another. I think I was the only coach Jack Ham and Jack Lambert ever had. I was in Pittsburgh for 11

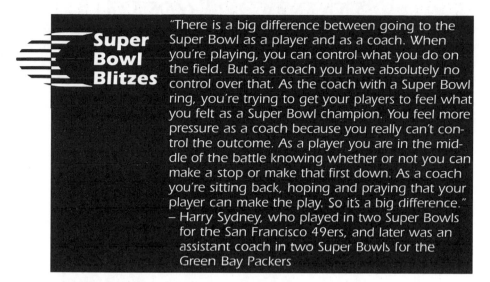

Super Bowl Blitzes

"There is a big difference between going to the Super Bowl as a player and as a coach. When you're playing, you can control what you do on the field. But as a coach you have absolutely no control over that. As the coach with a Super Bowl ring, you're trying to get your players to feel what you felt as a Super Bowl champion. You feel more pressure as a coach because you really can't control the outcome. As a player you are in the middle of the battle knowing whether or not you can make a stop or make that first down. As a coach you're sitting back, hoping and praying that your player can make the play. So it's a big difference."
– Harry Sydney, who played in two Super Bowls for the San Francisco 49ers, and later was an assistant coach in two Super Bowls for the Green Bay Packers

years. You end up being part of each player's family. You end up understanding the personal problems they have. It was that way with everyone. I think that's why we won. They were great players and we were innovative as coaches. We had great leadership and a great winning attitude.

I was part of four Super Bowls and the defensive coordinator in the last two. I was born in Butler, Pa. and lived there for some of my elementary years. We moved to Michigan, but all my relatives and family are from Pittsburgh and the Butler area. Going back to Pittsburgh and being part of a coaching staff that made that kind of impact was just one of the greatest feelings. As years go on you really thank God you had a chance to be part of history.

Super Bowl X

Date: January 28, 1976
Place: Orange Bowl, Miami, FL
Attendance: 80,187

AFC: Pittsburgh Steelers
Head Coach: Chuck Noll

NFC: Dallas Cowboys
Head Coach: Tom Landry

Dallas	7	3	0	7	17
Pittsburgh	7	0	0	14	21

Most Valuable Player: Lynn Swann (WR, Pittsburgh)

Super Bowl XI

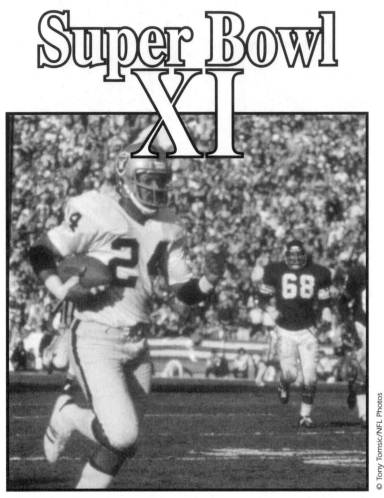

*B*y the time Super Bowl XI was played, the Minnesota Vikings had become a joke to some people, after losing three previous Super Bowls. Unfair but true, the tag of being the team that "couldn't win the big one" had already been applied to the Vikings before the 1976 season.

The Oakland Raiders had been to a Super Bowl, nine years earlier, where they lost to the Green Bay Packers. In Super Bowl XI, Oakland exploded for 429 yards, which, at the time, was a Super Bowl record. Another record that day was set by Oakland cornerback Willie Brown (No. 24) who picked off a Minnesota pass and returned it 75 yards for Oakland's final touchdown of the day. (Brown's record return was broken in Super Bowl XXX by another Brown, Larry Brown.)

One man who was a quiet key in the game was referee Jim Tunney, one of the league's most-respected officials from 1960-1991. He became the first referee to work back-to-back Super Bowls, XI and XII. Tunney, currently a motivational speaker, is a member of the National Football League Hall of Fame.

Jim Tunney

Every Super Bowl is strong in my memory bank, but Super Bowl XI tops the list, mostly because of all the history the Rose Bowl holds for me. I had worked Super Bowl VI (1972) when Dallas played Miami at the old Tulane Stadium in New Orleans. That was exciting, in part because 1972 was only my fifth year as a referee in the National Football League. But when Supervisor of Officials, Art McNally, called me about officiating Super Bowl XI (1977), I was thrilled, not only about having the opportunity to work another Super Bowl, but because it was being played in the Rose Bowl, about four miles from where I grew up.

My dad officiated high school and college football and basketball games and worked games at the Rose Bowl many times. From the time I was about 8 years old, big enough to carry his equipment bag, I'd tag along with my dad. He worked games for Pasadena Junior College when Jackie Robinson was playing there. Before the time I saw Robinson play for the first time, Dad told me, "Watch this guy. He's going to be something." Dad was right. He was a great athlete, even with his knocked-kneed and pigeon-toed run; and he was nice to the lucky little kid sitting on the bench, at the game as his dad's "assistant."

Years later, I played college games in the Rose Bowl, and after graduating, when I began officiating, I worked high school and college games there. Never during those years did I have a vision of working a Super Bowl there. I hadn't really formed a dream about it; still, when the call came from McNally saying I'd been chosen for the first Super Bowl to be played in that magnificent stadium, it felt like a dream come true.

I knew I might get the call, because I hadn't worked any of the season's playoff games and I'd had a good year on the field. Today, officials must work during the playoffs to be considered for the Super Bowl. Back then, an official was allowed to work only one postseason game, including the Super Bowl. You hoped to get "a call," but not until after the conference championships. Ten days before the Super Bowl, I got the call. Indeed, I was thrilled.

McNally had a strong edict about officials staying away from the press, which meant he also tried to keep the press away from officials. When he called, he said I couldn't tell anyone other than my immediate family that I would be working the game. I said, "Okay," and then asked which other officials were assigned to the crew. After all, I was crew chief and eager to get us started with preparations.

"No, no," McNally said, "Can't tell you, and you can't tell anyone other than immediate family. That's it."

In spite of McNally's efforts, word leaked out. Still, no one on the crew knew officially who else was on the crew until each person arrived at the game hotel Thursday before the game. The attempt at secrecy seemed impractical at the time, and seems quaint now. These days, officials assigned to the Super Bowl are introduced at the Commissioner's Press Conference the Friday before the game. I was glad to see the change come.

The next nice surprise was Lou Palazzi walking into the game hotel that Thursday. He was assigned as our umpire. Palazzi had played guard for the New York Giants in the 1950s and began officiating when his playing days were over. In 1967, my rookie year as a referee, Lou was on our crew. I learned a lot from him, especially about game control on the line of scrimmage, where things can get rough in a hurry. He would be retiring soon, so nothing was better in my mind than to have Palazzi working the game with me.

Also on our crew were Ed Marion as Head Linesman, Tom Kelleher as Back Judge, Armen Terzian as Field Judge and Pat Harder and Gene Barth as Alternates.

On Friday, I met McNally at LAX and we drove over to scout the Rose Bowl. We walked around, checking the locker rooms, the egress onto the field, the field itself, looking for anything that might create a surprise on game day. The walk-through gave me the chance to tell McNally how much the stadium meant to me. I couldn't wait for Sunday, to be on the field, with the stadium full of fans feeding the make-or-break intensity of a Super Bowl game.

I didn't care who won. Vikings. Raiders. Didn't matter. Impartiality comes with the territory for an official. In fact, it is the most important territory for an official, even more important than knowing the rules "cold" and having game control. If you aren't truly impartial, nothing else about an official's work can be trusted.

I never collected an autograph, pennant, jersey, helmet, photograph or any of that stuff. I wasn't a fan of a team, a player or a coach. I never looked at the over-under. It didn't matter which team was favored. True, I have great memories of particular moments in games, because you can admire the deftness or strength of an individual or team skill without holding a preference about who wins. My only focus was to officiate the game - which means enforcing rules designed to keep unfair advantage off the field, so that skill in coaching and execution are deciding factors, not somebody's preference.

Most NFL players (not the merely paid players, but the professional players) know that game officials are there to do a job; and more players than you might think appreciate the value of enforcing the rules. Officials aren't trying to "get" anybody or to set it up that a particular team wins. In fact, I always worked with the rookies - officials and players - to help them develop a rapport, the confidence that the official was there to do the job the commissioner mandated - make sure the game is played by the rules. Fairness is an advantage to everyone.

Super Bowl XI

In Super Bowl XI, Minnesota had Fran Tarkenton at quarterback and the "Purple People Eaters" on defense - Marshall, Eller and Page. Oakland had Ken Stabler at quarterback, guard Gene Upshaw and wide receiver Fred Biletnikoff, who turned out to be the game's MVP (now, there's a clue as to which team won...). And the teams were headed by two of the best coaches in the NFL - Bud Grant for Minnesota and John Madden for Oakland. The team organizations, our crew and the then-record crowd of 103,438 fans in the stands were ready for a good game.

Each play starts with the referee in position about twelve yards behind and to the side of the quarterback's throwing arm, watching the snap, the drop back, handoff to the running back or the pass, any fouls. This means I would have my eye on Stabler or Tarkenton all afternoon. Both of them were through-and-through competitors, willing to take a risk to get the play off.

Stabler liked to stand in the pocket, squeezing every millisecond to check through his options and make an accurate throw. The "Purple People Eaters" were intent on shortening those milliseconds, and maybe shortening Stabler. They came at him pretty hard from Stabler's first snap. One time after they had buried him, Stabler looked up at me and said, "Hey, Jim, count that defense. I think they've got fourteen over there."

Tarkenton preferred to scramble any which way he could. At one point in the fourth quarter, with Oakland leading 26-7, Tarkenton threw the ball to Willie Brown, which was a mistake because Brown played for the Raiders. He returned the interception 75 yards for a touchdown. As Tarkenton was walking off the field, he turned to me and said, "I'll be back," as if to say, "Okay, they got me on that one, but 'I'll be back.'" That kind of confidence and commitment always earned my respect.

Unfortunately for Vikings fans, Minnesota didn't come back. Oakland had led most of the game, but Tarkenton and the Vikings kept the pressure on and it seemed like with any play, the game might swing their way. Brown's interception and touchdown put the game out of reach for Tarkenton, no matter how confident he remained.

Super Bowl XI was Minnesota's fourth trip to the title game, without a win. They were the sentimental favorite for a lot of people, but they didn't win and, as of this writing, they haven't made it back since then.

There was no controversy in the game. We didn't have instant replay in 1977, but it wouldn't have been triggered any way. This game went along smoothly. Officials like a game without controversy. When a team edged toward getting out-of-control, I would tell the captain that either he could take care of things or I would handle it. That was plenty, even with the Raiders, a team known for its aggressiveness. Gene Upshaw was the Raider captain. I gave him the either-or statement once, and from then on we only had to have a couple seconds of eye contact and Upshaw took care of it, meaning, he took care of his team.

Always, though, an official's training is to expect the unexpected. As a crew, we prepared for this game by going over every conceivable play situation, checking ourselves for decisiveness and correctness. Each official must know where to be in

every play situation, be there, and then respond appropriately no matter how the play turns. When a ball breaks loose (e.g. is fumbled), you've got to watch for players batting or kicking the ball or any crazy thing. Super Bowl XI had only one "unexpected." Oakland punter Ray Guy, a No. 1 draft choice for the Raiders, had a punt blocked. Now, blocked punts happened pretty regularly and officials watch for it in every punt situation, but it had never happened to Guy. Even officials remember things like that. It was a great game. Oakland won, 32-14.

I am always asked, since officials don't care who wins, if we can enjoy the game the way fans do. Well, we don't enjoy any game, even a Super Bowl, like a fan does. We understand fan excitement: why fans dress in team colors, cheer and stomp; why they roar trying to take the audible away from the opponent; why they lean en masse trying to correct the arc of a field goal threatening to veer off line. We understand all this, but we see the game from a different perspective - simple fairness: no unfair advantage; by the rules; a field where consistency supports a team's valid preparation and execution.

Still, just like fans, players, coaches, even owners, officials feel high anticipation, even anxiety, at the start of a big game, and, no question, the Super Bowl is the biggest game in pro football. If your stomach isn't rolling, if you aren't a little uneasy, you ought not to be there: your senses are gone. And to work a game flawlessly, a game official needs every sense and every wit of game smarts on high alert, ready to be quick, but never hurried; decisive, but never at the price of certainty. You have to be pumped with preparedness so that you are immune to intimidation, even with the spotlight of millions of fans around the world, in the presence of twenty-two players on the field, a roughly equivalent number of players on the sidelines, a gaggle of coaches, trainers, owners staring and yelling; and your boss, the Commissioner, watching with binoculars to judge how well you do the job. Yes, it's exciting, but it doesn't require jumping up and down, clapping and screaming to express it.

That mentality is still with me today. When watching at home, or when I go to the stadium, I generally sit, arms folded, watching for effective execution and the little breakdowns that bust a play. Screaming doesn't improve eyesight. Nor does praying improve your team's chance that those smooth executions will be completed and those little breakdowns that bust a play won't happen.

Every official who has ever worked a game at any level – high school, college or professional – wants to work the Super Bowl. It's the highest praise for work well-done and the most serious chance to do what you know and do it excellently. To have that opportunity three times, plus a fourth as an alternate, is a terrific gratification.

Super Bowl XI

Date: January 9, 1977
Place: Rose Bowl, Pasadena, CA
Attendance: 103,438

AFC: Oakland Raiders
Head Coach: John Madden

NFC: Minnesota Vikings
Head Coach: Bud Grant

Oakland	0	16	3	13	32
Minnesota	0	0	7	7	14

Most Valuable Player: Fred Biletnikoff (WR, Oakland)

Super Bowl XII

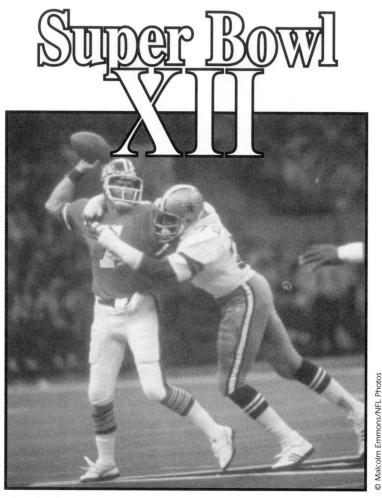

*T*he Dallas Cowboys had one of the toughest defenses, "Doomsday," throughout the late 1970s. In front of a sell-out crowd in the Louisiana Superdome, "Doomsday" met the Denver Broncos, and their "Orange Crush," in Super Bowl XII.

Dallas' "Doomsday" defense didn't disappoint. In the first half alone, the Cowboys intercepted two Craig Morton – a former Cowboy – passes, which eventually were converted into 10 points. By the end of the game, the Cowboys' defense had intercepted four Denver passes and recovered four fumbles.

For the first, and still only, time, Super Bowl XII produced co-Most Valuable Players, Harvey Martin and Randy White. Martin and White were nuisances to the Denver quarterbacks for the entire four quarters. Martin (above, right) collected one sack and several rushes against Morton and back-up Norris Weese.

Harvey Martin

After losing to the Pittsburgh Steelers in Super Bowl X in January of 1976, I was extra hungry facing the Denver Broncos in Super Bowl XII. As most teams do, we had a party after our loss to Pittsburgh. Even though we had just been beaten, we had so much fun at this party it made me wonder what the winners were doing in their celebration. In the loser's party we had all these country and western stars from Dallas and the Texas area, such as Willie Nelson. It was a festive atmosphere but I wanted to go to a winner's party. That was really important to me. It might seem trivial to some people, but to me it was paramount.

When we hooked up with the Broncos in Super Bowl XII, we were ready to play. Super Bowl X was like the circus for us because we were so happy to be there. That was my third year in the NFL, Ed "Too Tall" Jones' second. We were just babies. We were like, "Oh, my God, we're in the Super Bowl. I can't believe it." During the game we met a great Steeler football team. In XII we didn't have time to get caught up in the hoopla. We were there for business. We wanted to be world champions. And that helped us so much because we had been there, done that. We were no longer the starry-eyed kid in the Super Bowl. We were there to win.

A lot of that mentality was from the core group of guys that lost and didn't want to lose again. They wanted to go out and play ball. They were willing to pay the price to become the best. We all cried together after that loss to the Steelers, so against Denver we said, "Let's go out and play football." A lot of guys wanted the perks that went with being a Dallas Cowboy and being an NFL champion, but the only way you can get those perks is to win. The main thing we talked about all week leading up to the Denver game was that if you want all the adulation that goes with being No. 1, then you have to become No. 1.

The first thing I remember about walking onto the field in the Louisiana Superdome for the first time was seeing Denver's "Orange Crush" come out and all the people wearing that ugly orange. They figured the Broncos had a chance to win. (We didn't think they did.) The second thing that comes to mind was the concentration, the focus, on our side. The play of Randy Hughes. The play of "Too Tall" Jones, who could easily have been MVP himself. The focus on the sidelines. Knowing exactly what we had to do and not being satisfied unless we did that. Watching the rookies on the team get caught up in what the older veterans were doing, and playing their hardest ball. We all wanted badly to win this game.

By the time I went to midfield with the other captains for the coin toss, I was in a zone. Before each game, I would put my jersey over my head and – even though I'm a nice guy – transform. When I came out from under that jersey I was ready to go out into a violent world. The world of professional football. The world of "game day." And when I walked out on that field, I didn't speak to anybody. I didn't even look at the guys because it was my feeling that I was there to beat your butt. I was there to win the ball game. I wasn't there to shake hands. I let the other captains do the handshaking and stuff. I was at midfield to show you that I came to kick your butt. And that's the attitude I took into the Super Bowl ... I'm here with my team to kick your butt. I don't want to shake your hand; I'll shake it after the game. I'm not even going to tell you good luck because it's not going to happen.

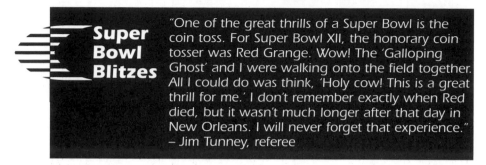

Super Bowl Blitzes

"One of the great thrills of a Super Bowl is the coin toss. For Super Bowl XII, the honorary coin tosser was Red Grange. Wow! The 'Galloping Ghost' and I were walking onto the field together. All I could do was think, 'Holy cow! This is a great thrill for me.' I don't remember exactly when Red died, but it wasn't much longer after that day in New Orleans. I will never forget that experience."
– Jim Tunney, referee

Specific plays or instances from the game don't stick out to me as much as the experiences surrounding the game. We just had a great game on both sides of the ball. Behind two interceptions in the first quarter to get things going, we jumped out quickly against the Broncos. By halftime we had a 13-0 lead. The fact that the defense played well didn't surprise a lot of people.

We had an excellent defense on those teams back in the 1970s. In fact, we ended the Super Bowl XII season as the No. 1 defense in the NFL. And we actually had the No. 1 offense in the NFL. Our defense was hungry. We were a bunch of oppor-tunistic guys. We had fought our way through one glorious season in the 1970s, when it was tough playing ball in the '70s. Today there are good football teams but there is free agency. In the 1970s, guys stayed with one team for the duration of their careers. It wasn't an easy chore for us to go through that season like we did. When we went on the football field, we could not let up until we finished that one game.

Our defensive group carried on what we had been taught by guys like Bob Lilly, Jethro Pugh, George Andrie, Lee Roy Jordan and D.D. Lewis. They taught us to go out and play very good, solid flex defense. Everybody plays their gap and then goes to the ball and uses their head. That's what we did.

The goal of our defense was to go in and win each ball game. We used to have a saying that if you can't score, you can't win. It simply meant defense. Defense is all attitude, and we had the attitude teams were not going to beat us. We weren't going to let them beat us. Also, though, we were blessed with superior talent. We had so much talent it should have been illegal. We had so much going for us on defense.

We also had some great stars on offense. Everyone remembers Butch Johnson's great touchdown catch against the Broncos. He was a superb wide receiver. But, of course, Drew Pearson was the man at wide receiver. In tough games, Drew was always there. In the backfield we had Tony Dorsett, who goes without saying. Robert Newhouse was playing wonderful football late that season. Then, last but

⊙CBS SPORTS Presents

In the Trenches with Dan Dierdorf

I'll be happy when the league goes to the Super Bowl being played with one week between it and the conference championship. I think we have a better chance of seeing more competitive ball games. Sometimes I think that the two weeks really grates on the players. They're used to playing every week, so to have that extra week breaks their routine. The longer you have to think about the magnitude of the game, about how many hundreds of millions of people are going to be watching, and what happens if you're the goat, that has a tendency to cause some players to lock up.

That extra week is just more time to reflect and think about the huge task in front of you. The extra week is good for the league; it's good for the people who are traveling. One week really rushes things if you are trying to make a hotel reservation and get to the site. I'm just talking selfishly about the players and their ability to perform at a higher level. I suspect the game would be consistently better with only one week in between. I don't think the hype would change at all. I certainly don't know how it could get any larger than it is.

not least, I like to say we cheated because we had Roger Staubach at quarterback. When you've got Roger, you're playing with a loaded deck.

Despite having a big 27-10 lead late in the game, we didn't feel comfortable until the last couple minutes. The memories of Super Bowl X, going down to the wire with the Steelers, was still in our heads. We wanted to be sure the Denver game was over before we celebrated. We started to count down the final few minutes of the game, and then we started to think, "OK, we got this one, baby."

The one thing that got me the most was at the end of the game when Randy White and I were standing next to each other, neither one of us having a clue we would be MVPs. We were just happy as hell we were winning the ball game. I'll never forget when then-CBS announcer Pat Summerall came out and said, "Folks, for the first time in history there are two most valuable players." Even at that moment, it was still totally far away from my mind. Then Summerall continued, "Harvey Martin and Randy White." I just lost it. I was not ready for that announcement. I was not ready for that at all.

I still get chills thinking about that because having co-MVPs might never happen again in a Super Bowl. That hadn't happened before us and it hasn't happened since. Randy and I worked well together in that game and throughout our careers. Before playing Denver we took time off to study game films together, just to be

sure our heads were in the right place. Now Randy and I have a special bond over being co-MVPs.

I consider that Super Bowl championship and the co-MVP a gift from God. In my "youth," when that happened, I had no idea of the far-reaching effect it would have. It is something that you get that you will have next to you for the rest of your life. It is a gift that I still appreciate today. It is very important to me. It is to be respected and it is to be cherished. Winning those doesn't happen to a lot of guys.

Playing in the Super Bowl and winning the championship, allows you to go into everyday life, whatever profession you're in after your playing career, and put that same drive and tenacity into your business. You know that you've been to the mountaintop in one profession. And you know that getting to the mountaintop in another profession is going to take that same kind of work, desire and faith. As head coach Tom Landry used to say to us, "What I'm teaching you guys here, you will use when you leave football. This is the basis for life."

Tom Landry was such an excellent coach, but a better man. We were so young in the beginning. The older we got the more we realized the same principles he taught us in football do work in everyday life. Playing in the Super Bowl and being around Coach Landry, I learned not to be afraid of success, but to know that to be success-ful, you have to take some hits. You have to get knocked down to get back up. That's very important. Just because you get knocked down doesn't mean you have to stay there. You can still win if you get up. But you have to get up and walk your-self through those defeats in life.

Since I've been retired, there have been times when I've sat back and looked at how much respect the Dallas Cowboys have around the country. I've especially noticed how much respect and love we have from Cowboy fans, not only in Dallas, but worldwide. Then I realize, my goodness, I was really there at a monumental time. I was able to be with the Cowboys at a time that people today close their eyes and see us playing. Money can't buy that. A lot of people talk about the huge salaries players have today. We made good money for the times we played, but as I tell people, we have millions of dollars worth of love. Money can't buy that.

By the way, there is a huge difference in the winner and loser's postgame parties. Winners have a hell of a lot more fun.

Super Bowl XII

Date: January 15, 1978
Place: Superdome, New Orleans, LA
Attendance: 76,400

AFC: Denver Broncos
Head Coach: Red Miller

NFC: Dallas Cowboys
Head Coach: Tom Landry

Dallas	10	3	7	7	27
Denver	0	0	10	0	10

Co-Most Valuable Players: Randy White (DT, Dallas) and Harvey Martin (DE, Dallas)

Super Bowl XIII

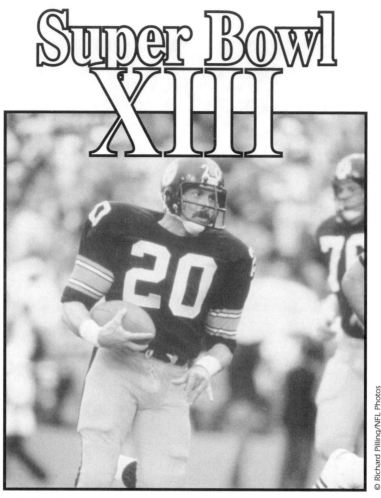

*A*lthough there had been exciting Super Bowls in the event's first 12 games, none matched the intensity and the excitement of Super Bowl XIII. The drama for the game had been set before the kickoff. The Dallas Cowboys were the defending Super Bowl champions, facing two-time winner, the Pittsburgh Steelers. Not to mention, the second installment to one of the Super Bowl's biggest rivalries.

The game was a battle of head coaches, Dallas' Tom Landry against Pittsburgh's Chuck Noll, and of quarterbacks, Dallas' Roger Staubach and Pittsburgh's Terry Bradshaw. It appeared as though it was going to be a game where the team that had the ball last would win. The Steelers held a halftime lead, gained on a 7-yard touchdown play from Bradshaw to Bleier with 26 seconds left in the half.

With 6:51 left in the game, the Steelers took a 35-17 lead. After a couple of breaks, and the passing efficiency of Staubach, the Cowboys cut the lead to 35-31 with 22 seconds remaining. However, Bleier (pictured above) snagged Dallas' onside kick attempt to seal the victory for Pittsburgh.

Rocky Bleier

I
f you look at teams that have won the Super Bowl, or even the teams that have reached the Super Bowl, a lot of the success is not only derived from talent but also from luck. Luck being that you are healthy and have everybody in tact for the entire season. Or, if injuries do occur, they don't arise at the end of the season. Looking specifically at our Pittsburgh Steelers teams, we were always healthy going into the playoffs.

Even though we had reached the Super Bowl, in my mind, 1978 and 1979 were coming of age seasons for us. I felt that nobody could beat us. If we were going to lose, we would have to lose by beating ourselves. We had the talent. The talent had been tested and we knew what it took to win. Heck, we already had two Super Bowl wins under our belts. As the 1978 season went along, a great expectation about going back to the Super Bowl was unveiled. That expectation came to fruition when we reached Super Bowl XIII to face our rival, the Dallas Cowboys.

Pittsburgh against Dallas has to be one of the best Super Bowl rivalries, if not the best. I think every team that plays Dallas is a great rivalry, especially during that period of time because it was "America's team." Everybody loved to beat the Cowboys. They were, are, and have been so dominant in winning to get to the playoffs and ultimately to the Super Bowl.

In the 1970s, we were two well-matched teams, especially for the Super Bowl. I recently ran into some Cowboy fans on the road and started talking to them about the "good old days." One of them made the comment that XIII was one of the all-time great Super Bowls because it was so exciting. We had some good games against Dallas, but I have to agree with that Cowboy fan.

Momentum seemed to be the key word in Super Bowl XIII. It really played a factor in that game, with each of us having it during the first half. After we scored first in the game on a pass from Terry Bradshaw to John Stallworth, the Cowboys struck twice. They scored on an offensive play to end the first quarter, then scored defensively following a fumble recovery. Bradshaw and Stallworth again hooked up for a 75-yard scoring play.

Toward the end of the second quarter we moved the ball down the field, with the game tied 14-14. With under a minute left, we found ourselves on the 6-yard line of Dallas in a third-down-and short situation. The play selected was a quick pass to me, the halfback, on a play-action. As we ran the play, I was headed toward outside linebacker D. D. Lewis, who came across the line of scrimmage to take away my path. All of a sudden with the broken play we had to become a little flexible, so I cut in and around Lewis, while Bradshaw spun to the outside and looked for other options. I drifted backwards. He continued to his right with very little running room and it quickly became one of those moments where, bam, we spotted one another. I always tell people that it was a *time-stood-still-as-our-eyes-met-across-the-field* kind of a moment.

Terry threw the ball but it was so high, I couldn't tell if it was supposed to be a pass or if he was throwing it away. As I leaped up, I felt the thud of the ball in my hands. I was as surprised as anybody else in the stadium that I caught it and somehow landed in the end zone. Quite frankly, I didn't know I could jump that high. By a fisherman's tape measure, I must've been in the air about 18-19-20 feet. I forget. In fact, thinking back, yeah, I had to come down to catch the ball. That play made the cover of *Sports Illustrated*, so people kid me about it by saying, "Well it doesn't look like you jumped 18 feet." I tell them, "Actually I was coming down into camera range as they clicked it." That play gave us the 21-14 lead heading into the locker room.

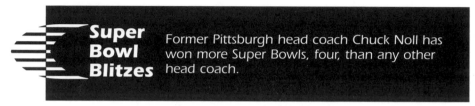

Super Bowl Blitzes Former Pittsburgh head coach Chuck Noll has won more Super Bowls, four, than any other head coach.

Catching that pass to give us the lead in the Super Bowl was incredible. It's a lot more special to catch a touchdown pass in a Super Bowl than in a regular season game. I think growing up we all had those Walter Mitty dreams in whatever we played in the backyard with our neighbors, or when we bounced a ball off the side of a building. In our minds we always put ourselves in that important situation ... the last play, with the clock ticking down, he dribbles to his left, now dribbles to his right, he's up, he scores and he wins! We've all done it. To have it actually happen makes it special beyond words.

That play gave us momentum going into halftime. We've all seen momentum change not only in halves and quarters, but also, on occasion, in minutes. Not a lot has to happen for momentum to change. All it takes is a fluke play, a broken play. In our game it was a great play or a great catch. It wasn't that Deede or anyone else made a mistake on that touchdown and blew the coverage, it simply was a broken play. Now we sit back and think, "Damn, how did that play happen for us to take the lead?"

We increased our lead in the second half to 34-17. Still, we couldn't count them out. All of a sudden, the momentum changed again on their part. They drove down the field in the fourth quarter and scored on a Roger Staubach pass to Billy Joe DuPree. The Cowboys were successful on the ensuing on-side kick when the ball bounced off our Tony Dungy and they fell on it. Besides having the momentum, the Cowboys also had the ball in the hands of one of the all-time great comeback quarterbacks in Staubach. They moved the ball down the field and scored to make it a 35-31 game with 22 seconds to play.

They were going to try another on-side kick. Our head coach, Chuck Noll, put in all his receivers and backs up front in hopes of one of us pouncing on the ball. There was a lot of pressure in that situation because of the Cowboys' capability and their momentum. No one wants to be the goat by having the ball bounce off them.

You kind of think, "Don't kick it to me, kick it someplace else." Of course the ball came straight ahead. I think they really wanted to bounce it, but it didn't work. Instead, it was a line drive right to me. That ball drilled the crap out of me. I pounced on it and then about 40 guys hit me all at once. Pure elation! That was the biggest hit I took in the whole game. That was such a relief because we got the on-side kick to win the game. It was over. We were once again Super Bowl champions.

Chuck was the driving force behind our success in the '70s. He was the man that was dedicated, and committed. He was a great teacher who understood both offensive and defensive schemes, and ran the show. Today, the head coach is the architect, but often the responsibility falls on the offensive and defensive coordinators. It's hard to tell if the offense and defense belong to the team, the head coach or one of the coordinators. Erase that thinking for us. At Pittsburgh it was Chuck Noll's offense. It was the same offense each year; from early in his career until the time he left. When you talk about Chuck Noll, you talk about continuity.

Unlike a lot of successful coaches, Chuck wasn't a workaholic. He wanted to have a normal family life. He wanted his assistant coaches to have normal lives. That was just as important to him as winning football games. For me specifically, I find myself saying some of the same things that Chuck used to talk about. And part of that philosophy carries over to everybody that he's ever touched. He certainly made a lasting impression on each of his players.

We had a lot of exciting times in Pittsburgh back then. It was incredible to be there and be part of what we now see as a dynasty. Going to the Super Bowl never became ho-hum or monotonous for me. The first one was special because it was the first one. That whole excitement of being able to be there and experience THE Super Bowl. And then to repeat the next year was great. Then, to win another one three years later, becoming the first team to win three, only to turn around the next year and win again to become the first team to repeat twice. Each Super Bowl took on a different significance. Each one was special.

Free agency has changed the complexion of football teams so much, that dynasties like we enjoyed are probably over. One reason for our success was that guys didn't change teams. We were able to establish continuity. I think if given free agency in the 1970s, some of our guys would have been gone. I don't think we would have accomplished what we did if there was free agency. The Steelers may not have been in Super Bowl XIII. Bradshaw and Franco Harris probably would have stayed there, but some other key personnel might have gone. Jack Lambert or

Jack Ham, for instance, might have left. It's the same thing that's happening today, where a guy comes up for a contract renewal and the team can't sign everybody, so that player leaves for a better offer. When that happens, continuity is gone.

With all the guys staying in Pittsburgh year after year, we knew what everybody was doing on the field and we respected their position. We had confidence in their abilities. It allowed us to just go out and play and have a great time. It's harder to do that today because everything is immediate. Teams have a two-to three-year window to develop continuity. If they don't capture it within that time frame, there's going to be turnover, because guys will sign with other teams. In our situation, we had 22 guys -the core- who played on all four of those Super Bowl championship teams in the 1970s. The glue keeping everyone together, as a part of that family, was Chuck Noll.

Chuck was one of the people who gave me a chance to stay in Pittsburgh. Ten years before I was in the Super Bowl, I had been injured in Vietnam and faced the possibility of not playing football again. At the time I never thought about it because my driving point was trying to go back and play. It wasn't as if I had other options or wanted to do anything other than play football. Ultimately for me, the opportunity was there to not only make the team, but to be an integral part of the offense. Every now and then I think how I've been pretty fortunate, pretty lucky, to be with organizations and their teams that allowed me to participate. That includes high school, college and especially the NFL with the Steelers.

Maybe in my case it's a story of perseverance, of not giving up. It's also a story of people who had faith in me and gave me opportunities, and how I tried to make the most out of those opportunities.

Super Bowl XIII

Date: January 21, 1979
Place: Orange Bowl, Miami, FL
Attendance: 79,484

AFC: Pittsburgh Steelers
Head Coach: Chuck Noll

NFC: Dallas Cowboys
Head Coach: Tom Landry

Pittsburgh	7	14	0	14	35
Dallas	7	7	3	14	31

Most Valuable Player: Terry Bradshaw (QB, Pittsburgh)

Super Bowl XIV

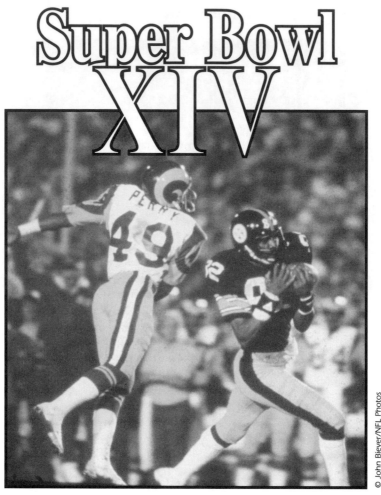

© John Biever/NFL Photos

*T*he Pittsburgh Steelers, three-time Super Bowl champions, were making their second bid at back-to-back NFL titles. They also were trying to become the first team in NFL history to win four Super Bowls. Behind the passing of Terry Bradshaw, who won back-to-back Super Bowl MVP awards, the Steelers were able to knock off the young Los Angeles Rams. Bradshaw, who threw three interceptions in the game, was 14-21 with 309 yards and two touchdowns. Steeler wide receiver John Stallworth (No. 82) caught the eventual game-winning touchdown pass early in the fourth quarter, a 73-yard catch and run play.

By the 1979 season, the Steelers were very much a veteran group. Except for one player. Kicker Matt Bahr was a rookie out of Penn State on that Pittsburgh team. He helped the Steelers get on the board first midway through the opening quarter with a 41-yard field goal.

Matt Bahr

The year leading to Super Bowl XIV was my rookie year with the Pittsburgh Steelers. I was like a college freshman working among men with multiple doctorates. Most had three Super Bowl victories in five years, many with more than 10 years in the league. Better than half of the starters should be in the Hall of Fame.

These guys won games whenever they really wanted to, at least that's how it seemed. There were so many offensive weapons; some were almost never utilized (tight end Bennie Cunningham comes to mind). There also were four or five guys who could score points any time they touched the ball. So many defensive standouts that rules were changed to compensate for their domination. Mel Blount was so defensive-minded that he wouldn't even let the wide receivers on the bus after the game. Quarterbacks knew there were at least 10 guys on our defense that could ruin a perfectly normal CAT scan. I have brought all this up to say how good these guys were. I never really appreciated their talent until many years and a couple teams later.

During my rookie season, as a sign of respect, I spoke to no one unless spoken to first. There was much of the typical rookie hazing that occurred (you were a "rookie" for your first four years, till you made pension) ... shaving cream, taping, picking up the bill, etc. -typical and good-natured. That all stopped when the game started. At that point you became a teammate regardless of the situation or your performance.

Super Bowl XIV was played in the famed Rose Bowl in Pasadena, Calif. One of the first things that immediately comes to mind when I think about that game is that the NFL provided each fan with a shiny, silver sheet of paper or cardboard, with something written on it. The sheet was about one-foot square. Nice idea, but with 103,000 fans using those shiny sheets in the Los Angeles sun all game, it was difficult not to be blinded.

Midway through the opening quarter we got on the board first against the Los Angeles Rams with my 41-yard field goal. It was nice to get that out of the way, but the thing that sticks out is that we tried an onside-type kick right after that field goal. Head coach Chuck Noll wanted me to chip the ball into a gap in the Rams' kick-off return unit. Unfortunately, it didn't work. They ended up getting the ball on our side of the field and eventually scored. By the end of the first half, the Rams led 13-10.

As strange as this may sound, I believe that game was won at halftime. There were many great plays and players in the game, but Jack Lambert (a man of few words) and Joe Greene (a man of many words) gave a halftime tongue lashing to all that were present. It was a wake-up call that we all needed. The play that sealed the game was early in the fourth quarter, with us leading 24-19, and Lambert made an interception on a play that, I believe, he was not sure what to do and just dropped back into coverage to help. Even champions sometimes get lucky.

Super Bowl Sunday: The Day America Stops

Jack had not said a word to me for my first eight weeks as a Steeler. The first game of the season was a Monday Night game for the defending champs on the road at New England. It went to overtime because I missed a field goal and an extra-point. Announcer Howard Cosell had written my epitaph and said everyone was witnessing my first and last game in the NFL. In overtime, a 42-yard field goal attempt on fourth-and-a-few yards was the decision presented to Chuck Noll. He asked the opinion of the great Jack Ham whether to kick or go for it. Ham said to Noll of me, "Have faith in him." We went out for the field goal and the Patriots called a timeout.

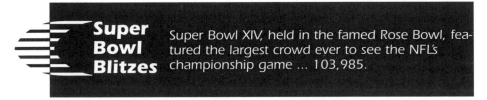

Super Bowl Blitzes Super Bowl XIV, held in the famed Rose Bowl, featured the largest crowd ever to see the NFL's championship game ... 103,985.

Lambert finally spoke to me for the first time. He was on the field goal protection team and he came back during the timeout and said, "We have all the confidence in the world in you." Those words mean as much to me today as they did then. Lambert defined why that was such a great team and he was such a great player, teammate and leader. As it turned out, I hit the field goal to give us the 16-13 win. It also was the 100th win of Chuck's career.

Yes, I was a dumb-ass rookie, deserving harassment, but I also was a teammate to be supported. All those guys were great teammates - Ham and Franco Harris; L.C. Greenwood and Greene; Blount, Rocky Bleier and Terry Bradshaw; Lynn Swann and John Stallworth; Mike Webster and the list goes on. Those guys are why that might be the best NFL team ever.

Toward the end of Super Bowl XIV, while the game was still in doubt, the Steelers started to put a drive together. Chuck Noll said he'd bet me 5-bucks on the likely field goal attempt. I agreed, though we'll never know who won the bet. We scored a touchdown to win the championship, 31-19.

Ironically, the next year, 1980, my brother, Chris, won a Super Bowl with the Oakland Raiders against the Philadelphia Eagles. Oakland was a team that, to my eyes, was like a motorcycle gang. They played hard on the field and partied hard off the field, dodging the law all along the way. They had fun winning wherever they were and whatever they were doing.

Chris is older and far wiser than me, so even though I had just experienced a Super Bowl championship, I didn't dispense any advice to him before their game. We've talked about our Super Bowls, but it isn't a main topic at the Thanksgiving dinner table. One thing I do remember, however, from their game with the Eagles is something that Oakland head coach Tom Flores told his team before the game. Dick Vermeil, an extreme workaholic, who had long, hard practices followed by 10 p.m. curfews and bed checks for his team, coached Philly. In the Super Bowl XV

⊙CBS SPORTS Presents

In the Trenches with Jerry Glanville

My biggest championship game memory is actually the NFL championship before the Super Bowl started. I was a 16-year-old sophomore in high school. This one goes back to 1957 between the Cleveland Browns and the Detroit Lions. I drove my car from Toledo, Ohio to Detroit. I didn't have enough money to park, so I had to pull the car into a bad neighborhood. Then, I didn't have a ticket so I stood at the corner of Michigan and Trumbull, and waited for halftime. At that time, the ticket price went down to $5.

I didn't know this when I bought the ticket, but my seat was behind a beam in the lower deck. (If the stadium were set up for baseball, I would have been behind home plate.) The lady next to me had fried all kinds of chicken. She looked at me and said, "I'll trade seats with you if you eat this chicken, because I think this game means more to you than it does to me."

And that was the first NFL championship game I ever saw. I never forgot that special feeling. I've never lost the feeling of sitting in that seat, splitting the chicken with that lady. No matter how long you live, you remember being at that first championship game.

pregame pep talk, Flores told his guys, "If they win, then his system must be correct." That motivation was enough for the free-spirited Raiders. (Chris got his second NFL championship two years later when the Los Angeles Raiders beat the Washington Redskins in the Super Bowl. I had to wait a few more years for my second championship.)

Super Bowl Blitzes

In Super Bowls XIII and XIV, each member of the Pittsburgh Steelers was truly a Steeler. Each player on those teams had played professionally for only the Pittsburgh organization.

In 1981, there was a period where I played for the San Francisco 49ers. Their kicker was hurt and they needed a temp for four weeks. After coming from the Steelers, you could see that Joe Montana, Ronnie Lott and company were a team destined for greatness. I said as much in a note I tagged to the team's bulletin board after I was traded to the Cleveland Browns, "GOOD LUCK IN THE SUPER BOWL". They didn't quite believe in themselves yet. When the Browns went into

---

◉*CBS SPORTS* Presents

In the Trenches with Mark May

On the first day of training camp in 1983, the camp following our Super Bowl XVII championship, head coach Joe Gibbs said, "Our goal [this year] is to get back to the Super Bowl. We're not a fluke team and there's no way they can say that we are a fluke team." We made it back to the Super Bowl but got crushed badly by the Raiders, 38-9. Gibbs told us the following year in training camp, "This is the goal. We're going to get back to the Super Bowl and we're going to win the Super Bowl. You guys did exactly what I wanted to do last year ... we got back to the Super Bowl, but you didn't win the game. Now our goal is to go back and win the Super Bowl." That's one of those memories of Joe that I'll never forget.

San Francisco that year and beat the 49ers, after the game I spoke to Eddie DeBartolo and told him, "You will win the Super Bowl." He laughed and said that if they did, he would definitely give me a Super Bowl ring. They did and he didn't. The 49ers dominated the 1980s with only five players being on all the teams.

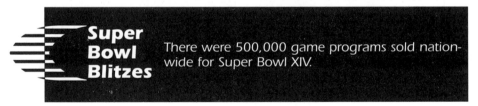

Super Bowl Blitzes

There were 500,000 game programs sold nationwide for Super Bowl XIV.

After 10 years with the Browns, I realized just how special that 1979 Steelers team was and how difficult it was to get that ring. In Cleveland, we had three championship game losses to those foul-bellied, stinking swine, bad-breathed and cursed Denver Broncos.

We had some terrific teams with the Browns, led by Brian Sipe and then Bernie Kosar. We played for the joy of the game but there also was great camaraderie on and off the field. Yet, realizing how hard it is to get to the Super Bowl, let alone how hard to win it, was a hard lesson to learn. In preseason of 1990, the year after their third championship game loss, the Browns fired me. If an NFL team firing me is the worst thing that happens in my life, then I have had one heck of a life.

Almost everyone I know who has won a Super Bowl says about the same thing. To win the conference championship game, the one that gets you to the Super Bowl, is the far more emotional high with great enthusiasm and excitement. To win the Super Bowl is exciting but there is an emotional low because you want to keep playing and keep winning. Instead, this terrific team that you've been with night and day for nearly six months, parts company and there are no more challenges until the next season.

The experience of winning Super Bowl XIV with the Steelers at the end of my rookie season was pretty incredible. It was great to get a Super Bowl ring; however, the most excited I got that year was when I saw myself on a bubble gum card. As a kid, I flipped cards (my Bob Feller card never lost) and put them in the spokes of my bike. Getting the Super Bowl ring was nice, but boy oh boy, that card...

Super Bowl XIV

Date: January 20, 1980
Place: Rose Bowl, Pasadena, CA
Attendance: 103,985

AFC: Pittsburgh Steelers
Head Coach: Chuck Noll

NFC: L.A. Rams
Head Coach: Ray Malavasi

Los Angeles	7	6	6	0	**19**
Pittsburgh	3	7	7	14	**31**

Most Valuable Player: Terry Bradshaw (QB, Pittsburgh)

Super Bowl XV

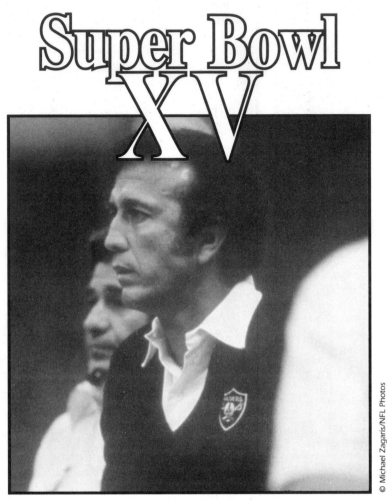

*I*n the history of the National Football League, there have been only two people who have played, served as an assistant coach, and as head coach in winning Super Bowls. One of the two, Tom Flores (pictured above), was fairly unknown early in his head coaching career. In fact, at a press conference for Super Bowl XV, his first as a head coach, Flores opened by introducing himself.

Making their first trip to the Super Bowl, the Philadelphia Eagles boasted a strong defense and a good offense. One member of the defensive line was Dennis Harrison. After a stellar career in the NFL, Harrison went into coaching. He was the head coach at Page High School in Franklin, Tenn. before becoming an assistant coach for the Vanderbilt Commodores under Woody Widenhofer. Super Bowl XV was Harrison's only trip to the NFL's championship game.

A few days after that press conference, behind quarterback Jim Plunkett's 261 yards passing and three touchdowns, Flores won his first head coaching Super Bowl ring.

Tom Flores

You're always surrounded by distractions (which isn't always bad) when you coach and play for the Oakland Raiders. You're always surrounded with innuendos. There was a lot of talk throughout the 1980 season about our pending move to Los Angeles from Oakland, and the debate between Al Davis and NFL Commissioner Pete Rozelle. Before Super Bowl XV against the Philadelphia Eagles, that turned into a big deal because there was a lot going on. It turned into one of the huge stories in the 1980s.

At the first press conference on Tuesday for the head coaches, I started off by saying, "I'd like to introduce myself. I am the head coach." Of course the reporters in that room had no sense of humor, nobody laughed. I thought, "Oh no, that bombed." One of the writers I knew from the Bay area, asked me why I introduced myself. I said because I didn't know if everyone knew who I was. All I read about was the Al Davis and Pete Rozelle feud, and Philadelphia head coach Dick Vermeil. It was always Dick Vermeil's Eagles but never my Raiders.

I had things to do to prepare for the Super Bowl and I couldn't be worried about Al. I know Al would never do anything to disgrace the trophy and the game. I knew Pete would be the same way. They both were friendly, but they were foes. Despite that they both had one thing in common, they loved the National Football League and they wouldn't do anything to degrade the league.

Even without that controversy, I knew it was anything but a typical Super Bowl week. Picture day was Tuesday at the Superdome, after which we were going to go to our practice facility for a light workout. The buses left me behind. I am standing there with two young players and we're looking at each other saying, "Well, there are no buses."

The three of us caught a cab and went to the workout at Tulane. Unfortunately, the cab driver didn't know how to get to the athletic department so when we got close I said, "There it is over there." I paid him and we walked across a muddy field. I was so ticked off; I didn't have time to even point fingers at anybody because I had to get practice underway. Then I started laughing. I couldn't help it after everything that could have gone wrong that week, did. Not only did the press not know who I was, I evidently needed to introduce myself to the team. How's that for humility. It was a humbling experience. To make matters more interesting before the Super Bowl, I got sick and didn't eat a solid meal until Thursday night. The week didn't start off very good.

We had played Philadelphia earlier that year, and lost to them in a close game. It was a defensive struggle all the way. I knew they were going to be very conservative, and I knew their defense was stingy, so, I didn't think the Super Bowl would be a high-scoring game. We were going to rely on some play-action and at some point go deep to Cliff Branch and utilize Kenny King's speed. By that time in the season, our defense was playing extremely well. It had gone from a loose defense early in the year to one of the stingiest. When that happened we played great. Still,

97

◉ CBS SPORTS Presents

In the Trenches with Lesley Visser

The great thing about sports and, specifically, the Super Bowl is that they're not scripted so you don't know what's going to happen. Super Bowl XXXIV, for instance, ended on the last play of the game. That's something great about sports. The other aspect of sports is that it is a wonderful passport ... for example, you can talk to a cab driver or a king about the Super Bowl. Everybody has an opinion.

I don't think anyone picked us to win, but I assumed we would.

Our defense continued to play solid in the Super Bowl. In the first quarter, Rod Martin had an interception, which we converted to the first points of the game. Martin finished with three interceptions.

There were a couple areas where we were sure we could get some big plays on the Eagles because of their style of defense. They played a zone-man principle, and we took advantage of that. One of the big strikes was a broken play where quarterback Jim Plunkett connected with Kenny King for an 80-yard touchdown play in the first quarter to put us up, 14-0. That was an improvised play because the guy we wanted to go to, who I think was Branch, wasn't open. Plunkett scrambled and found Kenny King. They adjusted well and King scored.

Jim was the last of the great warriors that called his own plays. He called all his own plays in both Super Bowls where he was the quarterback. I made the game plan, and I gave him plays from the sidelines. We talked about them in between series, and I gave him the first play.

I might have sent him a short-yardage play or a big play that I wanted, but more or less he called his own plays. A lot of people don't realize that Plunkett called his own plays. Other quarterbacks had plays sent in or signaled in. Plunkett called the game the way we wanted it. He had a good feel for the game, and he was in total control. He made big plays in big games. He did his whole life. That's my evaluation of great players; they play big and make big plays in big games.

To some people, Plunkett was an unlikely quarterback to lead our team. In fact, when we signed him in 1978, he had almost been out of football. While I was an assistant coach, he worked out for us under the eyes of Al Davis, John Madden and Ron Wolf. Plunkett became our third-string quarterback when we signed him that year, but when he played he did nothing but execute. He kept improving and helping the team win. In reality and retrospect, he probably should have been a starter for us two seasons later, 1980, but we traded a starter for a starter (Ken Stabler for Dan Pastorini), so Jim was second-string.

Even though we were up by 14 points after the Plunkett to King 80-yard touchdown play, it was still early; I wasn't ready to call off the dogs and bring out the starters. A head coach rarely feels confident about any lead. You feel good because you are in control of the game, but you worry that something might happen. The Eagles earned their right to be there by being the best in the NFC, so we didn't want to give them any life or any reason to rally back. We didn't, we just kept going, and we didn't alter our approach. I approached the game as if we were scoreless at halftime.

Another key for us was right before the half. Ted Hendricks blocked a field goal attempt by Philadelphia. That was huge because when the Eagles went to their locker room for the half, head coach Dick Vermeil was fuming, and they went in with their heads hanging down. That field goal would have given them a little bit of life. Instead, we held a 14-3 lead at the intermission.

We took the ball in the second half, moved it and put some more points on the board. The Eagles never really threatened and we won 27-10. I finally felt comfortable toward the latter part of the fourth quarter because we were in total control. Philadelphia was not a team that liked to pass a lot and come from behind. They were more of a ball-control type team with a strong defense. So when we went up by 17 points in the fourth quarter, I was pretty sure we would hold on for the win.

Winning the Super Bowl as a player, an assistant coach and a head coach is special in each situation, but it's also different. As a player you're involved in the actual execution of the game. As an assistant coach you're involved in making sure your guys are prepared. You also want to make sure you have all your stuff ready for the meetings and everything planned. As a head coach, you're overwhelmed with the media and you want to make sure the travel is taken care of. As I found out in Super Bowl XV, the responsibilities for a head coach are awesome.

Super Bowl Blitzes The 1969 Kansas City Chiefs, the 1980 Oakland Raiders and the 1997 Denver Broncos are the only teams that have won Super Bowl titles without winning their division.

Dennis Harrison

ate in the regular season in 1980, the Philadelphia Eagles defeated the
Oakland Raiders in Philadelphia. That win didn't really give us extra
confidence facing the Raiders in Super Bowl XV because in November, we
barely beat them, 10-7. We felt that we could control the game and it would be a
good one for us. Unfortunately, it didn't turn out that way.

We had some great players on that team and a great head coach, Dick Vermeil.
He is a tireless, hard-worker and a perfectionist. He was a great guy to play for.
That's why Brenard Wilson and I probably were the only two guys in Nashville
who were pulling for Vermeil and the St. Louis Rams against the Tennessee Titans
in Super Bowl XXXIV. My pulling for the Rams was nothing against the Titans,
because I was very happy for the season they had. However, for Dick to win that
Super Bowl was something special to see. I'm sure most of his former players felt
the same way that I did.

I worked a camp with Dick a couple of summers ago, so I knew a lot of those
guys on the St. Louis team. Working that camp was a great experience because
some of my old teammates were there working. Among those teammates were Carl
Hairston, Wilbert Montgomery and John Bunting. Three guys who I played with,
sweated with and bled with. It brought back a lot of great memories. Those friend-
ships that we built in Philadelphia, including with Dick, are everlasting.

If someone had told me before Super Bowl XV that the final score would be 27-
10, I wouldn't have believed them. Or, if I did believe them, I would have thought
it would be the other way around with us having 27 points. I felt that we'd be able
to score against the Raiders. We probably should have scored more. Three different
times when we drove down the field and were in range to score, Oakland linebacker
Rod Martin intercepted passes. Three times. Martin, I think, should have received
the most valuable player award. Instead, Oakland quarterback Jim Plunkett, who
threw for 261 yards and three touchdowns, was the MVP. I guess it was a quarterback thing.

The biggest key in the game, and it goes back to Martin and Plunkett, was
turnovers. We were in a position to score but didn't come away with any points
because of the interceptions; while Oakland's offense didn't commit any big
turnovers.

Late in the fourth quarter, it hit me that we weren't going to make a comeback to
win the game. Wide receiver Harold Carmichael usually was good for two big plays
each game and he hadn't had them yet. Until we were down by 17 points, after
Chris Bahr hit a field goal about halfway through the fourth quarter, we still had a
chance to win. Bahr's 35-yard field goal put the Raiders up, 27-10, which turned
out to be the final score.

A lot of people forget that Super Bowl XV was the same day when the hostages
in Iran were released. That was one of the few times when Super Sunday didn't
focus on the football game, and it shouldn't have been. More of the country's focus

100

was on the hostage situation, which is definitely where it needed to be. An amazing thing from that event was the big, yellow ribbon around the Superdome in honor of the hostages. It was great to see them honored with such an American symbol.

Even though we lost the game, it's still special to think that I was on a team that made it to the NFL's championship game. Think about all the great players who never reached a Super Bowl. When looking at the Super Bowl, everybody's hindsight seems to be better because when you're playing, you don't really think about the experience. You don't really think about the fact that you're one of a select few guys who have been in that game. Looking back, the Super Bowl was all that I could have imagined it to be.

Over the years, even in the 20 years since Super Bowl XV, the game obviously has gotten bigger and grander. It is broadcast to more countries, in more languages, and more money is involved. The game itself has stayed the same. I don't think the players like the media week. The teams that are playing well would rather just get right into playing and keep their momentum going instead of waiting two weeks. On the other side, having that extra week off helps the teams that have been banged up. It's still the Super Bowl and I shared a part of that history. To me that is something really special because not everybody gets to experience that game ... the biggest game in the world.

Super Bowl XV

Date: January 25, 1981
Place: Louisiana Superdome, New Orleans, LA
Attendance: 76,135

AFC: Oakland Raiders
Head Coach: Tom Flores

NFC: Philadelphia Eagles
Head Coach: Dick Vermeil

Oakland	14	0	10	3	27
Philadephia	0	3	0	7	10

Most Valuable Player: Jim Plunkett (QB, Oakland)

Super Bowl XVI

© Vernon Biever/NFL Photos

*A*s with Super Bowl IX, little did anyone know that while watching Super Bowl *XVI they were seeing the start of one of the greatest dynasties in the National Football League ... the San Francisco 49ers. Just like the 1974 Pittsburgh Steelers, the 1981 49ers were a young team with a bushel full of talent. At the top of that talent was head coach Bill Walsh, considered by many as the most innovative offensive coaches in the history of the game. His star pupil was quarterback Joe Montana, considered by many as best signal-caller in the history of the game. Walsh (far right) and Montana orchestrated a game plan against the Cincinnati Bengals in Super Bowl XVI that helped propel the San Francisco organization to its first of five Super Bowl victories. Even though he finished the game with an unimpressive 157 yards and one touchdown, Montana helped the 49er offense control the ball. For his efforts, "Joe Cool" was named the game's Most Valuable Player.*

Bill Walsh

When we defeated the Dallas Cowboys, 45-14, at home in the early part of the 1981 season, there was the feeling that it could be our breakout year. We had lost to the Cowboys by a huge score, 59-14, the previous year in Dallas, and at the time it didn't appear that we were establishing ourselves as a very competitive team or a team in competition for post-season honors, so to speak. With our young team we didn't know if we could go out every weekend and play the top teams with a very good chance of winning. We certainly were neophytes when it came to Super Bowls.

The week following the regular-season Dallas game in 1981, we went to Milwaukee and beat Green Bay. Then we came back two weeks after that and beat the Pittsburgh Steelers in Pittsburgh. They had defeated 17-straight NFC teams in Pittsburgh, but we went in and out-hit them and outplayed them physically. We won 17-14. Those were games that really established the foundation for our success in learning how to win key games.

We continued to take opponents, obviously, one game at a time and we kept winning. The Cowboys came back to San Francisco for the NFC Championship game. In those days, if the Cowboys lost, it was typical for them to say you didn't play the real Dallas team because their second-string guard was injured, or whatever excuse. There was always a reason why the real Dallas team didn't get beat. The NFL championship game was going to be the real Dallas against the only 49ers.

Although we outplayed Dallas the entire game, we found ourselves behind in the closing minutes, 27-21. Our offense drove 89 yards in 13 plays and scored with Dwight Clark making the now-famous catch on a pass from Joe Montana. Then we took ourselves seriously. Up until then we had no history of winning those kinds of games, so we were in the process of making our own history.

As the years passed, our attitudes changed as we matured and became more professional, in a sense. The next time we played in a Super Bowl, three years later, we were truly a great team. In games leading up to Super Bowl XVI, we managed to sometimes outwit or out-strategize the other team, or just make great plays. Virtually every game was tight, yet we came out on top, including the Super Bowl.

We were very confident going into Detroit for Super Bowl XVI against the Cincinnati Bengals. We liked our chances because we had beaten them 21-3 during the season, although we knew the Bengals really had a superior team talent-wise. There is no question they had an outstanding team. We were irrepressible, though, and thought nobody was going to stop us. Our guys were just young and innocent enough to think that we could beat anybody.

I arrived at the hotel before the player's buses, and to help break the tension I borrowed the bellman's jacket and cap. As the players were getting off the bus, I shook hands with them and welcomed them to Detroit. I'm not even sure if half of them recognized me. I looked ridiculous but it helped keep the attention away from the pressure of the Super Bowl.

Super Bowl Sunday: The Day America Stops

A disadvantage we had from the outset was that the NFL had not accounted for a West Coast team on the practice schedule in Detroit. There was a coin toss to see who practiced early in the morning. We lost the flip and were expected to practice at 8:00 in the morning, which is 5:00 a.m. our time. That means we were getting up at 3:30 in the morning our time, which was totally unfair. The NFL was callused not to appreciate the fact that we were from a different time zone. All week we were getting up so early in the morning that we were in a state of general fatigue as the game drew closer. Evidently, the halftime band took priority over the teams when it came to using the Pontiac Silverdome, because they had to use the field to rehearse during the day and night.

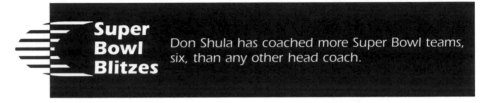

Super Bowl Blitzes — Don Shula has coached more Super Bowl teams, six, than any other head coach.

The Super Bowl week schedule is so hectic that you don't have a chance to adapt to the time zone switch. To accommodate our practice times, we had guys trying to go to sleep early in the evening. That was really a mess. I was operating on my last nerve because of the situation. The Bengals leisurely slept in and went over to practice in the afternoon. The weather was inclement, so we couldn't go outside to prepare. That really made it tough. But when game time came around, we were ready to play and did very well.

On the day of the game, we had three buses taking the team from the hotel to the Silverdome. The first bus made it to the stadium without any problems. The bus carrying most of the players and coaches (including me) was the second one. It just so happened that Vice President George Bush was in Detroit for the game, and his entourage of 30 cars had stopped traffic on all the freeways in the area, including ours. From where we were stopped, we could see the stadium just over the hill about a mile away.

Of course, it was probably 10 or 15 degrees outside with a strong wind and snow on the ground. (January isn't the best time to go sight seeing in Detroit.) Looking at that hill between the stadium and us I could see where cows had made a path over the top. We were so tight on time that I was ready to take the team cross-country on the cow path to get to the stadium. My biggest concern was how the guys would play in the game after taking that hike.

Once we were stopped, we had no idea when we'd start moving again. The only thing you know when you're stuck in traffic is that you could be there for an hour. We waited. We didn't move for probably 15 minutes. Then we moved a car length. It still didn't appear that we'd make it to the game. Just about the time I had decided we were going to make that cross-country trek in the frigid cold, carrying whatever gear was on the bus, the traffic began to clear a little bit. In the meantime,

⊙CBS SPORTS Presents

In the Trenches with Sam Wyche

Sixteen was a magic number for the 49ers in 1981. It was Super Bowl XVI. We won 16 games. If you took the ages of all the players and added them up, they were divisible by 16. The Super Bowl MVP's number was 16 (Joe Montana). Therefore, the Super Bowl rings were supposed to have 16 diamonds. The first set of rings from the manufacturer had 17 diamonds in it instead of 16. The first rings they made went to the people with short last names. My name only has five letters, so I got one of the rings with 17 diamonds. So all the hard work and planning that went into the ring to match-up with the magic number 16 got completely screwed up in the design. Sometimes there's no justice to any of this.

to keep everybody loose, I stated to everyone that the game had started and we were ahead 3-0, and that our equipment man, Chico Norton, kicked the field goal. It was pretty cute.

We were just young enough and crazy enough to not feel the pressure at all of the NFL's championship game. We had a number of players who were just outstanding in their first season that year like Ronnie Lott, Eric Wright and Carlton Williamson; guys who didn't know a Super Bowl from a Rose Bowl. Big games were nothing new to them after playing in the top college bowl games. All these different guys saw the Super Bowl as playing another bowl game with these stakes a little bit higher. Their attitudes were outstanding. That was really an enjoyable, exciting, fun moment and time in my life and in theirs.

We were supposed to open the game with possession of the football. Amos Lawrence returned the opening kick off 17 yards for us, but fumbled on the 26, giving the ball to the Bengals. They drove down inside the 10-yard line but were moved back on a couple big defensive plays. On third-and-11, Dwight Hicks intercepted a pass by Cincinnati quarterback Ken Anderson at the goal line. Dwight, who was an outstanding player, returned the ball to the 32-yard line. We drove the length of the field on that first drive and scored. For us, things went like clock work. The Bengals were an outstanding team, but with guys like Montana and Clark, and everyone else, we picked their defense apart and scored. On Cincinnati's opening drive of the second quarter, the Bengals made another run at us, but we got the ball, drove the length of the field and scored again to go up 14-0.

Joe wasn't affected by anything that day except playing football. He is such a great competitor and was so completely within himself when he played. He is the most unique human being who could function well under any circumstances. Joe

(14-22,157 yards) didn't have a great day statistically like Anderson (25-34, 300 yards), but he got the job done. Whenever we needed a drive, we got it from him. He didn't make any mistakes and was named the game's most valuable player.

Ray Wershing, our field goal kicker, had a great season. We won any number of games by three points. The last time we had been in Detroit for a game, Wershing didn't squarely hit the kick-off because he pulled a hamstring. When he missed the kick, the ball bounced and bounced. Nobody could field it because it kept taking crazy bounces on the artificial surface. I figured, what the heck, let's practice a few of those during Super Bowl week.

On our third and fourth kick offs that day, Wershing intentionally bounced the ball. It bounced up in the air and the Bengals weren't ready for it. The first time, our special teams buried the Bengals inside their 5-yard line. Our defense held them, and eventually Wershing kicked a field goal. On the ensuing kick off, Wershing again bounced the ball. This time, Archie Griffin couldn't hold on to the ball, and we recovered it. We came away with three more points to take a 20-0 lead into halftime. It was precarious; yet we were winning. Not only were we ahead, we were doing so on all these different devices that we were using.

In the second half, Cincinnati woke up. After the Bengals scored early in the third quarter, they got the ball back and moved it inside the 5-yard line. However, our defense did a remarkable job of stopping them on one of the great goal-line stands in history, from the 1-inch line. Our defense continued to hold off Cincinnati throughout the second half. Wershing kicked two more field goals, and we held on for the 26-21 win. Our first Super Bowl championship! I couldn't believe it. The atmosphere was crazy, euphoric.

One thing that Super Bowl coaches don't think about during their game preparation (or, at least, they don't admit it) is the post-game phone call from the President of the United States. I definitely wasn't prepared when President Ronald Reagan called. To worsen matters the noise in the locker room was deafening, you could hardly hear. Unfortunately, I had nothing to say; it was hapless. My first comment was something to the effect of, "I figured you might call." He mentioned something about winning it for the Gipper, and I said, "Oh, we could have used you today." I wish I had been a little more thoughtful or articulate when he called. I didn't handle that worth a darn. Oh, but I probably always will remember it.

When we went back to the hotel after the game, I left my briefcase in the bus and had to go get it. When I tried to get back into the hotel, the door was locked. They wouldn't let anyone else in the building, including me. My team was in there celebrating, but I was stuck in the freezing cold. It was so cold you couldn't even function. I was pounding on the doors, but nobody would look. I had to keep going back to the bus to warm up. It took me a half an hour to get back into the hotel! It probably would have felt a lot colder outside had we lost the game.

Before we went back to San Francisco, people told me there was going to be a victory parade. I said, "Oh no, don't have a parade. Nobody's going to go to a football parade." I really asked them to cancel it. The thought was ridiculous. We arrived in San Francisco the next day and rode in trolley cars with wheels on them.

There we were, riding along Front Street in San Francisco. There was a smattering of people on the street, but nothing to disprove my inkling. I just knew it was going to be so humiliating, tying up traffic with these silly cable cars on wheels while everybody was at work.

We turned the corner up Market Street and there they were ... about 200,000 people. Unbelievable! There were people hanging from every lamp post, every window, climbing on their stepladders. People of every ethnic group imaginable, every age group, rich and poor. They were all in this parade crowd together, in universal acclaim. The noise was incredible. If there is a tape around of that parade, I'd like to see it again some day. It was just unbelievable. That was definitely the greatest year of my life as far as football is concerned.

Super Bowl XVI

Date: January 24, 1982
Place: Pontiac Silverdome, Pontiac, MI
Attendance: 81,270

AFC: Cincinnati Bengals
Head Coach: Forrest Gregg

NFC: San Francisco 49ers
Head Coach: Bill Walsh

San Francisco	7	13	0	6	26
Cincinnati	0	0	7	14	21

Most Valuable Player: Joe Montana (QB, San Francisco)

Super Bowl XVII

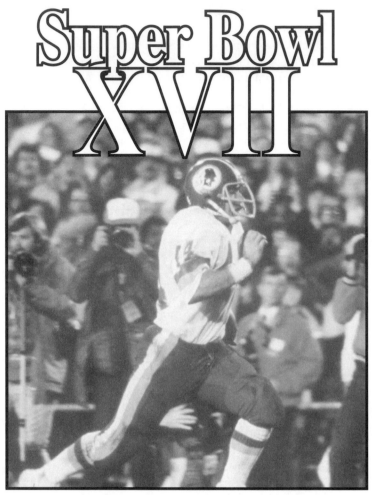

*U*nder head coach Joe Gibbs, the Washington Redskins were becoming a team that the San Francisco 49ers would have to reckon with in the National Football Conference. On the heels of the 49ers' Super Bowl XVI win, the Redskins headed into Super Bowl XVII behind a strong running attack featuring John Riggins (above). In the team's three playoff games heading into the Super Bowl, Riggins had rushed for more than 100 yards. Things didn't change in the Super Bowl. Behind the famed offensive line known as "The Hogs," Riggins amassed 166 yards and one touchdown in being named the game's MVP. In contrast, the Miami Dolphins had a total of 176 yards ... for the game.

One vital member of "The Hogs" was Mark May. However, May cracked two ribs in the NFC championship game against the Dallas Cowboys and saw limited action against the Dolphins. This was only the second time in 16 years that the NFL/NFC repeated as Super Bowl winners. Green Bay's victories in Super Bowls I and II was the other time it happened.

Mark May

Leading up to Super Bowl XVII, as Washington Redskins we were in awe because we didn't know what to expect since none of us had been that far in the playoffs before. We were a very young football team. At least 30 percent of that team was players with two years of experience or less.

For this to happen at such a young age for most of us was amazing. On the other side of the field was this Miami Dolphin team led by head coach Don Shula. Just the name of Don Shula at that time made people shake, because even at that time he was one of the best coaches in NFL history. There is a nostalgia that circles Shula. We had to figure out what he would come up with in that game to try and defeat us.

It was Miami's "Killer Bees" against "The Hogs" of Washington. It was one of those games where the fans were really into it. Ideally in that type of game a player needs to concentrate as much as possible on the game and the game preparation, but it was difficult because we were all 21-22 year old kids at the time.

Those two weeks before the Super Bowl are agonizing because there are so many plans with family and friends. People you haven't seen since junior high school call you for tickets, and everyone wants interviews. It's a long period. I liked the one week scenario because the day after the conference championship, you're on a plane headed for the Super Bowl but it's just getting ready for another game. There's not as much time with one week for people to track you down and distract you. They mean well, but they don't realize that your head is spinning in a thousand different ways thinking about the Super Bowl. A lot of players tend to forget that they are there to win the Super Bowl. Being as young as we were, it might have been easy for us to forget that fact before Super Bowl XVII, but head coach Joe Gibbs wouldn't let that happen.

The thing about Joe is that he was always straight and narrow. Here's a guy that you could pass in the hallways five times and he wouldn't say a word because he was concentrating and focused on something. Then, the sixth time you'd walk by him and he'd say, "Hey, Mark, how are you doing? How's your dad doing? I haven't seen him in awhile. Hey, how are your horses?" You're left scratching your head.

Joe was great at delegating to his assistant coaches exactly what he wanted them to do. He trusted Richie Petitbon on the defensive side, and Dan Henning and Joe Bugel on the offensive side. They were Gibbs' lieutenants to get things done on each side of the ball.

One thing about Gibbs, though, he would not shy away from calling plays. He let his coordinators call most of the plays but he still had a lot of input from the sidelines. For instance, there were times when Petitbon wanted to sit back in a prevent defense and Joe would say, "Let's go get 'em. If we've been successful at going after the quarterback and shutting them down, let's go get 'em." He didn't like trick plays but he had special plays installed every week.

I remember one time when we were first going to try the shotgun. Quarterback

Super Bowl Sunday: The Day America Stops

Joe Theismann said, "Yeah, we can use the shotgun, we can get rid of the ball, we can do this." In practice, Jeff Bostic snapped the ball, and it hit Theismann in the ankle, then on the chin. So they put Russ Grimm in to snap, and the ball hit Theismann in the side. Finally, Gibbs said, "We're not doing this. This is like a cheap suit; it's not us. We're never going to use the shotgun." We never did.

Gibbs and the staff he put together were great guys and great people to be around. It was a great time, a fun time. As players we were a very tight-knit group. Because we were so close and had such a great coaching staff, we were going to have a good football team.

One thing about our coaching staff before Super Bowl XVII is that our coordinators and line coaches were up for NFL head coaching jobs. Normally these guys ran around in T-shirts and shorts. Since they were up for head jobs, they were walking around carrying brief cases, going to practice wearing dress shirts and ties. That was kind of funny because we'd never seen it before. We didn't know those guys even owned ties.

We knew it was going to be a physical game with Miami. We knew the Dolphins' defense was very aggressive, but they were small. Joe Bugel told us before the game that if we kept pounding on them, since we were bigger than they were, they would wilt in the fourth quarter. As it turned out, he was right.

The game was tight until John Riggins broke for a 43-yard touchdown run early in the fourth quarter. Once he did that, even though we only went up by a 20-17 score, we felt like we had the momentum. We didn't necessarily feel comfortable, but we had the lead.

Riggins was always very quiet, particularly on the sidelines. He wouldn't say a word if he had a mouthful, but when he did say something everybody just stopped and listened. He would say maybe five words in the course of the game. He didn't have to talk much because he is a guy who knew what to do with the football. If he got the ball, he was going to pick up yardage. He picked up the yardage against the Dolphins. On his way to being named the game's most valuable player, Riggins ran for 166 yards -a Super Bowl record at that time. We went on to win the game 27-17.

Memories of Super Bowls are funny. Often, actual plays don't stick out as much as instances from the game. Little goofy things often stick out as much as anything else. For instance, the guy on the PA system mispronounced the name of one of our players when he entered the game. It distracted the player so much during the next play that he almost forgot he was on the field to play. The overall experience of the Super Bowl was great, but the little things and quirky things that happen on the field are things that I'll never forget.

There are various reception parties and all that stuff after the Super Bowl but guys don't realize yet that they're a Super Bowl champion. On the plane ride back the idea starts to seep in. The day you get your ring is when it hits. You know when you have the ring in your hand that no one can ever take it away from you. Well, almost. I'll turn the rings into pendants for my daughters to have when they graduate from college.

Thinking about it now, I appreciate the Super Bowl experience much more because I realize how hard it is to get there. I played with some players who were in the league 12-14 years but never went to a Super Bowl. Look at Bruce Mathews of the Tennessee Titans. He went to his first one in 1999 after 17 years of playing; and he still hasn't won one. Some players can go through a terrific career and never go to a Super Bowl, while others can experience a championship win during their first season.

My second year in the NFL was the first time we won the Super Bowl. I didn't take it all in because I was so young. Then to get back there the next year made it easy to think we're going to go all the time...it's no big deal. And then all of a sudden it was four years before we went again. I realized how hard it is to get there.

When we went to Super Bowl XXII, I took everything in, because I knew that I might never get back to another one. It was one of those situations where I wasn't going to forget anything. I was possibly the first player that started taking a camcorder and taping everything that was happening. There was no way in the world that I was going to forget the experience, because I knew how hard it was to get back.

I stick that tape in the VCR every once in a while. Sometimes my daughters will ask, "Dad, you played in the Super Bowl, right?" To which I proudly reply, "Yeah, come back here to the television; let me show you something..."

Super Bowl XVII

Date: January 30, 1983
Place: Rose Bowl, Pasadena, CA
Attendance: 103,667

AFC: Miami Dolphins
Head Coach: Don Shula

NFC: Washington Redskins
Head Coach: Joe Gibbs

Miami	7	10	0	0	**17**
Washington	0	10	3	14	**27**

Most Valuable Player: John Riggins (RB, Washington)

Super Bowl XVIII

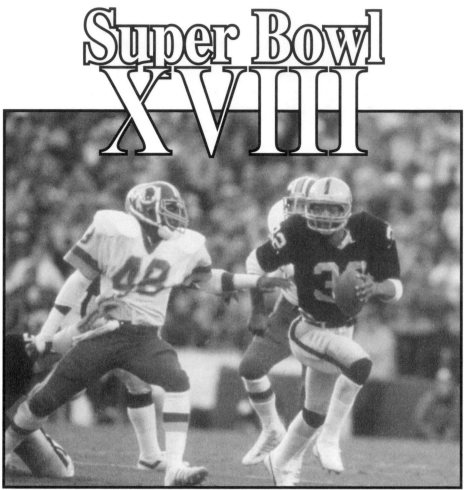

*R*emember the idea from Super Bowl XVII that the Washington Redskins appeared to be a team headed for dynasty status in the NFL? In 1983, the Redskins once again put together an impressive run through the regular season, finishing with a record of 14-2. On the other side, after a two-year absence, the Oakland ... uh, Los Angeles ... Raiders returned the NFL's showcase event, again under head coach Tom Flores. The Raiders went into the game with a record of 12-4. The two teams played each other during the regular season, as Washington won 37-35 on their home field. On paper, Super Bowl XVIII was a super match-up.

In the most lop-sided Super Bowl, the Raiders demolished the Redskins, 38-9. Raiders' running back Marcus Allen (above #32) was the star of the game with 191 yards and two touchdowns on 20 carries. His most exceptional run was on the last play of the third quarter when he set a Super Bowl record with a 74-yard touchdown sprint.

Tom Flores

We had a great team in 1980 when we won Super Bowl XV, but we didn't start out as a great team. Cliff Branch was already on that team and we picked up Burgess Owens, Kenny King and Bobby Chandler. We had Dwayne O'Steen and Cedrick Hardman. We picked up guys that had a year or two left and they gave us a great year. Then we went through a quarterback controversy. We were 2-3 when our quarterback, Dan Pastorini, broke his leg. All of a sudden a guy who hadn't played since who knows when, Jim Plunkett, resurrected us. We got it done, and that was, I think, one of the great stories in the history of the game.

However, in 1983, the regular season leading up to Super Bowl XVIII, we were loaded with great players. We had great defensive and offensive big-play guys such as Lyle Alzado, Howie Long, Matt Millen, Ted Hendricks, Rod Martin, Lester Hayes, Mike Haynes, Vann McElroy, Marcus Allen, Todd Christensen, Branch and Plunkett. We also had a punter named Ray Guy, who turned out to be one of the best punters in the history of the NFL. We were a great team.

Going into the Super Bowl, I thought it was going to be a wild game with the Redskins because we had already played a wild one with them that season. They had just broken the scoring record in the National Football League, and I didn't know if we could stop them. Once again, as in 1980, by the time we reached the Super Bowl, our defense was playing exceptionally well.

Our incentive going into the game was that we had played Washington earlier in the year; just liked we had played Philadelphia in 1980 prior to Super Bowl XV. We lost each of those games, but we came back and beat both teams in the Super Bowl. The fact we had played them both in the regular season is what helped us, not the fact that we had lost to them.

On special teams and defense, we had two key plays that took everything out of the Redskins. One play people don't think about being big, if they even remember it, was earlier in the second quarter. Ray Guy was punting from the 30-yard line. The ball sailed over his head, went up in the air, he grabbed the ball with one hand, came down, and not missing a step punted it inside their 20-yard line. That ball would have gone over any other punter's head.

Right before halftime we held a 14-3 lead but the Redskins had the ball deep in their own territory. They had been in a similar situation in our loss to them earlier in the year. At that time, the Redskins ran a screen play to Joe Washington, who ran 67 yards to inside our 10-yard line. Late in the second quarter of the Super Bowl, our defensive coordinator, Charlie Sumner, remembered that screen earlier in the year. He took Millen out of the game, sent in Jack Squirek, and called a zone, which was a defense where everyone dropped off, but we locked on Washington. Millen was furious, hotter than a pistol, because he came out of the game. About 10 seconds later he was picking up Charlie off the ground and hugging everybody because Squirek picked off the Joe Theismann pass and ran it in for a touchdown. It's funny how emotions will change in this world. That play gave us a 21-3 lead at

⊙**CBS SPORTS** Presents

In the Trenches with Jerry Glanville

When I went in to coaching, I refused to go to the Super Bowl unless my team was playing. I boycotted it. If I wasn't going to be coaching in the game, I didn't want to be there. As a result, I missed a lot of Super Bowls. The first time I went was after I got into broadcasting.

halftime. That was huge.

I was surprised we were able to do what we did against the Redskins' defense, especially Marcus Allen. He wasn't going to be the main go-to guy in Super Bowl XVIII, but he always was our main runner. We threw to him a lot because that was part of our offensive style. His main responsibility was being the main ground gainer. The normal big-play guys were Branch and Christensen. Marcus had a great game. He finished with a Super Bowl record 191 yards and two touchdowns. Marcus Allen turned regular plays into big plays because of his talent.

In the postgame ceremony, Commissioner Pete Rozelle said that I was one of the greatest coaches in the game. That meant a lot because I had not received a lot of recognition in my coaching career even though that was my second Super Bowl in five years as a head coach. I was proud of that fact, but you never heard my name mentioned. And still you don't. So Pete's comment meant a lot to me because he said it on national television. Al Davis reinforced it by saying that I was one of the greatest coaches in the history of the game, and the Raiders team is one of the best in the history of football. It felt good to be recognized.

In 1980 we barely won the wild card against a pretty good Houston team. We barely beat Cleveland in Cleveland. And had we not had the ball last in San Diego, we might not have been able to stop the Chargers' great offense. Ted Hendricks came off the field and said to Plunkett, "Don't give them the ball back. We can't stop them." We held it for eight minutes at the end of the game because they were so tough offensively. That wasn't the case in 1983. The 1983 Oakland team was as good of a team as I have ever been associated with as a player or as a coach. We annihilated every team in the playoffs. Our games weren't even close. In our last four games of the season (including one regular season and three postseason), we scored at least 30 points while our opponents scored no more than 14 points.

In each Super Bowl, it hit me the next day that I was a Super Bowl champion. The night of the game you're still numb from the game. You go to the party, you get up in the middle of the night to be on television, and then you're exhausted and you're flying home. There is just this warm glow of knowing that you're the best. And then sometimes you're sad because it's over. It's a pretty good roller coaster ride.

Super Bowl XVIII

It's hard to put the fact that you're a Super Bowl champion in words because there is one every year. However, that year you were the best in the world at what you did. They can't ever take that away from you. They can never take this game away because you are the best in the world and it's in the history books. When a guy wears that ring, he's part of history. That's a tremendous feeling.

Super Bowl XVIII

Date: January 22, 1984
Place: Tampa Stadium, Tampa, FL
Attendance: 72,920

AFC: L.A. Raiders
Head Coach: Tom Flores

NFC: Washington Redskins
Head Coach: Joe Gibbs

Washington	0	3	6	0	9
L.A. Raiders	7	14	14	3	38

Most Valuable Player: Marcus Allen (RB, Los Angeles)

Super Bowl XIX

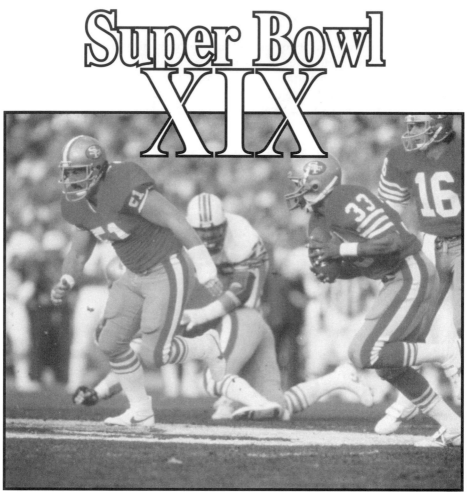

© George Rose/NFL Photos

*R*ightly so, going into the game, Super Bowl XIX was billed as Miami head coach Don Shula against San Francisco head coach Bill Walsh; and Miami quarterback Dan Marino against San Francisco quarterback Joe Montana. Even at that time, those were four of the best in their respective positions to step onto the football field. Unfortunately for the Dolphins, the 49ers were too explosive on offense and too stingy on defense. San Francisco finished the game with 537 total yards.

Super Bowl XIX was San Francisco's second championship.

Randy Cross (left #51, along with Roger Craig #33, and Montana #16) was a key component to the 49ers' offensive line. Cross is currently a key component of CBS Sports' NFL team.

Randy Cross

During my career with the San Francisco 49ers, I played on three Super Bowl teams. Each of the three teams was so unique, just in personalities. The first team, in XVI, was very much a young team. I always call them the "happy dummies," because we didn't know any better. The best example of our attitude was on the bus after the game and Dwight Clark looked at me and said, "Who's next?" We didn't have much of an idea. In Super Bowl XXIII we were a pretty crummy team halfway through the year. A record of 6-5 after 11 games doesn't really scream Super Bowl.

The 1984 team was flat-out dominant. We just threw the balls out as if to say, "O.K., we're going to kick your butt." Our mentality going into games that whole season wasn't wondering if we were going to win but rather by how many. The 1984 San Francisco team was the best team I played on.

There are some strange things that stick out from Super Bowl XIX. For instance, the fact the game was being played at Stanford Stadium. Stanford was actually a lot closer to our facilities than Candlestick was. Stanford was right in our back yard. Literally. After the experience of Super Bowl XIX, I wouldn't wish a home Super Bowl on anybody. You have more friends, more family, more business acquaintances, more everything at home. It's hectic enough to be in the Super Bowl, but if you do it at your own place, in your own city, watch out. You'll have friends and contacts that you never even knew you had.

I remember the media, in general, making such a huge deal out of the Miami Dolphins, in spite of the fact that we were 15-1 and they were 14-2. It was like we were the underdog. We had Joe Montana, Roger Craig, Wendell Tyler, Dwight Clark, Freddie Solomon, a lot of excellent football players, and we were sort of the "other" offense. That was actually the best thing that could have happened to us. We had stormed through opponents that year. For all the hype about our offense, we had some great talent on defense, which we always thought was something people didn't understand. Miami quarterback Dan Marino learned to appreciate those guys up close and personal in XIX.

I still contend, and every time I get around former Miami Dolphin Nick Buoniconti or any of those other undefeated guys, I have to remind them, "How many times did you guys win 18 games? I know you were 17-0, but how many times did you win 18? Let's put a short list together of the teams that have done that. Who was the first team to do that? Oh, yeah, it was the 49ers, thank you very much."

Early, it was a close game. We were behind a freckle or two in the first quarter. After we started hitting them and physically started getting after the Dolphins in the second quarter, they never reacted. Our defense slammed them back and then their defense went from the "killer bees" to just the "bees." We didn't see many killers. That is a less intimidating name when you drop that one word.

Montana had the ability to make a lot of defenses seem less intimidating. When

117

fans think about Joe, they imagine him as this inspirational guy in the huddle with all these great ideas; epic, like something out of the "Iliad and the Odyssey" with the quotes and the heroic measures. In reality, Joe was just Joe. He was a normal person until he strapped on the helmet and started playing quarterback. Then a lot of times it wasn't fair. We had a lot of great players, Hall of Fame players. But Joe was the guy that we knew if he played anywhere from his average -which was career best for some guys- we had a 90 percent chance of winning from the get-go. Now, if a defense could frustrate him through the offensive line and the rest of our offense, the opponents had a shot. If we could protect him, he would just carve teams up. That's when it reached the not fair stage.

I remember one instance when we were watching game films with our offensive line coach, Bobb McKittrick, who had probably seen the tape umpteen times already. He said, "Guys, you're about to see a play you're never going to believe. But this play is going to show you why you've got to protect our quarterback every single time for as long as you possibly can." He got up and drew the play on the board, and then said, "Now, the x is supposed to do this and the z is supposed to do this. The tight end is supposed to curl over the ball and the last receiver in this deal is the running back. Just a little dump out in the flat. Now watch what Joe does with this."

He turned on the tape and everybody started watching their routes. On the play, Joe bought a little extra time and suddenly on the back side, a safety kind of stumbles. He didn't fall down, just stumbled. Suddenly, Joe planted and threw the ball back across the other way to the x, the receiver across the other side of the field. I don't remember if it was a touchdown or a gigantic play, but Bobb was sitting there laughing. There you go. The defense ran that play perfectly. That one guy just sort of hesitated a little bit and he was dead.

We got almost callused to Joe's abilities after awhile. To be honest, that way of playing football, that way of running an organization, that way of performing as a quarterback, I was around it so long, I figured everybody did it that way. Then I got into TV and started going around the league and said, "Hmmmm, I guess that was pretty special back then."

Each Super Bowl was equally special to me because they were so different. The first time, of course, was the first time and that was an unbelievable experience. That team had more fun than most states allow. The 1984 team was dominant. And that's as dominant of a three-year period as we've seen in the league, considering the 1984 49ers, the 1985 Chicago Bears and the 1986 New York Giants lost a total of four games. That was something incredible.

It's pretty amazing, when I look back on the focus that we had to find and maintain in that ever elusive and mythical zone that teams really have to be in. Teams don't sort of happen into that area. It takes a certain mentality, a certain determination. It's hard to describe. Teams also have to have the type of owner who is obsessed with winning because it all trickles down. We had an owner that was obsessed with it, we had a coach who was obsessed with it, and they built an organization where winning was the only idea. Eddie DeBartolo was a wonderful owner for this franchise. Bill Walsh is the best coach on paper, in person, at halftime, and probably during the week of game-planning that I ever saw.

The first day we went to camp, we didn't talk about having a winning record, we didn't talk about going to the playoffs, we talked about winning the Super Bowl. We won it three times when I was there, and the organization won the championship five times in a stretch of about 15 years. It takes that single-mindedness and obsession that starts from the top.

Like the Pro Bowl, there's only one thing worse than having never played in one Super Bowl... it's playing in only one. Then you know what you're missing. If you have no point of reference, you can just sort of longingly say, "I'd like to someday play in the Super Bowl." Until you've played on that stage and in that game, and especially until you've won one, there is no other description than to say it's bigger than the World Series and the NBA finals.

It's the only format short of golf and tennis where you just sort of put it up there and say let's go get it, and it produces consequently some of the more memorable moments both in the positive and the negative in sports.

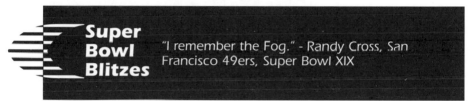

Super Bowl Blitzes

"I remember the Fog." - Randy Cross, San Francisco 49ers, Super Bowl XIX

Super Bowl Sunday: The Day America Stops
Bill Walsh

The fact that we were playing Super Bowl XIX in Stanford Stadium didn't really hit me at first. Sure, I knew it was Stanford and that we would be playing close to home, but my personal history didn't enter in the picture. Once we walked in and I had a minute to reflect, I looked across that stadium and the emotion of it struck me. Nobody saw, but I broke down a little bit. Of course my college teams had played there when I coached at Stanford. With the Cardinal, we had some great victories and some tough losses in that stadium.

What a return "home." After all the incredible memories I had of that place as a college coach, I was standing there as a NFL coach, in the biggest game in football. The emotion was incredible when I saw that stadium and thought about it in those terms. I couldn't help but wonder, "What am I doing here? Just a couple of years ago, I was in here playing Illinois or somebody. Now here we are playing for the world's championship." It was overwhelming.

The 49ers had improved since our Super Bowl XVI championship. We had such a good team. Miami, our Super Bowl XIX opponent, was a very good team, but wasn't as complete as we were. Of course, they had quarterback Dan Marino and his receivers. And they had a great record of 14 - 2. They may have even been favored in that game; however, going into it, we didn't concern ourselves with that. We knew what we were capable of doing. Our defense was faster, bigger and better than theirs. Offensively we were very comparable, but we could move the ball on the ground much better than the Dolphins could. We definitely had a better ground game with Roger Craig and Wendell Tyler.

The game started out close in the first quarter. Actually, at the end of the first quarter we trailed 10-7. Our offense started rolling in the second quarter and we took control. Quarterback Joe Montana put up some big numbers with 331 yards passing and three touchdowns (he also ran for a touchdown). Craig and Tyler also had very good games. Really, as I suspected, we had a great team performance.

We dominated so much, I had to hold down the score. On one drive we had the ball on the 2-yard line, and instead running a play to circle around the line for a walk into the end zone, I tried to run up the middle. There was no question in my mind that we could have easily put more points on the board. I just didn't think the score should go higher. As I look back now, after seeing some of the other Super Bowl blowouts, I wish we had scored another touchdown. Instead, we won 38-16.

We're not likely to see another dynasty in the NFL like we had in San Francisco, although the St. Louis Rams look like they're headed toward one. Green Bay looked like it was headed toward just a couple of years ago, as did Denver. It's so hard to tell what is going to happen with organizations from year to year. I don't know how to predict whether or not there will be any more dynasties in the National Football League. You definitely have to keep the same people together for a period of time and not be distracted by contracts and things of that nature. Our players were well paid, yet we had contract problems.

Today, so many different things come in to play such as agents, free agency and the salary cap. It's much tougher to sustain a winning tradition. It's not as hard to get to the top, there's no question about that. Teams today can get there in a hurry. As far as holding it year after year, it is very difficult. We are fortunate to have what we did in San Francisco.

The Super Bowl is such an intensely involving event. As a coach, you don't have time to look up and enjoy it. There might be a press conference or two with the opposing coach or some accolade you receive, but otherwise you don't have time to think about anything but the next game (which happens to be the Super Bowl). In my particular case, I was the team's offensive coordinator as well as the head coach. My focus was on planning practices and game planning, so I didn't look up until the game was over. When the final horn sounded, I looked up and saw we were ahead. That's when it really settled in that we were Super Bowl champions. It was fantastic. It's a feeling I could never forget. Not at all.

Super Bowl XIX

Date: January 20, 1985
Place: Stanford Stadium, Stanford, CA
Attendance: 84,059

AFC: Miami Dolphins
Head Coach: Don Shula

NFC: San Francisco 49ers
Head Coach: Bill Walsh

Miami	10	6	0	0	16
San Francisco	7	21	10	0	38

Most Valuable Player: Joe Montana (QB, San Francisco)

Super Bowl XX

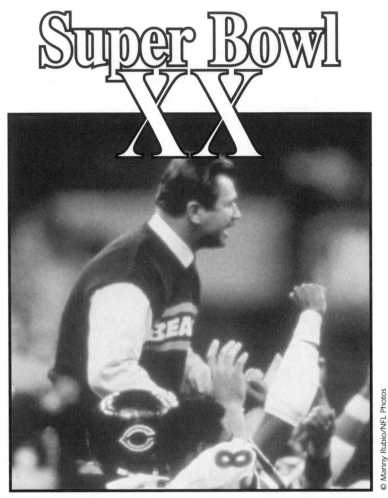

© Manny Rubio/NFL Photos

To say the least, the 1985 Chicago Bears was a team full of personalities. As head coach Mike Ditka points out, defense was not the team's strong suit early in the year, but the offense was good enough to win games. By the end of the season, the Bears' defense was one of the best in the league. As Chicago's defense improved throughout the season, they gained confidence. That confidence reached a new level in December of 1985 when some members of the team produced a music video known as the "Super Bowl Shuffle." Once the video came out, the team had to live up to its bold prediction. They didn't disappoint. As they marched through their schedule, it became glaringly obvious that they could stop any offense.

After an exhilerating mashing of the New England Patriots in Super Bowl XX, some of the Bears paraded Ditka off the field (above). Ditka is now on the CBS Sports team. One of his sidekicks on The NFL Today pregame show is Craig James, a running back for the Patriots in Super Bowl XX.

Mike Ditka

In the 1984 National Football Conference championship game, the Chicago Bears got hammered by San Francisco, 23-0. I wanted our football players to remember that. After the game, I told them I was so proud of them for what we had accomplished. I said, "I don't think there's any shame in getting beat. We got beat by a better football team, but that doesn't mean we can't become a better football team."

Then in 1985, we started out kind of crazily because our defense wasn't the strongest part of our team yet. Then all of a sudden they started hitting on all cylinders. Our guys felt like nobody could score on them, that nobody could hurt them. They almost felt like they were invincible on defense. Take nothing away, they were good. Buddy Ryan, who was a great coordinator, did a super job with them. We didn't always see eye to eye, but that's not important. The main thing was that we did what was best for the Chicago Bears and we won a Super Bowl. He had a great rapport with his players and I think he was an old-fashioned coach in the way that he made those guys earn the right to go out on the field each week. Because of that, when they got out there, they played their butts off. They didn't take many prisoners on defense.

While it was happening, I never really thought about the different personalities we had on the team. I thought it was important to have a little bit of fun, and we did. Now, I had no idea what the "Super Bowl Shuffle" was. The guys asked me about it but I couldn't decide if it was a good idea or not. Then somebody said, "Coach, it's for charity."

I said, "Do what you want to do." They asked me if I would be in it with them. Could you imagine me doing the "Super Bowl Shuffle"? Needless to say, I declined their offer but I told them to go ahead and do it if they wanted to, since it was for charity. We had a day off, so they made the video. It was no big deal.

Looking at it in retrospect, it sounds a little bit arrogant the way they did it, but that was how these guys felt. I don't believe people can achieve things in life until they believe they can do it. If you are going to go around saying, "Wow, I think the other guy might be better," he probably will be better. That's the way it is. Our guys put a chip on their shoulder with the "Shuffle," but the Super Bowl became our motto and they worked hard to make it happen.

They put a lot of pressure on themselves with the video coming out during the regular season, but they responded very well. We went through a lot of adversity with the injuries. The guys just stepped in, especially back-up quarterback Steve Fuller, who filled in quite a bit because Jim McMahon was hurt a lot of the time. It was just amazing that we were able to do what we did. People can say what they want to about McMahon, but as great of a running back as Walter Payton was, and as great as the defense was, we wouldn't have won the Super Bowl without McMahon.

Jim didn't handle authority very well when he was a younger player, but his teammates loved him and they played for him. I don't know that a coach could ask

⊙ CBS SPORTS Presents

In the Trenches with Lesley Visser

Super Bowl XX will always be one of my most memorable Super Bowls. Bears' quarterback Jim McMahon had a bad cramp or pain at the very top of one of his hamstrings. My main assignment for that Sunday morning was finding his acupuncturist, who was flown in to help make the day work for McMahon. That was a pretty funny assignment.

That was the same year that some of the Bears made their famous "Super Bowl Shuffle" music video. One of those guys told me they thought that song was the first rap. They think they invented rap. I'll have to ask Mike Ditka about that.

It's fun to work with Ditka, the Bears' coach in that Super Bowl, and who I now work with on The NFL Today; and Craig James, a running back for that Patriots' team, and who works with us as well. We've all sort of come together after 15 years. Super Bowl XX was a really a memorable game.

for much more than that. There were some strange things that happened with him that season, and all the talk about his having acupuncture to cure some of his injuries. Early in the season, in a game at Minnesota, we got a glimpse of what Jim could do. The kid couldn't play. He couldn't even throw the ball during the week in practice. Yet he was begging to get in the game.

We put him in finally, because we weren't playing well. The Vikings knew he couldn't throw the ball, so they blitzed him. Well, he did throw it and completed a pass for a touchdown. Over the next four minutes, he threw for three touchdowns. Not only did he ignite the offense, but I think he also ignited the defense. They figured that if we got the football back quickly enough, McMahon would help us score again. And that's basically what happened. We came back and won 33-24.

There wasn't much of a difference between the New England Patriots and us going into Super Bowl XX. The final score was lopsided, 46-10, but the Patriots were a good team. I don't say this to slight anybody, but our defense intimidated their starting quarterback, Tony Eason. I think that's why they didn't have very much success after the first two series. Then they brought in back-up Steve Grogan, who played the majority of the game. I can't help but wonder if Grogan would have played the whole game, would they have been more successful? I don't know, but I don't think it would have mattered a lot. I think we would have still won the football game. Standing on the sidelines and watching our defense was almost like watching somebody put a piece of raw meat in front of a bear ... pardon the expression.

Our opening drive of the second half was one of the key moments in the game. We were backed up on our own 4-yard line, but McMahon hit Willie Gault on a

Red Cashion, Referee

The coin toss doesn't always go as smoothly as officials would like. There were some problems in Super Bowl XIX because of the ceremonial coin. In Super Bowl XXX, one of the two Super Bowls I refereed, one side of the coin had a teepee and the other side was a train station. Can you imagine me saying to Troy Aikman, "Troy, please call teepee or train station." So you have to come up with an agreement with the team captains of what's heads and what's tails.

The coin toss of Super Bowl XX got pretty exciting for a different reason. Ideally, the script went like this: I would hand the coin to honorary coin tosser Bart Starr, then Bart would toss it. Walter Payton of the Bears would call it. Well, I handed the coin to Bart and he tossed it up in the air. My eyes watched the spin of the coin. As my eyes followed the coin down, they met Walter Payton's. Walter's eyes were about the size of saucers. It occurred to me that he didn't know he was to call heads or tails. The coin hit the mat, but nobody said anything. Of course, it is pretty loud inside the Superdome, even when it is supposed to be quiet. I didn't hear anybody and the coin came up heads. The New England captain said, "He said tails." I didn't hear anything but Bart Starr jumped in and said, "No, he didn't; he said heads."

I said, "He did?"

Bart said, "Yes he did."

"Great, Walter it's your choice," I said.

By that time I was a nervous wreck. I then ran to where I was supposed to be and suddenly realized that there were 300 million people watching around the world, 67,000 in the Superdome, including the supervisor of officials who was up in the press box. I've got a yellow flag sticking out of my pocket, I'm wearing silly-looking knickers, a two-inched striped shirt and I've got a bigger problem because I'm at the wrong end of the field. Now all I had to do was get to the other end of the field without being seen.

I looked up and my old friend Tony Franklin, who'd I known as a high school kicker in Texas, an all-American at Texas A&M, and an all-pro in the NFL, was about to kick off for New England. As I walked up Tony said, "Red, what are you doing out here?"

"If you want to know the truth, Tony," I said, "I'm at the wrong end of the field. And if I say something to you maybe people will think it's something different as far as the Super Bowl is concerned and I can go on down there where I belong and I might get away with it."

Tony looked at me and said, "Well, how are things in College Station? And I said, "Well, they're fine, Tony. When are you coming back to see us?"

long play-action pass to reach New England's 40-yard line. We went on to score to go up 30-3. A guy that never got very much credit, but who played outstanding in that game, was Matt Suhey, who ran for 52 yards. He did a lot of nice things on offense.

There were a lot of big plays in the game, but it seems like there were more on defense. Every time you turned around, our guys were sacking their quarterback (seven times), stopping a run or causing them to punt. I would have to say that most of the big plays were on defense. Our defense held the Patriots to 7 yards rushing ... total.

One play that everybody seems to remember from that game is the touchdown that William "the Refrigerator" Perry scored in the third quarter. We had run that play a lot with Perry. Sometimes, however, it didn't work. Basically, there were three options on the play for McMahon. He could keep it, give it to Walter Payton, or give it to Perry. Obviously, that day, he chose to hand it to Perry and it worked. Probably the only thing I regret is that we didn't have Perry leading for Walter. As a coach I guess it's my fault, but I never thought about Walter not scoring a touchdown; that never dawned on me. Then after the game, when someone asked me about it, I really felt bad because here I had one of the greatest players that ever played the game, and he didn't score a touchdown in the Super Bowl. That really hurt me and I know it hurt him.

As great as Walter was on the field, he was even better off it in the sense that he was a catalyst for enthusiasm and he kept people loose. He was a practical joker. You never knew what he was going to do and he did some of the darndest things. One of my favorites was when he would take over for the receptionist and answer the phones into the Bears' offices. He had that high voice, so we never knew it was him. And then he'd pull pranks on me where he'd call and tell me his name was Yolanda and he was waiting for me at the motel. He usually did that late at night when I'd be in the office working. Finally, after a while, I caught on. I think he had more fun than most people. He was unbelievable. I really do miss him.

Late in the game, Jim Morrissey intercepted a pass and returned it 47 yards. It started to dawn on me at that time that we were in good shape. I didn't pay much attention to the scoreboard during the game, but when I did look up, and saw that it was 46-10, I said, "I think we're pretty safe right now."

After we won, even though I asked them not to do it, the players put me on their shoulders and carried me off the field. Steve McMichael and Perry were the main ones who hoisted me up. Then the other guys got beside them. As much as I say I didn't want them to do it, in retrospect, that was really a very flattering moment in my life and it was something I was very proud of.

People ask me what was my greatest feeling about the game. Honestly, it was relief that the thing was finished. There was so much hype and pressure going into the game with all the things that we had accomplished (plus the Super Bowl Shuffle). I was glad it was over and that we won it.

Most people forget that we won Super Bowl XX on Sunday and the Space Shuttle Challenger blew up on Tuesday; so everything has to be put back into the real world. We are probably the only professional sports team that did not go to the White House after winning a championship. The Challenger exploding was such a colossal tragedy in our country that it rightly took a lot of the focus and celebration off the game.

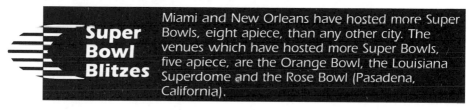

Super Bowl Blitzes

Miami and New Orleans have hosted more Super Bowls, eight apiece, than any other city. The venues which have hosted more Super Bowls, five apiece, are the Orange Bowl, the Louisiana Superdome and the Rose Bowl (Pasadena, California).

Winning the Super Bowl as a player, an assistant coach, and a head coach is kind of unusual when you think about it. I don't know if when it's all said and done, anybody is going to care a lot about it, but I'm very honored by that accomplishment. I was fortunate enough to be in a great organization like the Cowboys, then I was fortunate enough to have the opportunity from Mr. George Halas to coach the Bears. So it worked out.

The first one as the player was terrific. The one as an assistant coach I was completely happy for the team and the players. The one as the coach it's a combination of everybody in the organization. I think winning the Super Bowl as a head coach is a lot more satisfying than winning it as a player.

A head coach is a product of all the good people around him. If people asked me how good of a coach I was, I said, "How good are my players? That'll tell you how good I'm going to be." And I really meant that; I'm not being facetious. I'm not saying you can't make people be better than they think they can be, you can do that, but still you've got to have good players.

When I think about the Super Bowl, I think about my teammates when I was a player; and I think about the players when I was an assistant coach; and I think about everybody in the organization when I was a head coach. While I was with the Bears, we became a family. There was a lot of mutual respect throughout the entire organization. Losing will destroy anything, so when we ended up losing at the end and I was let go, I understood it. It hurt, but I understood it. Football is a very simple game. The formula is, you win or you don't work. But we created a family atmosphere in Chicago and I'm very proud of that.

Super Bowl Sunday: The Day America Stops

Craig James

As a player in the National Football League, you don't really buy into the hype of any other player or team. In 1985, a lot of the fans had bought into the Chicago Bears' "Super Bowl Shuffle," all the hype of William "the Refrigerator" Perry and Walter Payton. As players we were focused on our job of winning the Super Bowl. Our opponent didn't intimidate us.

Super Bowl XX was the first Super Bowl I'd ever attended as a player or as a spectator. I could not get over the amount of Hollywood that went into the game. It was not a regular game. The hoopla was a distraction. The media, the fans, the pregame ceremonies, everything collectively took it away from being a normal game. There is a lot to be said for teams who have experience in dealing with those festivities. Super Bowl XX was the first time for both teams, so I'm not using the distraction of the Super Bowl as an excuse, although coming from Chicago, the Bears were a little more Hollywood than us.

Some of our guys battled the flu during the two weeks. It has been suggested that affected us. I don't buy in to any of those ideas. The Bears, first of all, had a great team. We would have had to play really well and them have an average day for us to win. They featured a dominating defense. Also, the adrenaline level that you get by playing in the Super Bowl will take care of any kind of physical weakness you may have going into the game. In my mind, if anything hurt us, it was the two-week layoff between the AFC championship game and the Super Bowl. If we had played on a one-week schedule, I believe we would have been a much better team.

We made it to the Super Bowl by running the ball. Throughout the season we were very physical and would wear our opponents down by continually pounding the ball with our running game. Plus, we were opportunistic on defense; we created a lot of turnovers. We felt, as a team, we needed to run the ball against the Bears and maintain what we'd been doing to reach the Super Bowl. We needed to be patient and create some opportunities. Unfortunately, in the game, we did not run the ball like we had during the regular season. We tried a strategy of seeing if we could beat the Bears through the air, but we had trouble protecting our quarterbacks. Therefore, we had trouble scoring and the Bears beat us 46-10.

There have been far greater players than me who have never ever walked on a Super Bowl field. To start in a Super Bowl was something I never dreamed of doing. Even though we didn't win, there is still a tremendous feeling when I think about that season. I wear my AFC championship ring with a lot of pride. It was an honor and a privilege to represent the Patriots and the AFC in the Super Bowl. We had a special team. People in New England will never forget what we did. Neither will I.

There are a lot of people now who forget that I played football. I guess that means I've made it as a broadcaster. I've been to Super Bowls since Super Bowl XX against the Bears, and have covered them for local stations or for ESPN. Super

Bowl XXXV is my first time covering the Super Bowl with the network that's broadcasting the game. It is a ton of fun for all of us at CBS Sports.

Super Bowl XX

Date: January 26, 1986
Place: Louisiana Superdome, New Orleans, LA
Attendance: 73,818

AFC: New England Patriots
Head Coach: Raymond Berry

NFC: Chicago Bears
Head Coach: Mike Ditka

Chicago	13	10	21	2	46
New England	3	0	0	7	10

Most Valuable Player: Richard Dent (DE, Chicago)

Super Bowl XXI

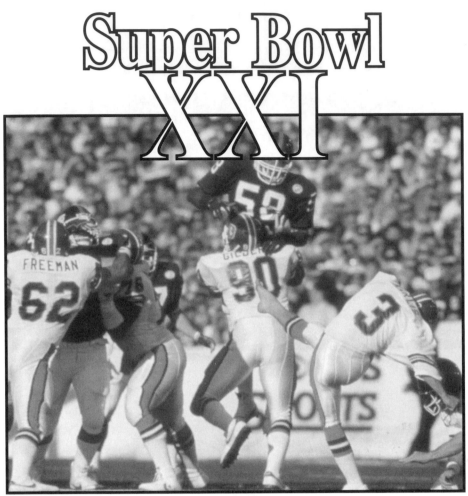

© Manny Rubio/NFL Photos

*O*ff the foot of placekicker Rich Karlis, the Denver Broncos reached the Super Bowl with an overtime victory at Cleveland in the AFC championship game. Denver quarterback John Elway placed his name in football lore by manufacturing a 98-yard drive late in the game to force that game into overtime. The Broncos' momentum carried over to the Super Bowl XXI hoopla. The hype being placed on the Broncos may have helped the New York Giants, winners of the NFC, focus easier on the game.

The Broncos were able to score on their opening drive of the game, thanks to a then-record 48-yard field goal the bare-footed kicker Karlis (No. 3). After holding a 10-9 halftime lead, the Broncos couldn't stop Phil Simms and the Giants' offense, as the New York team scored 30 points in the final two quarters. Simms threw for 268 yards and three touchdowns. During the second half, the New York quarterback completed 10 passes in a row.

Rich Karlis

I am often asked about the nervousness around kicking the game-winning field goal in overtime against the Cleveland Browns in the AFC championship at the end of the 1986 season. Believe it or not, the extra-point attempt to tie the game in regulation was the harder of the two kicks, mostly because of where we had to kick it. The old stadium at Cleveland had one end known as the Dawg Pound. This playoff game was before the league outlawed people bringing garbage bags full of dog bones into the stadium and throwing them at the opposition. In pregame we had gone down there to warm up and had to quit because there were so many bones flying out of the stands and hitting people. Obviously, missing an extra point would have been a terrible way to end the game.

The thing I remember most about the game is it was almost like stepping back in time. The stadium was such an old place with the worst facilities and terrible locker rooms. The field was as bad as any field I had known at the time. It was just dirt painted green. That day it was extremely cold, icy and snowy. It was like stepping back in time to when the Giants played at the Polo Grounds, a black and white television game. That's the way I remember it. It was such a gray, cold, snowy day, reminding me so much of old-time football.

Even though the ground was icy and the wind-chill was 5 degrees, my bare kicking foot didn't feel too bad. I was wearing a boot on that foot during the game, so it stayed fairly comfortable. Because of the elements, if I wanted to kick a few into the net we would wait between plays, then drag the net from the sideline to the field because there was slush and mud from where normally I would kick.

In overtime I had a chance to kick a 33-yard game-winning field goal. We were at the end away from the Dawg Pound. I went out and tried to clear a smooth kicking spot. When I moved the frozen dirt, I made a big hole. Finally I figured the heck with it. I stomped the dirt back down and just went with it as it was. Looking back now, I wasn't overly nervous about the attempt.

I grew up in a small town outside of Youngstown, Ohio. Every time I go visit, people give me an earful. For 13 years people have been telling me, "I know you missed that kick." I say, "Yeah, I probably did." Regardless, the record books show that we won the game, 23-20.

As one might guess under those conditions, I slid into the kick. Try kicking out of a sand trap sometime. That's what it was like. The ball was definitely moving quickly right to left. I didn't respond when it passed the goal posts. Instead, I looked straight down at the referee that stood down at that post. He didn't hesitate. He took two steps forward and put his hands up. There was no doubt in his mind that it was good. That's a pretty vivid memory.

That was such an ecstatic time! There was a picture on the cover of the January, 19, 1987 *Sports Illustrated* with me jumping in the air after the kick. I get teased about that. People say, "I never knew you could jump that high." Another thing that most people don't know about that picture is that before the attempt, Gary Kubiak, who was the holder, said to me, "When you make this I'm going to jump into your arms." I was sitting there thinking that this guy was way ahead of himself. I was concentrating on kicking the thing and the holder was talking about jumping into my arms.

When I made the kick, I looked, and Kubiak was running to the sidelines. Rick Dennison was standing there so I ended up jumping into his arms. The only problem was that he fell on top of me. So we were face mask to face mask with what felt like 30 guys jumping on top of us with me saying to Rick, "Rico get off of me, I can't breathe." Of course I was having this conversation, three inches away from him, while feeling like I was being crushed to death.

As a professional athlete, you never know if or when the script's going to be written for you to make your mark in history. You just hope it ends in a good way. For me, a good script couldn't have ended better. The Browns were a team I followed growing up. My dad used to take me to the Brown's training camps. To be from that area and win that game against them, in front of the 50 people there to see me, is amazing. It's not a bad story for a guy to be headed to Super Bowl XXI, who was just a walk-on kicker in 1982.

We felt like we could play with the New York Giants in the Super Bowl. We had played them in New York two months before the championship and lost 19-16. So, they may have had an edge on us, but we knew they were beatable. They had such a great defense with the likes of Harry Carson, Lawrence Taylor and George Martin. For us, it was such a shock to win and get in the Super Bowl. To go to Cleveland, the way we beat the Browns, was such an emotional high, almost like we had won the Super Bowl. Then for most of us, that was our first time to a Super Bowl, so we didn't know what to expect. I was so overwhelmed personally coming off the kick against Cleveland because I had never gotten that much attention before.

The Super Bowl is not a game for the players, it's a game really for the fans and the corporations. Going to the game is a blast. But as a player, it's a period of constant distractions. The atmosphere is very disruptive to the athlete. The only time it's really a blast for the players is if their team wins. Heck, family and friends and the fans have a lot more fun during that week than do the players. Players are trying to concentrate on work while everybody and their brother is calling you up saying, "Hey, in case you get a couple more tickets..." You just want to yell, "Leave me alone." I heard from people I hadn't heard from in years. They were just like bloodhounds. Those people tracked me down. Long, lost friends and distant cousins mean well, but that's a distraction that players generally aren't prepared to face.

I remember my first kick in Super Bowl XXI. It was a 48-yarder in the first quarter to give us a 3-0 lead. I was so relieved to hit my first attempt that well because I hadn't really kicked that great in practice during the week. Needless to say, I was frustrated going into the game. The one good thing that helped me right before that attempt is the Giants called a timeout. That helped me calm down a little bit and make that kick. Still, I was hyper. It felt like I drank 30 cups of coffee. I could not get myself settled down before the game and I never did settle down during the game, but that kick certainly helped ease some tension. At the time, that

◉CBS SPORTS Presents

In the Trenches with Phil Simms

I don't get too upset when people say I was in a zone that day; but, come on, I was in a zone for 10 weeks that season. It didn't just come to me that week.

kick of 48 yards tied a Super Bowl record set by Jan Stenerud of the Kansas City Chiefs in Super Bowl IV. (The current record is 54 yards set by Steve Christie of Buffalo. Stenerud and I still are tied for third on the list).

As a team we did poorly that entire game. One of the biggest keys was our inability to put the ball in the end zone. For instance, we were first-and-goal at the 1-yard line and moved backwards. Had we scored a touchdown, the complexion of the game would have changed because that would have put the Giants on their heels down by 10 points. That's a big deficit in any game, but especially in a Super Bowl. We had a terrible offensive showing. The Giants had such a great defense, but we hurt ourselves.

On fourth down of that series when we were pushed back several yards from the one, I missed a short field goal attempt of 23 yards. Talk about adding insult to injury. I was devastated. I just could not believe I missed such a chip shot. I hate the thought of missing that field goal. Throughout my career, I was such a long shot; a kid who was never, ever supposed to play in the NFL. I kicked during my senior year of high school, my senior year in college at Cincinnati -where I walked on- and then I walked on in Denver through a 475-player tryout camp. Everything was personal to me. I train hard and expect myself to do well. The thought of letting people down, letting my team down, kills me. To this day, even the thought of that miss is a sore spot. Each player wants to feel that he did everything he could to help the team win.

I came back later in the game and missed another short one. It was a nightmare. It really felt like my team needed me to kind of stop the bleeding and I wasn't able to stop it. I really felt like I had let down the team a lot. Obviously in Super Bowls you need to score touchdowns, not field goals. Even if those field goals were good, we still may have lost. But if you can't get it in the end zone then you need to make the field goals.

A real turning point of the game was a controversial play in the second quarter when the officials ruled a catch by Denver's Clarence Kay to not be a catch. He did catch it. On the next play, George Martin sacked John Elway in the end zone for a safety. So, instead of us possibly driving down the field, the score was cut to 10-9 heading into the locker room for halftime. We had such a sick feeling at the half knowing that we had our chances and blew it. The attitude in the locker room was that we were in trouble. It was very solemn in there, although, I'm not sure that it

133

should have been. Despite missing those opportunities, we still were up by a point.

Bill Parcells, who was coaching the Giants, is obviously a great coach, a great motivator and a great psychologist when it comes to firing up his teams. Who knows what he said to his team at halftime, but it worked. To add to their tough defense, quarterback Phil Simms lit things up offensively for the Giants in the second half. Our team came out flat in the third quarter. The second half, to me, was kind of blurred.

For whatever reason, in Super Bowls XXI and XXII we turned guys who were average quarterbacks, Simms and Doug Williams, into Most Valuable Players. We still sometimes joke about that today.

Simms finished the game 22-25 for 268 yards and three touchdowns. During one stretch in the second half, he completed 10 passes in a row. It was obvious, he must have been living right when early in the fourth quarter, his pass went off the hands of New York's Mark Bavaro and into the hands of his teammate, Phil McConkey, for a touchdown. McConkey's unbelievable catch gave the Giants a 33-10 lead and almost put the game out of reach for us. The Giants went on to win, 39-20.

Losing the Super Bowl is disappointing, even though you're on one of two teams that season to reach the championship game. I have a tape of Super Bowl XXI somewhere, but never have watched it. A friend of mine gave it to me saying, "You need to watch this because it's not as bad as you think." I just can't bring myself to put it in the VCR and possibly never will. I'll just hold on to the great memories that I have of the experience.

As a player you excel to be the best, and every year you start training in February to make that goal attainable. The feelings for the teams that don't win the Super Bowl are interesting because you feel like you were the worst team in the league. That's almost how you are treated, like you were the worst instead of the second-best team in the league. Just reaching the Super Bowl is an accomplishment. It certainly was for us considering our AFC championship game in Cleveland.

Growing up, boys dream about being the hero in the Super Bowl. Since I didn't play organized football until my senior year in high school, and didn't attempt a field goal until my senior year in college, those dreams were far away for me. I wasn't the hero in a Super Bowl but I helped my team reach that plateau. So, being a part of the AFC championship game by kicking three field goals, in a game considered the world's introduction to John Elway -and his signature moment- as a comeback quarterback, is very special for me and always will be.

Today, the feeling of losing two Super Bowls doesn't bother me as much as it did after the games. I have a lot of friends who kicked in the NFL who never even got close to the championship game. I had dinner before Super Bowl XXII in San Diego with older kickers Eddie Murray and Rolf Benirschke. At that time, neither had been in a Super Bowl. They reminded me of how special it is to play on that last Sunday of the season, and how many guys go through their whole career and never have that experience. They taught me to embrace the experience. They're right ... I played in the NFL for nine years, and on two Super Bowl teams in that span. That is very cool.

Super Bowl XXI

Date: January 25, 1987
Place: Rose Bowl, Pasadena, CA
Attendance: 101,063

AFC: Denver Broncos
Head Coach: Dan Reeves

NFC: N.Y. Giants
Head Coach: Bill Parcells

Denver	10	0	0	10	20
New York Giants	7	2	17	13	39

Most Valuable Player: Phil Simms (QB, New York)

Super Bowl XXII

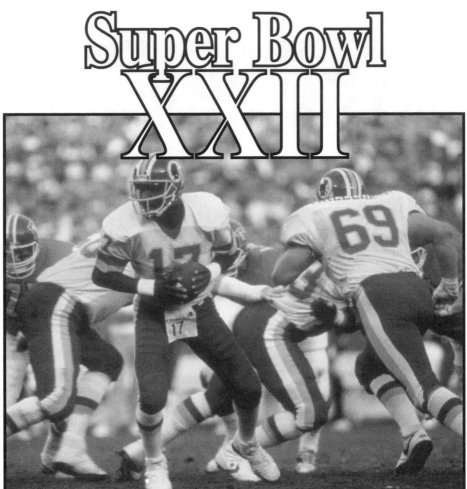

© Vernon J. Biever/NFL Photos

*A*fter losing Super Bowl XXI, the Denver Broncos made a return trip to the big
game as the representative of the AFC. Their task was to take on the
Washington Redskins, a team that had lost Super Bowl XVIII to the Los Angeles
Raiders.

The Redskins featured a quarterback who was a star before he led the team to a
touchdown in the Super Bowl. Even though he grew tired of the questions, the fact
was that Doug Williams was the first African-American quarterback in the Super
Bowl. On top of that, Williams racked up 340 passing yards as he became the the
game's MVP.

R.C. Thielemann (on right, #69) was a member of Washington's "Hogs" offensive line. After playing eight years with the Atlanta Falcons, Thielemann played the
final four years of his career with the Redskins, helping to protect Williams (with
the ball, #17).

R.C. Thielemann

T he 1987 season was a tough one for everyone in the National Football League. That was the season of the strike and the replacement players - although we arrongantly referred to them as "scabs." For all of us in the league, we played the first two games of the regular season as if things were normal. Then there was a threatened strike, which turned out not to be a threat. Our head coach, Joe Gibbs, called us into a team meeting and said, "If you're going to strike, you've got to do it as a team. If you come back in, you have to do it as a team; not just one or two guys." The Redskins and the Philadelphia Eagles each stuck to that philosophy. It basically solidified us and probably saved us.

We stayed together during the strike, which helped make us a tight-knit group. Excluding the replacements, if ever there was a war, I would want those teammates to be on my side. They're a loyal, good group of guys. Whether or not it was part of Gibbs' doing, his whole run of championship teams was assembled with great guys. Atlanta, where I started my NFL career, had great guys too, but the whole organization in Washington was just fantastic.

The strike was silly. Looking back, it's silly to envision us thinking we were actually a labor union like the teamsters, like we had coal dust all over us. I'm not sure what purpose we served in throwing water balloons at the replacement buses as they went to practice, and picketing outside Redskin Park.

The true credit of our success that season goes to Gibbs. He put that team of replacements -I don't want to call them "scabs" because that's a union thing- together and turned them into winners. They were a pretty darn good team for the three weeks we were out. They actually went into Dallas for their last game and won. Dallas had some big names that had crossed the line earlier in the strike, such as Randy White and Danny White. Some of their other starters were on the team. Joe's replacement guys went in there and beat the Cowboys on Monday Night Football!

The acumen that Gibbs showed by getting the best replacements possible under the circumstances certainly helped our cause of trying to win the division. Those replacements helped put us so far ahead in the standings when the regular players came back. All of that was because Gibbs was prepared. We already had a three-or four-game lead when we returned, with the season almost half over. We ended up with a record of 12-4.

Gibbs' ability to work with people is incredible. He's the main reason I wanted to finish my playing career in Washington. We actually had a relationship before I went to the Redskins. Joe was the offensive line coach at Arkansas, and is the one who recruited me out of high school in Houston. One of the reasons I picked Arkansas was because of Gibbs. Unfortunately for me, as soon as I signed with Arkansas, he started his NFL coaching career. Then we both had long careers and it ended up that I worked out the trade to get to Washington and finally play under Joe. He's one of the few coaches I've played under, that when he walks into the

---

◉CBS SPORTS Presents

In the Trenches with Mark May

We were standing on the sidelines before the game, geeked up about playing, when all of a sudden the Blue Angels flew over Jack Murphy Stadium. We had no idea they were going to fly by. My heart just stopped. I looked up and started to shiver because it was so neat. I looked around and realized that is what the Super Bowl is all about.

---

room, the team shuts up. Tom Landry, who I played for in a couple of all-star games, is another one. Coaches like Joe and Tom have a certain presence that commands respect.

Our team won the NFC East, and was playing well, at the end of the year when we reached the Super Bowl to play Denver. George Rogers was our running back pretty much through the last half of the year. For whatever reason, Gibbs had a hunch and went with a kid named Timmy Smith at running back. Smith, a rookie, came out and set a Super Bowl rushing record that probably will never be broken. He ran for 204 yards, breaking Marcus Allen's previous record of 191 yards. (Ironically, Allen set the old record in Super Bowl XVIII against the Redskins.) A year later, Smith was out of football. He'll probably be one of the great trivia questions ... who holds the all-time rushing record in a Super Bowl?

Going into the game, we were 10-point underdogs. Sure enough, at the end of the first quarter, Denver led 10-0. The way the two teams were playing, it looked like it was going to be the typical Super Bowl blowout with Denver routing the Redskins. The first quarter was somewhat affected by our quarterback situation. Doug Williams twisted his knee and came out. Then our backup Jay Schroeder, who was off and on as the starting quarterback that year with Doug, came in and got roughed up. Doug came back in the game at the end of the first quarter.

For some reason, in the second quarter something clicked. Williams had one long 80-yard strike to Ricky Sanders to quickly get the thing going for us. All of our counter-plays worked as if we were blocking the scout team. It was surreal for one quarter. That one quarter was something. We had 35 points in a matter of five possessions. I can't explain what happened in that second quarter. All of a sudden, Doug hit the big pass to Sanders; Timmy Smith ran like he was Jim Brown; and everything worked as designed. The game plan was perfect. Our blocking schemes were perfect against Denver's defense. Everything we did worked. The game was over by halftime, which I guess is what you want if you're on the winning side. We led 35-10.

In the locker room at halftime, we had a feeling the game was in control, but there is always that uneasy feeling. If you play the game long enough, you know there's always a let down for the team that is way out in front. There's always a

⦿ **CBS SPORTS** Presents

In the Trenches with Charles Mann

One thing I'll always remember as a defensive end in Super Bowl XXII is covering John Elway ... the receiver. During the 1987 season, the Denver Broncos ran a quarterback throwback twice. On the play, out of the shotgun Elway would get the ball and hand it off to Steve Sewell, who would run a sweep, stop, turn and throw it to Elway as a receiver. So out of 16 games, four pre-season games, they had two quarterback throwbacks. Our defensive coach, Torgy Torgeson, told Dexter Manley and me that we would see the quarterback throwback in Super Bowl XXII. From the two times they ran it during the year, we knew Elway would be coming to Dexter's side of the field. We talked about it all week long.

Then in the game, here it goes. Elway was in the shotgun with Sewell in the backfield. Before I got down into my stance, I looked over at Dexter and told him to lookout for the throwback. We both got down in our stance. The Broncos did the quarterback throwback, however, they ran it my way. Elway got the ball and handed it to Sewell, who ran towards Dexter, while Elway brushed by me. I looked ahead to see if a reverse was coming my way. As I did that, Elway bumped me a little bit, when all of a sudden the light goes off. I thought, "Hmmm. This looks like the...oh no!..."

I turned and sprinted to try to catch Elway. The ball was in the air for what seemed like 10 minutes. It goes over my head and lands right in Elway's arms. I was racing after him with all I had. Along with a couple of defensive backs, we stopped him at about the 10-yard line. We ended up holding the Broncos there and they had to kick a field goal, but that field goal put them up 10 0. They didn't score another point. We scored 42 points and won the game.

By the end of the game, I sacked Elway and put all sorts of pressure on him. We won the championship, so I got all kinds of payback for getting burnt in the Super Bowl. That is one of my fondest memories. I got burnt, but it was neat seeing how the teams reacted. The cat and mouse game that is played during the course of a football game is unique.

chance the other team is going to come back. But our defense was playing so well. On offense, we were just telling everybody to stay in bounds to keep the clock running and get the thing over with. In the back of your mind though, you're always thinking that anything can happen. Truth be told, deep down we pretty much thought the game was done at halftime.

That game, especially that second quarter, was most of the world's introduction to Doug Williams. People seem to forget a little known fact that Tampa Bay had been to an NFC championship game against the Rams with Doug as its quarterback. Everybody thought Tampa Bay was a lousy team in those years. I knew Doug could play. What I didn't know about Doug was he was hard to understand, speaking-wise, in the huddle. Nothing against Doug because he's one of the best guys I've ever had a chance to meet or play with. The only problem is that he's a rural-sounding, black Cajun. When all three of those dialects are combined, it can be hard to understand. That's how it was sometimes with the different plays.

There are a lot of letters and numbers in any one particular play, and it may take 10-15 seconds to call the whole thing. The process is more difficult when the quarterback is hard to understand. Back in those days, the play that Gibbs wanted to call was signaled to Doug through a series of hand signals. Plays were signaled to Doug, but we also had our offensive line coach, Joe Bugel, signal in the plays to us so we knew what was going to be called. That way we really didn't have to decipher what Doug was saying. It's funny because coaches are always paranoid that the other team is trying to steal those hand signals and then relay that on to the defense. Although it's amusing to think they could pick up the play from the hand signals, get it to the defensive captain and tell him what the play was going to be to my knowledge, it has never happened.

We never had a problem doing it that way. All of us "Hogs" were pretty smart guys ... we just didn't look good in the shower. We picked up on the signals and knew what was going to be called before Doug even uttered a word.

Relatively speaking, the second half of that Super Bowl was pretty quiet. The only other points put on the board came early in the fourth quarter on a 4-yard run by Timmy Smith. That capped off his day and our season. We beat the Broncos 42-10. With his 340 yards passing, Doug was named the game's Most Valuable Player.

That game also marked the end of my playing days. It worked out well to end my career after that Super Bowl, with an experience I will never forget. In fact, I wear the championship ring almost daily as a constant reminder. I have all the memorabilia from that game in my sport room, including my Super Bowl jersey - still with the dirt of the stadium on it- framed. Those are just good memories. It would have been nice to play a couple of more seasons, but God didn't intend knees to be pushing around 300 pounders for too many years.

Super Bowl XXII

Date: January 31, 1988
Place: San Diego Jack Murphy Stadium, San Diego, CA
Attendance: 73,302

AFC: Denver Broncos
Head Coach: Dan Reeves

NFC: Washington Redskins
Head Coach: Joe Gibbs

Washington	0	35	0	7	42
Denver	10	0	0	0	10

Most Valuable Player: Doug Williams (QB, Washington)

141

Super Bowl XXIII

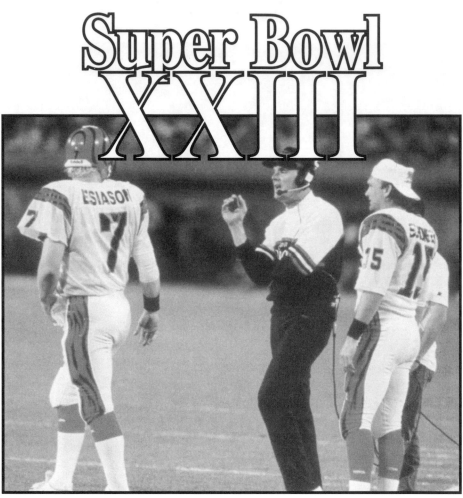

© Dave Boss/NFL Photos

*S*uper Bowl XXIII started out as an intriguing match-up; it ended up with one of the most fantastic finishes in Super Bowl history. The San Francisco 49ers and the Cincinnati Bengals were meeting in a rematch of Super Bowl XVI. The Bengals were one of the big stories in the 1988 season, going from a dismal 4-11 record the previous year to champions of the AFC. The other intriguing part of this game was on the Cincinnati sideline. Bengals' head coach was Sam Wyche (with headset), who almost lost his job after the 1987 season, was involved in Super Bowl XVI as an assistant coach ... with the 49ers.

With 3:20 left in the game, the Bengals took a 16-13 lead on a 40-yard field goal by Jim Breech. It appeared as though the Bengals were on the verge of winning their first Super Bowl, with the lead and the 49ers starting at their own 8-yard line. Wyche, having coached San Francisco quarterback Joe Montana, and under head coach Bill Walsh, felt he may have left too much time on the clock. He was right.

Sam Wyche

In 1987, the Cincinnati Bengals went 4-11. I often joke that in 1988 I was on a one-week renewable contract. Every week that I coached, as long as we won, I'd still have a job the next week. Once we lost, I'd be gone. Thank goodness we ended up winning our first six games of the season. We continued to play well throughout the rest of the year, and earned a trip to Super Bowl XXIII to face the San Francisco 49ers, where I had been an assistant coach from 1979-1982.

Going into Super Bowl XXIII, the AFC had a tremendous losing streak against the NFC. AFC teams had won only one Super Bowl in the previous seven years. Dan Reeves, who was coaching the Denver Broncos at the time, had seen his team lose in Super Bowl XXII. Since it was my first Super Bowl as a head coach, Dan offered me the notes that he had made to himself before and after the game, his Super Bowl schedule, things that he had faced in preparation, etc. That was invaluable to me. Unfortunately, it couldn't have prepared me for what I was going to face less than 24 hours before the game.

The night before the Super Bowl, we decided to move our team to another hotel that was quieter so the guys could get some rest. NFL Films had a 15-minute segment about the Bengals in an hour special that was going to air that night. Normally, we would eat dinner at 6:00, have a meeting around 6:45, and then have bed check at 10:00. The show was on at 7:00, so I told the guys I wanted them to go back into their rooms, relax, and watch the show because it was about them. I thought those pictures would do more than I could say to them in person. Then we were going to meet at 8:00. During that time period, running back Stanley Wilson decided to turn to cocaine. I don't blame myself. My feeling is if he's going to do it that night, he's going to do it. However, because I moved the meeting back, he did it before the meeting.

Earlier that night, Stanford Jennings, who was another running back for us, and would later run the kick off back for a touchdown, was excited. His wife had given birth to their first child and the local television station had somehow (by satellite or something) sent pictures of the baby right after it was born in the mother's arms. We were all sitting around looking at the photos of Stanford's new baby, everybody was excited and happy and everybody's motor was running for the game anyway.

We got ready to start the team meeting, and everybody was there except Stanley Wilson. The running backs coach, Jim Anderson, waved at me from outside the hall and said, "Stanley's up in the room, actually standing in the tub, and he's been into the cocaine again." I went back in and I think I might have had a tear in my eye, and I told the team. Stanley even had an author following him around to write a book about how he beat drugs. He had a great week of practice, and a terrific day. His son and his ex-wife had come in, his mom and dad had flown in to see the game. He was so proud, showing everybody, introducing everybody. There was no hint of a problem. I went back into the meeting and said, "Stanley's not going to play tomorrow; he's gotten back into the cocaine."

Guys started throwing their books on the floor and putting their heads in their hands in disgust. They were as upset as I was. Then I told Stanford Jennings, "You're going to do this in place of Stanley." We substituted up.

I went to Stanley's room to tell him. By that time he was out of the tub, soaking wet with sweat, sitting on the edge of the bed. I sat on the other edge of the bed and said, "Stanley, you know you're not going to play tomorrow. You may never play again, because you know this isn't your first time. You can't do this and I can't let you play."

He just kept looking at me and saying, "I'm so sorry, I'm so sorry." That was it. I had to go back to the meeting, so I had a security guard stay with Stanley. He apparently thought his parents were coming down the hall, so he ran from the security guard and left the hotel. We didn't see him again that trip. We didn't even hear where he was until days after the game.

Stanley's running style was short, wide, choppy steps. Our other running back, Ickey Woods, had a long, bend-back style. James Brooks was pure "quicks." I think Stanley's running style would have stood up better than the other two guys that particular day. It would have made it tougher on the 49ers' defense. We might have made some first downs that we didn't make. We'll never know that.

I actually got criticized after the game for not letting Stanley play. "Why didn't you wait until after the game and then punish him?" some asked. Of course, I wasn't going to do that, that wasn't the answer. I often wondered if I had gone ahead and had the meeting, and then said catch the show, Stan probably would have gone and done the same thing, but I wouldn't have known about it because he would have fallen asleep in his bed that night and the next day we probably wouldn't have gone around and checked everybody. Everybody was so ready to play. If I never would have known, he probably would have played O.K. We'll never know what the outcome of the game would have been. The problem would have still been there. Stanley's problem would have still been there.

Early in the ballgame the next day, we lost one of our best defensive players. Tim Krumrie broke his leg early in the first quarter. Still, the defense played well. The game went down to the final 34 seconds. That was a tough game and a tough situation. Jim Breech kicked a field goal to put us up 16-13 with 3:20 left in the game. It had been a close game, back and forth.

After Breech hit the field goal, Cris Collinsworth, who was a wide receiver for us, came over and elbowed me and said we may have left too much time for No. 16. (Of course, No. 16 was Joe Montana.) Having coached Joe in a winning Super Bowl [XVI], I knew that we were going up against the toughest challenge you could put on the field. There wasn't another quarterback, except for maybe John Elway, with a better chance to move the ball 92 yards in 3:20. I knew Bill Walsh's system, because it was the same system we had when I was an assistant at San Francisco. I had learned from him. I knew with that much time, they could dink and dunk, and move the ball down the field.

Two plays stick out from that series. We had them with a second-and-20 at the 50-yard line. We triple-teamed, not double, but triple-teamed Jerry Rice. That was the guy we wanted to stop. We had Lewis Billups, our cornerback, bumping Rice, with David Fulcher, our safety, over the top and Ray Horton in a lurk position. We were guessing that they were going to try to get part of the yardage back with Rice.

NO HUDDLE BY SAM WYCHE AND J.D. CROWE

Sure enough, they threw the ball on an inside move to Jerry. He beat the bump-and-run and he broke the coverage underneath. The turf was coming up in chunks that day which affected both teams during the game, but I can still see a little square of turf come up on that play causing Horton to miss a step. That was enough for Montana to get the ball to Jerry who made the first guy miss, as he gained 32 yards on the play. So on second-and-20, he gained 32 yards versus triple-teamed coverage.

We were trying to confuse Montana with different coverages. We were expecting him to throw the ball to the right, I think that was to Rice again. Joe threw into the coverage like we'd hoped. Billups was standing there and the ball hit him in the chest and bounced out. Within the next two plays, with 34 seconds left, Joe threw a pass to John Taylor on the left side for the game-winning touchdown. The ball was perfectly thrown, perfectly timed and of course a good catch.

We got beat on as near a perfect play as you will ever see. We allowed that play to take place by making a mistake on two other plays. We really defended them well on both of those plays, but didn't get it done. If we had, we were going to take a knee and win the world championship that year. That was a heart breaker.

The loss was especially tough on me because of the legendary Paul Brown. I played for Paul Brown and coached under him. He is the one who gave me a chance to make it in the league. He had never won a Super Bowl. I felt worse for him than I did for me, for our players, or anyone else. We had played a good game, a very competitive game, against a good football team. They won the game on a good play, not on a botch play or anything. Paul was sitting in the press box, and I have since heard from people that were sitting next to him that at the end of the game he got up and said, "Well, that's football." And he walked out. That was it. He didn't throw a fit even though he'd come so close and still not won the Super Bowl.

I was a free-agent walk on at Cincinnati in 1968, one of the original Bengals, but I was in graduate school at the time at the University of South Carolina. Coach Brown gave me a try-out in the middle of final exams. They decided to give me a contract. I was the fourth-string quarterback. They didn't have any investment in me at all; my contract was for $16,000, but I felt like the richest guy on earth. Paul Dietzel, who was my coach at South Carolina, called me and said, "I need to know if you're coming back or not. We need to get someone else to take your place if you're going to stay up there in Cincinnati."

⊙CBS SPORTS Presents

In the Trenches with Randy Cross

Super Bowl XXIII was going to be my last game as a player. Everyone knew that going into the game. On the Wednesday before the Super Bowl, I told my teammates in our meeting and the media at the Super Bowl press conference, "I'm not a boxer; I only intend on doing this one time." You always want to go out on a positive note.

Quarterback Joe Montana helped see to it that I went out on a championship team. We had the ball at our own 8-yard line with about 3:45 left in the game, trailing 16-13. There was a TV timeout, which at a Super Bowl is clocked in dog years. You have a lot of time to dwell on your situation. Everybody was sort of anxious, sitting in the huddle. Joe Montana, of course, was over with head coach Bill Walsh. Harris Barton, who was a second-year player at the time, was such an intense guy, just really uptight. Joe ran back to the huddle, looked over Harris's shoulder and said, "Hey, H, is that John Candy over there?" Harris got a funny look on his face, turned around and says, "Wow, I guess so; yeah."

It's not like it was a very important situation, I mean we only had to go 92 yards to win. It was a strange moment. When you figure the context the comment was in it sounds strange, but it was the perfect thing at the perfect time. That was Joe being Joe.

I went to Paul Brown and I said, "Coach Brown, I'm the fourth-string quarterback. Can you tell me if I got any chance to make this team? If I've got a chance, I'll stick it out, and I'll work at it. If I make it, fine and if I don't, no obligations. I just want to know if I have a chance or if I'm just a body here until cut down day."

Paul said, "Meet me after lunch and we'll talk about it." Here's a guy who had a thousand obligations, but he sat down with me and said, "I think you have a chance to make the team. If you've got a deadline to go back to school, I'll start you this week against the Buffalo Bills in a preseason game. After the game I'll tell you whether you've got a legitimate shot or not." Dietzel agreed to wait until after the game. I had a good enough game that Brown told me I had a chance. Well, I ended up making the team. A lot of coaches would have said to get the heck out of Dodge. Paul, instead, gave me a chance.

When we were playing Super Bowl XXIII, I remembered things like that. He had done a lot of things for a lot of people, not just me, and I really regretted not being able to win that game for him, because I knew at his age, he might not get another shot at it.

That 1988 Super Bowl year was the first time that during training camp I paired black players with white players, defensive players with offensive players, as room-mates. For example, a black offensive player roomed with a white defensive player. In the next room there might be a black defensive player rooming with a white offensive player. My reasoning was that once the season started, they were in separate meeting rooms, offense at this end of the hall, defense at the other end, separate ends of the field during practice, separate individual drills. The only time they saw each other was when they were going at each other in scrimmages. I wanted them to know more about each other, so that when they got down there at fourth-and-one, they could look each other in the eye and know what was important in his life - those kinds of things.

The guys didn't like it at first. We at least tried to pair them up with someone who had something in common so there would be some common ground. But I did that every year after that because I thought it brought the team closer together than it ever had before.

I think every player understands, and every coach understands, that if you get to a Super Bowl once, you may never be back there again. A guy like O.J. Simpson, who, regardless of what's happened post-football, was one of the greatest running backs ever to play the game, never played in the Super Bowl. Barry Sanders never played in one. We are talking about great players that never played in a Super Bowl.

When you get to the Super Bowl, you're treated in first-class style. Going to practice was as much fun as anything because all the police motorcycles, sirens going, and people running outside waving at us. All we were doing was going to practice. We were kings for a week, the center of attention.

Whether it is your first, second, third, or fourth Super Bowl, it's always going to be a special time because it may be your last one. Sometimes I think in life that the first time is always better than anything that follows. But in the case of the Super Bowl, it works the other way around. You're always saying to yourself, the end is just so close all the time, I better enjoy every moment of this.

Super Bowl XXIII

Date: January 22, 1989
Place: Joe Robbie Stadium, Miami, FL
Attendance: 75,129

AFC: Cincinnati Bengals
Head Coach: Sam Wyche

NFC: San Francisco 49ers
Head Coach: Bill Walsh

Cincinnati	0	3	10	3	16
San Francisco	3	0	3	14	20

Most Valuable Player: Jerry Rice (WR, San Francisco)

Super Bowl XXIV

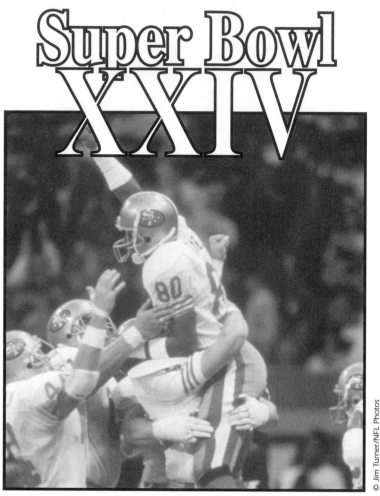

© Jim Turner/NFL Photos

*A*fter a close call in Super Bowl XXIII, the San Francisco 49ers wouldn't have minded if their fourth Super Bowl championship was a little easier. That's exactly what happened against the Denver Broncos in Super Bowl XXIV. The 49ers had plenty of chances to celebrate with Jerry Rice (top of pile), as the wide receiver caught seven passes, three of which were good for touchdowns. San Francisco never trailed in the game en route to a 55-10 destruction of the Broncos. Joe Montana, who became the first three-time Super Bowl MVP, threw for 297 yards and five touchdowns.

Montana was the team's co-captain with Ronnie Lott and Harry Sydney. After driving a forklift in North Carolina just a few years before joining the 49ers, Sydney is a wonderful example of perseverance. Sydney played for two of the 49ers' Super Bowl winners before serving as an assistant coach on the Green Bay Packers' Super Bowl XXXI and XXXII teams.

Harry Sydney

I have been around a lot of different teams in my football career, including four that went to Super Bowls, but the only game I've ever been in with a team clicking on the highest cylinders possible was Super Bowl XXIV with the San Francisco 49ers. All 45 guys were on the same page as the coaches. That was the only game in my life I felt if we wanted to go out and score 100 points, we could have. The crazy thing about it is our opponent, Denver, knew that. From looking into their eyes, they knew we could score at will that day.

The fact I was in the NFL was crazy to many people, considering where I had been just a couple years before that Super Bowl. I never had what you would consider a "normal" NFL career. After finishing my collegiate career at the University of Kansas, I bounced in the NFL from Seattle to Cincinnati without really getting a chance to prove myself. I played briefly in the United States Football League (USFL) for the Denver Gold and the Memphis Showboats, and in the Canadian Football League (CFL) for the Montreal Alouettes.

Shortly thereafter, I was back home in North Carolina working odd jobs. Even though I never gave up my dream of making it in the NFL, there were times I couldn't help but doubt whether or not that'd be a reality. Finally, while I was teaching school, I decided to give football one more shot. I sent my resume tape out one more time and figured if something happened, it was meant to be. If it didn't happen then I could always call myself a professional football player who never really played.

That realization was the hardest part because I always knew deep down that I was a professional football player. I was working in this one factory in North Carolina, driving a forklift. I'd tell everybody how I was going to try to play football because I was an athlete. They'd look at me like, "Yeah, you're an athlete; but you're driving a forklift right now." My ego really got abused at times. But every experience was a learning experience. Unfortunately at the time I didn't see it that way. The only person and team willing to take a chance on me was Bill Walsh of the San Francisco 49ers. As I said, not many people could have imagined that just a couple years after driving a forklift in North Carolina, I would be a member of the defending Super Bowl champion 49ers.

Going into the 1989 season, coming off a Super Bowl championship, there was a lot of pressure on us, but most of it was self-imposed. We knew we were a good team, and we had all the components there to win. The main change was that George Seifert took over as head coach after Bill Walsh stepped down. As players we wanted the world to know that not only was the coaching good, but the players also were. We thought we had the players and the veteran leadership to win three Super Bowls in a row, even though it didn't happen. We felt there was no reason why we couldn't be in a Super Bowl. The only team that could stop us was ourselves.

During the week leading up to Super Bowl XXIV, we were so intense that a couple of our guys got into a fight in a hallway. Of course there was some talk in the

◉CBS SPORTS Presents

In the Trenches with Brent Jones

All week before Super Bowl XXIV, our offensive coordinator, Mike Holmgren, was building up Denver's defense every time we looked at game films. We were a pretty sharp group of guys and we saw that Denver did a lot of things that were fundamentally exploitable. Still, he kept telling us how good they were. Finally, he stopped me on Friday and said, "You know what, I'm sick and tired of saying how good this defense is. We're going to kill these guys." I said, "Hey coach, thanks for saying that because I'm getting tired of hearing all this other baloney." We weren't going to be stopped that day.

media about it, talking about how we weren't getting along as a team. We had a team meeting to clear things up. Ronnie Lott stood up and said, "You know what? There are guys in here I like and there are guys in here I don't like. We don't have to get along. I don't have to like everybody. I'm not going out to dinner with everybody. Everybody's not coming over to my house for dinner. But when I line up on Sunday, I've got to look in your eyes and respect you, and know that you're going to fight and give it your all." Once we reached Sunday, we were ready.

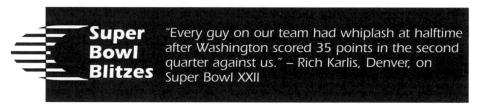

Super Bowl Blitzes

"Every guy on our team had whiplash at halftime after Washington scored 35 points in the second quarter against us." – Rich Karlis, Denver, on Super Bowl XXII

When we walked out of the locker room before the game, we honestly felt like we had the championship wrapped up. Bill Walsh and George Seifert used to say, "When you're a champion, you have to have a certain swagger about you; not cockiness or conceitedness, but a certain amount of self-confidence." When we walked out of the locker room, it was not a matter of whether we were going to win or how we were going to win, but by how many points we were going to win. I'm not saying that to downplay Denver. We just knew our plays were designed to attack the Broncos, and we had a heck of a match-up. We knew that once we scored, the floodgates were open.

One of the most incredible experiences for me from that season was being a captain and going out to midfield before the game for the coin toss of Super Bowl XXIV. I still can't believe it actually happened. It made me feel like a little kid. All my life I dreamed about being a professional football player. All of a sudden I was

⦿CBS SPORTS Presents

In the Trenches with Jerry Glanville

While I was in Houston, we won a heck of a playoff game in 1988 at Cleveland, 24-23. When Marty Schottenheimer and I met at midfield after the game, I said, "Gee, Marty, It's too bad you didn't get to win also." And he said, "It wouldn't matter, because whoever won this game can't win next week, because we just killed each other's teams off." I lost four starters, he lost six. He was right. Buffalo beat us the next week.

You play so hard in the playoffs with hopes of advancing, that sometimes you lose so many players you can't play at 100 percent the next week.

standing at midfield between two of the greatest people who ever played their positions, Joe Montana and Ronnie Lott, as tri-captains before the biggest game in the world. It was such a moment of "I told you so." It was a self-fulfilling dream. It was vindication of everything I had gone through. Everybody that said I wouldn't make it. Every time I doubted myself. All of sudden, "I can believe." It was no longer wishing to be there, it was not wanting to be there; at that particular moment in time I was standing there. The goose bumps were running.

To think I could be a contributing factor, that I could make a difference in what happens with the guys around me, that they look at me as their teammate, made all the stuff that I went through previously, well worth it. You talk about shivers and an unbelievable feeling. I was on top of the world. That was incredible.

Playing with Joe Montana was outstanding because his standard of excellence was so incredibly high. But it was high because that's how he did it. He went out and proved himself. Joe has a great sense of humor. The greatest thing about him, though, was his class. For being who he was, he could have been a jerk, but he was just Joe. Ronnie Lott could have been anything, but he was just Ronnie. They had different personalities, but the greatness just oozed out of them.

There was such a sense of obligation to each other on our team because you didn't want to be the weak link in the chain. There was greatness around there and you didn't want to be the reason that it wasn't great. There was a whole lot of pressure, but nobody ever embarrassed you or put you down. We had a true amount of respect from the top brass, to the coaches, to the equipment guys. Everybody wanted to do his best. There was no room for not doing so.

There were a lot of different situations that happened during that week before the Super Bowl, from the build up of the game to personalities on our team clashing. We decided in that team meeting that we had to protect each other. We had a thing

◉CBS SPORTS Presents

In the Trenches with Lesley Visser

I had to do some reports from the field during Super Bowl XXIV. As I started to do one of my reports, "Jet Man," the guy with the jet pack on his back, took off right next to me. I had no idea that was coming. Of course, "Jet Man's" fumes were blowing in my face and no one could hear what I was saying because "Jet Man" took off right next to me. I've definitely had to develop a sense of humor over the years.

called one heartbeat, where we had to be able to look each other in the eyes and know that everybody could count on everybody else. Going into the Super Bowl, there was an air of intensity that nothing could stop us. It was just a matter of how much we could score.

As expected, we rolled over the Broncos. In the third quarter, with a 41-10 lead, Joe came out of the game. We pulled off the "dogs" in the third quarter of a Super Bowl. Looking across the line at Denver's eyes, they knew we could do whatever we wanted to do. They knew they were in an eye of a storm.

Sometimes that game clock ticks so slow, and sometimes it goes fast. When you're up 55-10, the clock takes forever. The same enthusiasm was there for us, but it became, "OK, let's get this over. It's the Super Bowl, we've got to do some celebrating. Let's get out of here, take a shower and nobody get hurt."

I will never forget the Super Bowl. It's a game, an event, in which millions and millions of men who love the game of football would give their right arm to have played. Then you look at all the great players who don't have Super Bowl rings, or who never got a chance to do something like that. It's true what they say that until you've been to that event, you can talk about it and think you know about it, but until you've lived through that, it's not the same.

The only truly intimidating experience about the Super Bowl is all the craziness that goes with it. The media is a circus, the commercials, the hype, the Super Bowl tickets, the family's wanting to come and all the craziness that goes with it. Before the kickoff happens, it's a Super Bowl. Once the kickoff happens, it becomes a game. As the game winds down in the second half, it becomes the Super Bowl again. Late in the game you look up at the clock and you realize there are 15 more minutes to either win and become Super Bowl champions, or lose and be forgotten.

The game is almost secondary until two nights before and then the day of the game. The week before, the focus is on tickets. Then the players start looking at what the Super Bowl can do for them in terms of endorsements and bonuses. When the day of the game comes, a player has one game to determine how his life will be. One day -three hours, actually- to determine the legacy you will leave your kids.

"What's your dad do?" "He played on a Super Bowl team," blah, blah, blah. There's a sense of pride there.

When you get that championship ring that you can show your kids and grand-kids, it shows, at some certain point of time in your life, you were the best at what you did. You were on the team that was the best in the world. And once you are successful in that, nobody can ever take it away. I might lose my ring, but as long as there's a world and there's history, on that page where it lists the Super Bowl champions, there's our name ... the San Francisco 49ers. That's cool.

There are great memories from each Super Bowl, but that was a group that, even though people may not have been best friends, they would have died for each other. And you don't see that anymore. That was a special time.

Super Bowl XXIV was in New Orleans, which is a great place for a celebration. However, we had so little private time with our families or loved ones during the week, after the game I went up to my room before the craziness, and sat back and cherished everything I had gone through. I tried to imagine what I was going to go through as a Super Bowl champion, what the future was going to hold. It's amazing. You think about every broken bone that you had; every obstacle; every time you've been cut; every time you weren't good enough for this or for that. At that exact moment in time, all is forgiven because those negative opinions don't matter anymore. At that moment in time, everything that you ever dreamed of is right in front of your face. That's an awesome feeling.

Super Bowl XXIV

Date: January 28, 1990
Place: Louisiana Superdome, New Orleans, LA
Attendance: 72,919

AFC: Denver Broncos
Head Coach: Dan Reeves

NFC: San Francisco 49ers
Head Coach: George Seifert

San Francisco	13	14	14	14	55
Denver	3	0	7	0	10

Most Valuable Player: Joe Montana (QB, San Francisco)

Super Bowl XXV

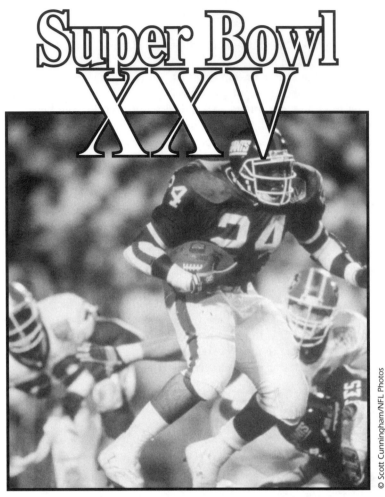

© Scott Cunningham/NFL Photos

*E*leven days prior to Super Bowl XXV between the New York Giants and the Buffalo Bills, the Persian Gulf War broke out. For the first time in the history of the Super Bowl, there were some discussions of cancelling the game. The game went ahead as scheduled. From singer Whitney Houston's rendition of the National Anthem to the final play of the game, Super Bowl XXV went into the history books as one of the most moving and most memorable Super Bowls ever.

Giants' running back Ottis Anderson (No. 24 with ball) rushed for 102 yards and was a key component in New York controlling the ball for 40:33. Matt Bahr, who played in Super Bowl XIV as a rookie for the Pittsburgh Steelers, kicked the game-winning field goal midway through the fourth quarter. Buffalo's Scott Norwood missed a 47-yard field goal attempt in the final seconds, wide right.

Ottis Anderson

When I was drafted out of the University of Miami in 1979 by the St. Louis Cardinals, I always told my roommate, Kenny Johnson, if I ever was on a Super Bowl team and that Super Bowl was played in Florida, and I was the featured running back, I'd win the most valuable player award. That was 12 years before Super Bowl XXV.

We played the San Francisco 49ers in the NFC championship game on their field. We trailed 13-12 late in the game. Matt Bahr had kicked four field goals to score all 12 of our team's points. With 2:36 left to play, we got the ball after Lawrence Taylor recovered a 49er fumble. I told Mark Ingram on the sideline, "Mark, we can't lose."

He said, "Why is that?"

"Because this is the only dream that's left in my career and I think God is going to fulfill it for me."

He asked, "What dream?"

I explained the dream to him, "If I am the feature running back and play in a Super Bowl in Florida, then I will be most valuable player."

Bahr hit a 42-yard field goal as time expired to give us the win and send us to Super Bowl XXV in Tampa, Fla.

When we showed up at the hotel in Tampa after defeating San Francisco, the 49ers had already sent their ticket information there, their computers, everything. They were sure they'd be in Florida for a chance to repeat their Super Bowl title. The city, itself, had banners of Jerry Rice, Joe Montana and Roger Craig all over. In the city's minds, Buffalo and the 49ers were going to be visiting for the Super Bowl. They did not have any intention of us being a part of the festivities.

Mathematically, or in terms of our team's playing output, we, maybe, weren't supposed to be in Super Bowl XXV. In terms of heart, spirit and the will to win, then we were supposed to be playing.

Based on what the Bills did in the playoffs when they beat the Oakland Raiders by 48 points in the AFC championship game, we were seen as the underdogs in the Super Bowl. The Bills had a breeze all the way through the playoffs, plus they beat us late in the season at home, 17-13. So, it's understandable that people saw us as the underdogs.

During our week of preparation for the Bills, the Gulf War started. Of course there was a lot of concern about safety at the Super Bowl. Security was heightened, but it was especially unique for one reason ... each time we entered Tampa Stadium it was just "mad" security. Back in the days of our team's first Super Bowl, XXI, Lawrence Taylor and a lot of other guys liked to go over to the stadium early on game day or picture day so they could get familiar with the area; take pictures; and really go out and have fun. That didn't work this time. Those guys showed up about 20 minutes before the buses arrived and they couldn't get in.

Basically, every item we brought into the stadium had to go through some sort of

---

◉CBS SPORTS Presents

In the Trenches with Brent Jones

We knew we had the Giants beat in the NFC championship game, and we were going to be playing for our third-straight Super Bowl title. Instead, after recovering a fumble with a couple minutes left in the game, New York drove down the field against our defense and kicked a field goal with no time left. That just crushed me. That made me realize how special it is to go to the Super Bowl. It's easy to take it for granted when you've won two in a row.

X-ray or security check. I even heard they were discussing not playing the game because of terrorism and bomb threats. Security measures were enforced to make sure the game was played. We weren't really concerned for our safety because we figured we were probably in the most secure place in the country other than the White House.

In terms of preparation for the Bills, we knew how explosive their offense was, considering their track record, the points they put on the board, the way quarterback Jim Kelly was able to move the ball down the field and the way Thurman Thomas was running the football. We knew, if they had opportunities, they would score and they would score lots of points. Our only advantage, and only weapon, was to make sure they didn't get on the field. Sometimes your best defense against a high-scoring team like the Bills is your offense. To us that meant ball-control and clock management.

We nailed home that idea with our first drive of the second half. We ate more than nine minutes off the clock to go 75 yards for a touchdown to give us a 17-12 lead. At one point in the second quarter, we were down 12-3. The key play to keep that drive alive was on a third-and-13 situation. Quarterback Jeff Hostetler threw a short pass to Mark Ingram, who made a great catch and an unbelievable run. He eluded eight or nine people as he worked for the first down.

I capped off that drive with a 1-yard touchdown run to the left side of the field.

Scoring that touchdown was truly special, largely because I am the only player who scored in both of the Giants' Super Bowl games. I guess every time you play in a major event, in a limited or major role, and you're able to contribute in a big way, then you have to feel happy. Plus, if it helps your team win, that makes it even more special to you.

Earlier in the game, in the second quarter, there was a situation that didn't seem as significant until we saw the final score. Basically, it was a play where Hostetler was tackled in the end zone by Bruce Smith for a safety. How is giving up two points a good thing? Well, Jeff had the ball in his right hand when Smith started to grab him. Hostetler had the mind and the ability to use his left hand to grab the ball

◉CBS SPORTS Presents

In the Trenches with Dan Dierdorf

Super Bowl XXV has been one of my most memorable games. As a broadcaster, I worked the game, which was between the Buffalo Bills and the New York Giants, during the Gulf War. Everyone had to go through metal detectors to go into the stadium because of the threat of terrorism. When Whitney Houston sang the national anthem, I have never seen such a bursting at the seams of patriotism and enthusiasm. From the moment she sang that memorable rendition, we knew what we were witnessing was only a football game; that American men and women were putting their lives at risk in the Persian Gulf. There was a sober mood to the entire proceedings. And then we ended up with one of the greatest Super Bowls of all time with it coming down to the very last play of the game and Scott Norwood's missed field goal, wide right.

It's so unfair that because of a missed field goal, Scott becomes part of Super Bowl history. It's unfair because if the Bills had lost the previous game, he never would have been subjected to that. The losers, the guys that never made it that far, never have to pay that price. If you ask Scott Norwood, I'm sure he would tell you that it is a stiff price, indeed.

and take the safety to prevent Smith from stripping the ball or knocking it loose. If that had happened, it could have easily been seven points for the Bills.

Late in the fourth quarter, trailing 19-17, we put together a nice drive, taking the ball inside the 10 yard line. We felt we should have scored a touchdown. In fact, I'm surprised I didn't have two touchdowns that game. Unfortunately the blocking assignment didn't go the way we had practiced. Had that not happened, it would have been a walk into the end zone for me. Instead, with a couple minutes left in the game, Matt Bahr kicked a 21-yard field goal to give us the 20-19 lead. To get something on the scoreboard every chance you get in the red zone, whether it's a touchdown or a field goal, is something you have to feel good about.

When the Bills got the ball back, they took it down to our 30-yard line. With less than five seconds remaining, Scott Norwood came out to attempt a 47-yard field goal. It was do-or-die. I was at the end of the field toward our locker room ready to run in had we not won the game. Fortunately for me, the people from Disney were standing next to me, saying, "If he misses this field goal you're the most valuable player." I found out that the Disney people also were on the Buffalo side of the field talking to Thurman Thomas, saying, "If he makes this field goal you're the most valuable player."

From the angle that I had, being so far behind the kicker, when Norwood kicked it, the ball looked as if it was going through the uprights. I immediately looked over at the Bills sideline, and I saw head coach Marv Levy and everybody else with their hands going up in the air. From my angle, it looked like it was going to be a good field goal. Then I looked on the field and saw one of our cornerbacks, Roger Brown, jumping with joy and doing cartwheels. That showed me we won the game. The Disney people confirmed that I was the most valuable player. I had a lot of help watching that field goal go too far to the right.

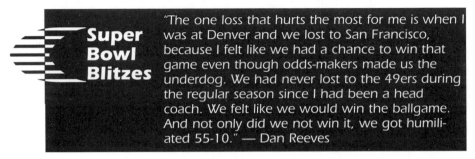

Super Bowl Blitzes

"The one loss that hurts the most for me is when I was at Denver and we lost to San Francisco, because I felt like we had a chance to win that game even though odds-makers made us the underdog. We had never lost to the 49ers during the regular season since I had been a head coach. We felt like we would win the ballgame. And not only did we not win it, we got humiliated 55-10." — Dan Reeves

When I look back at the previous Super Bowl MVPs, I realize I'm in a very elite class. Bart Starr won the award ... Franco Harris ... Terry Bradshaw ... Joe Namath, and the list goes on. To actually see my name in there, knowing that I will always be part of history and the record book is overwhelming. To actually be part of that elite group is like being part of a private SWAT team that nobody knows about but you and the special agents of the government. The Super Bowl MVPs are a protected group of people. It's not a big fraternity, but it's an elite fraternity with a limited membership. Many are called, but few are chosen. It felt good to be a part of this special group.

Even if I never see another record book, I don't think the Giants' fans will allow me to forget that I was a part of their two championship teams (XXI and XXV). They're constantly reminding me of it. That makes it seem like I did it by myself, but winning the Super Bowl was a team effort. I was just part of one of the spokes in the wheels. That's all I was. But the fans love their football in New York and they especially love a winner. They love those two Super Bowl titles because they don't know when the Giants may win a third. Dreams will always be there along with hopes and wishes. I'm living proof of that.

Matt Bahr

I had a good playing career in the National Football League with really nothing left to prove when the Cleveland Browns fired me in the preseason of 1990. But when the New York Giants called after their kicker, Raul Allegre, got hurt, since taking the risk of failure is the spice of life, I said sure. Allegre was only slightly hurt and rookie Matt Stover, in head coach Bill Parcells' eyes, was not quite ready. I'm sure that either one could and would have been successful that season. There were no illusions of my future, though. Ron Barnes, the team's trainer, once asked why I was so serious before a game. I said, "I've got to stay as long as I make field goals." He said, "You better believe it!"

I joined the Giants in 1990 when their record was 3-0. When our record reached 10-0, people started hyping our Monday Night meeting two weeks later with the 10-0 San Francisco 49ers. Even though each of us lost the week prior to our Monday showdown, there still was as much media coverage for that night as there was for Super Bowl XIV. We lost that night in San Francisco, 7-3, but the game was a precursor to the NFC Championship game five weeks later -low scoring, big plays and whichever team blinked first would lose.

Phil Simms and Ron Lott got into a scuffle after the game in the middle of many 49ers. I saw it and jumped in (although about the only use I would have been is if Phil picked me up to use as a shield of life or a sacrifice until he got some real help). Phil Simms got us that far in the year but he got injured and missed the last third of the season. Jeff Hostetler took over and the team rallied to support him.

The NFC Championship game in San Francisco (and the Super Bowl) took place during the Gulf War. Tight end Howard Cross asked us all to show our support, thoughts and prayers for the troops by wearing yellow wristbands during the game. The NFL forbade us to do that. The league also wouldn't let us do it during the Super Bowl, though they did include a United States flag patch on the jerseys. Incidentally, the Super Bowl ring also has a United States flag on it.

The Giants received some bulletin board material for the NFC championship when the 49ers announced that their Super Bowl headquarters had already been setup in Tampa. (We packed for an extra week, just in case.) Those things do help motivate. The middle of the field had been re-sodded; the weather was perfect with a steady wind from one direction. That is unusual for San Francisco because the wind typically swirls and is consistently inconsistent.

The game lived up to its hype with Montana and the 49ers going for the Super Bowl hat trick, three in a row; and us trying to screw up their travel arrangements. It was a game marked by great plays all over the field. Mark Collins virtually smothered Jerry Rice the entire afternoon. We ran a fake punt on the one play the 49ers were short a player and right over the spot where he was supposed to be. Many plays went our way like that and we still barely beat the defending NFL champs. I had made four of five field goals, missing early in the fourth quarter. Late in the game, we trailed 13-12.

159

Montana was injured and it turned out to be his last game as a 49er. The 49ers had only to make a first down to run the clock out. However, new quarterback Steve Young and Roger Craig had a less than clean exchange on a hand off, and either Leonard Marshall or Erik Howard shot the gap put a helmet on the ball to jar it loose. Lawrence Taylor was just there to get the fumble. Trailing by one point, it was obvious we were playing for a field goal with little time remaining. Again, great plays and extra efforts got us into position. There was a particularly good catch and run by tight end Mark Bavaro during that final drive.

On my missed attempt earlier in the quarter, we were sent out late, I rushed the kick and missed it. Nevertheless, it was my fault entirely. I mention that not as an excuse but merely to state the following ... I am continually amazed when opposing coaches call timeout to "ice" the kicker. It actually gives kickers a chance to relax, take a deep breath, prepare the spot (which in this case needed to be prepared because the re-sodding had come up or left gaps or loose spots on the field) and say to yourself to simply keep your head down and follow through. The 49ers called timeout and it helped us.

Incidentally, during the timeout snapper Steve DeOssie came back and said to me, "They can't ice you." I replied jokingly, "Steve, they're trying to ice you." He told me later he had a death grip on the ball for the crucial snap. The snap was good, Hoss put down his usual good hold, I hit it and immediately felt it was a good hit ... maybe too good. I hit it hard and it started to pull left, but it straightened out. The 42-yard field goal went through the uprights with room to spare. Good thing, too, because the 49ers had a clever rush scheme from the right side that likely would have blocked a kick over the middle. We were headed to the Super Bowl!

San Francisco and Buffalo were significantly favored in both conference championship games, as well they should have been. Yet my father had a most telling experience in his life that has always been an example to me. He played for the United States in the 1950 World Cup in Brazil. They beat the best team in the world, England, 1-0, and he had the assist. That has always been a lesson to me that the best team doesn't always win, that's why they play the game. Upsets happen. The 49ers were going for three Super Bowl victories in a row, and Buffalo had just scored 51 points in their championship. Both teams seemed unstoppable. The Giants knew those would be tough games. At no time were we fatalistic about being beat; we just knew we couldn't make any significant mistakes and expect to win.

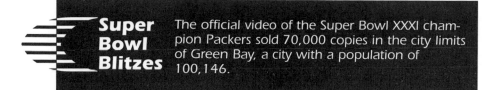

There was only one week between the conference championships and Super Bowl XXV. In addition, the Gulf War was on so security was tight in Tampa. We heard later that there were more than 30 snipers on top of the stadium, just in case, as well as the metal detectors, etc.

In Cleveland, the ball boys knew to throw in the most beat up football to the referees for kick-offs, field goals and punts, because they travel better. When I came to the Giants, Raul and Sean Landetta showed me how to "doctor" a football -how to make a new football behave like an old one, while still looking new. At the Super-Bowl, we were the "home" team and therefore had to provide the footballs for the game. Because the kickers had little to do during practice, we spent all week getting the 36 balls ready. A new football has a coating on it that makes it slick and it must be brushed.

After we were finished with the footballs, they were a benefit to both teams, even though the quarterbacks had the final say since they handled the ball the most. Unfortunately, the NFL had a different logo applied to the ball just before the game and used 36 new balls. All of our preparation went for naught. This meant shorter kick-offs, punts and probable fumbles and interceptions.

Because of our five field goals against San Francisco, including the game winner, the most popular question both kickers were asked during Super Bowl week was some variation of, "Do you hope the game will come down to a field goal?" All week I said, "Hell, no. I hope we are ahead by three touchdowns and we can enjoy the game. It's much less nerve racking that way."

I believe Buffalo's Scott Norwood said he did hope it came down to him. I do not mean to seem shallow, but be careful what you wish for. Regardless, all kickers know how much of a team effort the field goal is and that everything has to be right. A good snap, a good hold, perfect protection ... without these first three things, the fourth (a good kick) can never happen.

Buffalo probably would have won this game 80-90 percent of the time against us. They were a great team that scored countless points. How do you stop that offense? On the first series of the game, Buffalo was three and out, the first time it happened to them all season. Again, though, there were so many individual efforts at all times during the game. Mark Ingram had a third-down catch and run which kept a drive going, and eventually led to a touchdown. More importantly, it kept Buffalo's offense off the field.

Hostetler's will to hold on to the ball while Bruce Smith was sacking him for a safety. The replay showed Smith had his arm on Hoss's arm, and more often than not would have been able to strip the ball for seven points instead of two. Steven

◉CBS SPORTS Presents

In the Trenches with Lesley Visser

I grew up loving the Packers and I was raised on that Lombardi ethic. I always wanted to cover pro football. I was fortunate enough to be the first woman to cover the NFL as a beat writer with the Boston Globe, a very progressive newspaper, back in the mid-1970s.

When I left the Globe in the early 1980s and went to CBS Sports, I found out CBS was real visionary. The network gave me a lot of responsibility being the first, and still the only, woman to handle the Super Bowl post-game trophy presentation after Super Bowl XXVI. It was an enormous honor to be the first woman to do that.

To add to the experience, it was Joe Gibbs' third Super Bowl with his third different quarterback, Mark Rypien, who was the MVP. People had so much respect for Gibbs and the "Hogs." It was a privilege to do that. That was when they had the presidential inauguration and I remember thinking when I started the presentation, that the orderly transition of power had occurred twice in Washington, with the inauguration and with the Redskins. Making that presentation was really an honor and a pleasure. I felt like I had things to ask these guys and I felt like I was in control. It was extremely exciting. That's one of my favorite memories in my almost 30 years of covering sports.

halftime. O.J. Anderson's continual extra efforts on runs were a big key. Our offense continually sustained drives to keep Buffalo's offense off the field. During one stretch, Buffalo's offense was off the field for an hour and a half. So much for warm-ups.

The defense played as one and limited Buffalo's chances, forcing the Bills to play with a sense of urgency every time their offense got on the field. The defense also had to figure a way to slow the Bills' no-huddle offense, so seven or eight times during the game someone "accidentally" kicked the football after the referee set it down. Bill Belichick's defense held Buffalo to less than 20 points (19) for the second time that season.

And of course, we had head coach Bill Parcells. "Get me to the playoffs and I'll find a way for you guys to win." Like Joe Paterno, my college coach, Parcells loves football. Each of them knows what your best is and they expect to see it during the week. Since they know what to expect, they continually, maddeningly, demand that you get better. That is why they are great coaches. There is no doubt in my mind that if there was an MVP for the 1990 season, it was Bill Parcells.

Some of my fondest memories in the NFL were making tackles. First, because in those moment I really felt a part of the team; second, because most people believe

162

those moments I really felt a part of the team; second, because most people believe kickers are unsuitable to make tackles; and, third, because it was fun. Super Bowl XXV was no exception. I am more proud of the two tackles I made in that game, than of the two field goals -including the game-winner.

The Giants needed to make every play in order to win. And they did. Buffalo had a chance to win at the end with a field goal attempt, but it's a great disservice to the Giants, the Bills and to Scott Norwood to reduce the game to that attempt. I vividly remember standing on the sidelines, arms crossed, wishing for anything to happen except for Scott to miss that kick. Obviously I didn't want him to make it, but a fumble, an interception, a bad snap, a bobbled hold, a block, anything else would have been a perfect end to that game. A 47-yarder at any time is chancy. Combine that with a turf kicker on natural grass and the Super Bowl on the line, and you have an unfortunate focus. Also, the football's laces did appear to be turned out slightly (that does affect trajectory, and to Scott's credit he would never -nor did- make an excuse like that). The focus in this game must be on the extraordinary efforts made by both teams. The players, the coaches and the staffs created a magnificent game to watch and be a part of at the end of a long season.

Super Bowl champions are made of all these parts. The reason certain teams dominate is that the ownership is as much a part of the victory as anyone. The Maras and Rooneys created those legacies. The DeBartolos and Al Davis learned and built lessons for others to follow. Though I believe the main ingredient that most championship teams have is the ability of all the players to create an atmosphere that says, "We can count on you and you and can count on us. We are teammates."

Super Bowl XXV

Date: January 27, 1991
Place: Tampa Stadium, Tampa, FL
Attendance: 73,813

AFC: Buffalo Bills
Head Coach: Marv Levy

NFC: N.Y. Giants
Head Coach: Bill Parcells

Buffalo	3	9	0	7	19
N.Y. Giants	3	7	7	3	20

Most Valuable Player: Ottis Anderson (RB, New York)

Super Bowl XXVI

© Paul Spinelli/NFL Photos

Washington head coach Joe Gibbs took the Redskins to their fourth Super Bowl in less than 10 years. With some of the dominant teams over the years, four Super Bowls might not be seem like such an overwhelming feat except for one variable ... quarterback. Super Bowl XXVI not only marked the fourth appearance for Gibbs and his Redskins, but it also marked the third different quarterback to lead Washington into the NFL championship game. Mark Rypien followed in the footsteps of Joe Theismann and Doug Williams, and, like Williams, won the game's MVP award.

Charles Mann was a long-time member of the Redskins' defensive line, shown above, trying to make a goal-line stand against the Bills in the third quarter. This was one of the few times the Redskins didn't stop their opponents' offense. Mann is now a member of the CBS Sports team.

Charles Mann

The Super Bowl is the biggest game in the world and everyone watches it. This might sound strange, but knowing that everyone is watching, during the four Super Bowls in which I played, I always wondered who from my past was seeing me. For instance, maybe one of the kids I went to junior high school with is watching the football game.

Our Washington Redskins of 1991 were a very disciplined Joe Gibbs coached team. By that I mean that we realized and knew that Super Bowl XXVI could be ours if we executed, played smart and let Buffalo do all the talking during the pregame hoopla. It was falling right into place for us. We heard a lot of stuff out of their camp but I don't believe they heard a lot of stuff out of our camp. In fact, they probably didn't hear much of anything out of our camp. Most of our talk and conversation was about how great Buffalo was and what a wonderful team they were.

We always felt we had a chance to win under Joe Gibbs. We might not always win from executing but we knew no teams were better prepared than ours. Joe did things unlike a lot of other coaches. He wanted a good person, a sound individual, and a guy with good character, who was upstanding in the community. If the guy could play football that would be a plus. Joe felt that he could mold good guys into believing in themselves, and win a lot of football games that way. He knew that if he had a lot of superstars on the team, then egos came into play. We never thought we were superstars; we saw ourselves as blue-collar workers.

Joe's philosophy and how he prepared us was sound. We knew we were a good football team if we played together; but if we didn't play together we would stink. We felt no differently going into Super Bowl XXVI.

Throughout the entire time of preparation and the game itself, I don't remember not being confident. There were arguments coming out of their camp about which one of them was going to be the Super Bowl MVP and the one who was going to be saying he was going to Disney World. At least that's what we heard. There were a lot of myths in their camp, and we heard everything. Unfortunately we had to answer to a lot of it for the media. We simply said that the Buffalo team was the greatest thing since sliced bread, and how we didn't stand a chance against the Bills. Everything played right into our hands.

The first thing I remember from Super Bowl XXVI is how Buffalo running back Thurman Thomas "lost" his helmet. He didn't get to play in the first couple of plays because he couldn't find it. Now that is part of your war gear in the biggest game of your life. How could you misplace your helmet, unless you've got other things on your mind? At that moment, most guys are only thinking about having their helmet strapped on and being ready to go. It was kind of interesting that Thomas had "misplaced" his helmet.

Thomas was an important part to Buffalo's no-huddle, run-and-gun offense. In that system, quarterback Jim Kelly and company scored quickly and often. However, their offense would score so fast that their defense would be left on the field for most of the game. That was the weakness of that run-and-gun offense. Their offense only played 45 plays a game but their defense played 70-80 plays. Our normal offensive strategy was to run the ball down the other team's throat. So we pounded the football for 70-80 plays and beat them into submission. On defense we would stay fresh because we were only going to play 45-50 plays. The Bills were probably going to get some big plays on us, but they were going to get a lot of three-and-out series, also.

We really got after Kelly. We banged him around, hit him late; we just roughed him up. I was waiting for the time where he would quit. There's a transformation that happens a lot of times in a game where you see the team finally give up. We knew Kelly was close to doing that. He didn't, though, in that game. He hung in there.

During halftime, Richie Petitbon, who was the best at making halftime adjustments, thought there was a play we could run against Kelly. We had about 80 defensive plays in the scheme every week, although 50 percent of those were usually on the back burner. Petitbon pulled out one of those "50 percent" plays at halftime. Even though we had the game under control, leading 17-0, he said, "Hey guys remember this play we put in during training camp?" Then he drew it up on the chalkboard and brought it back to everybody's mind.

He said, "Well, we're going to run that." Kurt Gouveia was our middle linebacker on nickel situations. "Kurt, I want you to sit down in the middle here. What we're going to do is force Jim Kelly into this throw. We're going to make him throw to this particular guy based on what we've seen so far in the first two quarters. So, if you sit here, you're going to have a chance at a pick." Petitbon continued to go over that play making sure everyone had their responsibilities.

In the first series of the second half, Buffalo had a third-and-long situation and we ran that play. Kurt sat in the spot where he was told to sit, and here comes the pass. Kurt intercepted the ball and returned it 23 yards to the 2-yard line. Gerald Riggs scored a touchdown on the next play. It was pretty much smooth sailing after that. I remember walking off the field thinking Petitbon was a genius. He drew up this play in the sand, in the dirt, at halftime and it worked exactly how he thought. We had so much confidence in our defensive coaches. It really paid off in that Super Bowl.

Before that Super Bowl, one thought I had was whether or not all the hoopla at halftime would choke us. Sure enough, when we came running back onto the field after halftime, we could hardly breathe because there was so much smoke inside the Metrodome from all the halftime hoopla. Besides wondering when we'd be able to breathe again, I kept thinking, "Man, we missed a great half time show." We were fresh the whole game, except when we sucked in all that smoke. It took a while for that stuff to clear up.

The first thing that comes to mind when I think about playing in four Super Bowls is the feat. Just the fact that I did get to play in four in 12 years is amazing to me. Four Super Bowls is almost unheard of for players other than Charles Haley. (But I didn't have to jump from team to team to do it. I guess some guys had to do it that way.) I was blessed with an opportunity to play in four Super Bowls with one team, the Washington Redskins.

Super Bowl XXVI

The camaraderie that we shared on the team was special. We had so many good guys on our team and we were so close. We would go over to each other's homes, black and white hung together; offensive and defensive hung together. We didn't have a bunch of clicks. We genuinely liked each other. It was something fantastic.

We didn't have too difficult of a time not answering back all of Buffalo's talk before the Super Bowl. After the game, for the next six months, the media could write and talk about our fantastic season and the fact that we were Super Bowl champions.

Super Bowl XXVI

Date: January 26, 1992
Place: Metrodome, Minneapolis, MN
Attendance: 63,130

AFC: Buffalo Bills
Head Coach: Marv Levy

NFC: Washington Redskins
Head Coach: Joe Gibbs

Washington	0	7	14	6	37
Buffalo	0	0	10	14	24

Most Valuable Player: Mark Rypien (QB, Washington)

Super Bowl XXVII

*A*s with the Minnesota Vikings in the 1970s and the Denver Broncos of the 1980s, the Buffalo Bills were hoping that the third time would be a charm in Super Bowl XXVII. The Bills were making their third-straight appearance in the Super Bowl, a feat no other team has done in the history of the event. The Bills' opponent was the Dallas Cowboys, a team with a rich history in the Super Bowl, but they hadn't been the season's final game since Super Bowl XIII, a loss to the Pittsburgh Steelers.

Trailing 7-0 in the first quarter, Dallas quarterback Troy Aikman found tight end Jay Novacek for a 23-yard touchdown play (left, No. 84). On Buffalo's opening play on its next possession, quarterback Jim Kelly fumbled the ball on his team's 2-yard line. Dallas' Jimmie Jones picked up the ball and ran it in for the touchdown. The Cowboys didn't look back as they routed the Bills.

Jay Novacek

Even though the Dallas Cowboys hadn't been to a Super Bowl in 13 years when we went to XXVII to face the Buffalo Bills, we wanted to keep that tradition going of "America's Team." We were a completely different team, different style of team, than the older Cowboys were. Our group was pretty cocky. I hate to say that because I didn't particularly like it, but we were also able to back it up and produce a lot of excitement.

I personally didn't like it when players would strut around, like Michael Irvin. He's a good friend of mine but I made fun of him (and others) whenever he did that. That's kind of how our team was made up. We had a lot of different personalities. As much as our personalities sometimes clashed, that also helped us cling together. We were all good friends. Winning is about going out there with good friends, trusting them and supporting them in what they do and knowing they are definitely backing you up on what you do.

Reaching a Super Bowl is an enormous feat. To do it four times in a row, as was the case with the Bills, is incredible. They turned the impossible into possible. In order to do that you have to be a good team. At the same time, it had to haunt them when they were there. There almost had to be that something in the back of their minds saying, "Can we win this time?" Any time you have a little bit of doubt like that, it's awfully tough to win. We went into the game thinking we could win. That's not being cocky or arrogant; it was just the honest way we felt.

Super Bowl XXVII was the third-straight NFL championship game for Buffalo. The Bills came out like a team ready to finally win. In the first quarter, they were leading 7-0 when we started to put a drive together. Those first few plays in which you're involved in a Super Bowl are incredibly emotional. You'd like to say it's just another game, but everyone in the world knows that it isn't. Since the Cowboys hadn't been to a Super Bowl in more than a decade, most of us had no idea how great of a feeling it really was to play in the championship.

The football was slippery that day, which caused our quarterback, Troy Aikman, to throw more bad balls -translated, not real tight spirals- in that game than in any other game we played together. He is such a great player, though, that even when he isn't throwing tight spirals, he's still incredibly efficient. That's the one thing I remember about that game, especially because Troy threw one of those passes to me during our first drive of the game. It turned into a 23-yard touchdown.

I'm not exactly sure what went through my mind when I crossed the goal line. However, way before the ball was thrown, I just knew it was coming to me. I was very much a prime read on that play. It just kind of opened up like, oh this is going to be easy. Guys often play on fear in a Super Bowl. No fear was involved on that touchdown. There were a lot of other passes in the game where I had a little fear of dropping the ball, but on the touchdown, everything was extremely relaxed. You hear about the ball coming in slow motion. That happened. And I will never forget turning around after I scored, and seeing old knucklehead Michael Irvin with arms spread out wide, ready to give me a bear hug. That's just an incredible feeling.

I talked to Troy afterwards about that play. He said, "I just saw where you were going and kind of kept the ball in my hand and let her go. It was one of my worst passes ever." I said, "It may not have looked real pretty, but I think it was one of your greatest passes ever." People don't realize little things like that, and don't know what actually happens on the field. That's what makes the game special. There are so many little things that happen; things that we, as players, forget. People bring up that play or that game and it kind of sparks a memory. And that's what's neat about being a part of a Super Bowl team.

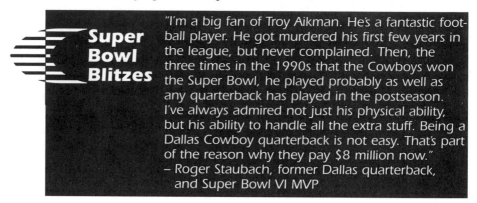

Super Bowl Blitzes

"I'm a big fan of Troy Aikman. He's a fantastic football player. He got murdered his first few years in the league, but never complained. Then, the three times in the 1990s that the Cowboys won the Super Bowl, he played probably as well as any quarterback has played in the postseason. I've always admired not just his physical ability, but his ability to handle all the extra stuff. Being a Dallas Cowboy quarterback is not easy. That's part of the reason why they pay $8 million now."
– Roger Staubach, former Dallas quarterback, and Super Bowl VI MVP

Troy is such a great quarterback that he can sense his receivers. One of my favorite plays happened a couple different times, although not in Super Bowl XXVII. There were instances when I would come out of my break in a passing route, and I couldn't see Troy because of the offensive and defensive linemen. The next thing I knew, there was this hand with a ball coming out of it, throwing a great pass. Watching films the next day I'd say, "Troy, I didn't even see you. Did you see me?" He'd say, "No, I didn't. I just knew you were going to be there." It always brings tears to my eyes to tell that story, knowing the simple fact that someone had that much confidence in me.

Running routes isn't necessarily an art, it's more of a feel. You just have to kind of feel your way to being in the right place at the right time. Sometimes it doesn't matter how that happens and sometimes it matters a lot. It obviously helps if you have a quarterback and a receiver that have a lot of confidence in each other. That's what Troy and I had; we just knew.

Most of the balls I dropped when we played together were because I thought he was going to hit me higher or lower than he did. Even though I might go back to the huddle and tell Troy it wasn't a very good pass, usually it was a great pass. I was so used to him being so accurate and almost knowing exactly where he was going to put the ball for me to catch it, that I'd be surprised if it wasn't right there. Troy was, and still is, an incredible player and person.

That first quarter touchdown in Super Bowl XXVII relieved a lot of pressure. We needed that drive. Earlier in the game we had a punt blocked, which eventually resulted in Buffalo's first touchdown. The momentum was in their favor, but we

⦿CBS SPORTS

In the Trenches with Jerry Glanville

The biggest pain you feel as a coach is when you lose a game in the playoffs and you realize you're not going to the Super Bowl. In fact, when I was with the Atlanta Falcons and we lost to Washington in the playoffs in 1991, I didn't leave the house for 10 days. The pain was just unbearable. You think you have a shot. You think you can keep winning. I found out that when you lose a playoff game on the road, the flight home seems a little longer. That's a sick feeling because all the hard work everybody has put into winning, then you realize it's over. When you win a playoff game, it raises your belief that the Super Bowl is a possibility.

stayed calm and knew exactly how well we could play. As long as we moved the ball and didn't make any mistakes, we felt we could be successful. And we were.

We had a 28-10 lead at halftime and felt, at that point, like we had the game under control. The reason we felt in control at halftime wasn't because of our lead as much as the fact that the minute we walked into the locker room, we all wanted to be back on the field playing. Halftime was entirely too long. It seemed like it lasted two days. Everyone was ready to play again. I think right then we knew that the faster we got back on the field, the quicker we were going to control the game.

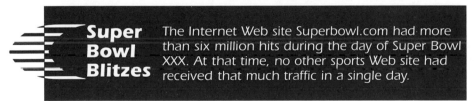

Super Bowl Blitzes The Internet Web site Superbowl.com had more than six million hits during the day of Super Bowl XXX. At that time, no other sports Web site had received that much traffic in a single day.

As the game wore on, we gained more control. Things fell apart for Buffalo in the fourth quarter as we scored 21 points and won 52-17. I think 90 percent of the Super Bowls are won by the team that makes the least number of mistakes. That was the case in XXVII. By the end of the game, our defense had intercepted four Buffalo passes and recovered five fumbles.

Our offensive and defensive lines played incredible against the Bills. The way our defense was able to rotate linemen put a huge stress on Buffalo's offensive linemen and helped force a good number of those nine turnovers. Plus, our guys were able to stop Buffalo's running game. On the other side, we had a good running game with Emmitt Smith and Daryl Johnston. Troy, on his way to becoming the game's Most Valuable Player, completed a lot of passes in crucial situations. All of that was because of our offensive and defensive linemen. Of course, it seems they never get the credit they deserve. They sure deserved it that day.

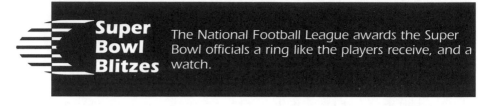

Super Bowl Blitzes The National Football League awards the Super Bowl officials a ring like the players receive, and a watch.

That was the first of three titles we won in Dallas while I was with the team. All three championships are close to the top for me. Super Bowl XXVII, our first one, is so much bigger emotionally because we were so doggone happy to be there. It's an incredible feeling. The second one was a challenge, just because few teams have ever won back-to-back. And then the third one was something that we proved to ourselves. We were older, more mature, even though some people didn't act like it (myself included.) We proved that we could still win; that we still had that desire.

Knowing that I was a part of three Super Bowl championships with the Cowboys is an incredible feeling. I don't necessarily concern myself with the Super Bowl rings we received. In fact, I always call them "stupid rings." I've never worn them. My normal response when someone asks me about them is to say that I traded them in for a good horse. A surprising amount of people who know me well enough, evidently kind of believe that. Everyone knows we won those Super Bowls, so why do we have to show off the ring?

If I were to have anybody wear it, it'd be my dad. And some day I'll probably let him. Knowing that we won is all I need to know. And we were able to be good at what we did. That's what is special to me. Buffalo did the impossible by going to four Super Bowls in a row, but we also did the impossible by winning three Super Bowls in four years. It is more special for me to know that I was associated with that, than to sit there and show people the ring on my finger. We proved that we were the best team those years. That should be enough.

Obviously playing in those Super Bowls is something I will always remember. Now, whenever January comes around, I know what type of seasons those postseason teams have had. I know what it takes in terms of mental preparation to win a playoff game. There were times when I played and the playoffs basically meant extra money to us. It's really more than that. Once you start winning those playoff games and you start getting closer and closer to the Super Bowl, it's a heck of a lot more than just playing for money ... it's playing from the heart.

Super Bowl XXVII

Date: January 31, 1993
Place: Rose Bowl, Pasadena, California
Attendance: 98,374

AFC: Buffalo
Head Coach: Marv Levy

NFC: Dallas Cowboys
Head Coach: Jimmy Johnson

Buffalo	7	3	7	0	17
Dallas	14	14	3	21	52

Most Valuable Player: Troy Aikman, (QB, Dallas)

Super Bowl XXVIII

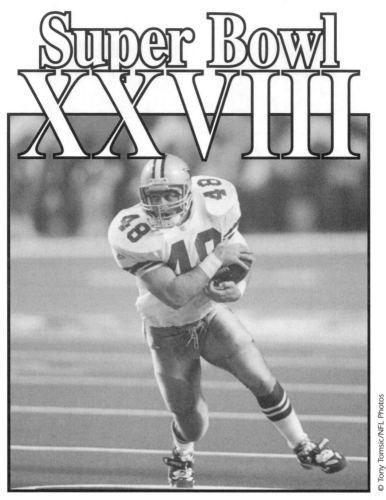

© Tony Tomsic/NFL Photos

*A*s baseball legend Yogi Berra might say of Super Bowl XXVIII, "It was deja vu all over again." The Buffalo Bills did the near-impossible by going to their fourth-straight Super Bowl, while the Dallas Cowboys, who defeated the Bills the previous January, were going for back-to-back titles.

The Cowboys had trouble getting their offense going in the first half, and trailed at the intermission, 13-6. After a couple of small adjustments, the Cowboys marched downfield on their first offensive possession in the third quarter behind the running of Emmitt Smith, who carried the ball seven-out-of-eight plays, including a 15-yard touchdown run. On the other play during that drive, fullback Daryl Johnston (pictured above) ran for three yards.

With the win, the Cowboys became the sixth team to capture back-to-back Super Bowl championships.

Daryl Johnston

I have always loved the game of football, but I didn't gear my life toward becoming a National Football League player. I didn't even think I was going to have an opportunity to be a part of the NFL until late into my college career. Syracuse was the only Division-I school that offered me a scholarship out of high school. Not until some of my friends were drafted in the NFL during my junior year, did I think that I might have the opportunity to be a professional player. Then, to end up with one of the most storied organizations in professional sports, the Dallas Cowboys, makes my road even more special.

As players with the Dallas Cowboys, we never went into a season expecting to be in the Super Bowl. That even held true in 1993, the season after we won Super Bowl XXVII. We hoped to get back there and have a chance to defend our title, but we didn't expect to be there. After a challenging season, we were fortunate enough to have that opportunity to defend our title against the Buffalo Bills. We beat Buffalo the year before to win our title.

Our offense usually put a lot of pressure on defenses and how teams wanted to defend us. We were effective at running the football, and we had the ability to throw the ball down the field or underneath. We had a great offense with Troy Aikman at quarterback; Emmitt Smith and me in the backfield; tight end Jay Novacek; wide receivers Michael Irvin and Alvin Harper; and a solid offensive line. Defenses tried to figure out a way to take a little bit of everything away and hope we would make mistakes. They couldn't commit to stop one entire part of our offense, because we could always come back with another option and exploit them.

For whatever reason, we had problems getting our offense going in the first half of Super Bowl XXVIII. As a result, the Bills led 13-6 at halftime. Despite that, it was a pretty controlled locker room, actually. I don't think any of us panicked. Buffalo had done a nice job of taking away our base running game. We liked to run between the tackles but they were stunting the defensive line and doing some run blitzes that really took away our blocking angles for the plays that were the foundation of our running game.

At halftime we talked about a play we thought would take advantage of what the Bills were doing. In the play, the tight end and tackles block down, the fullback kicks out and the guard pulls around into the hole. It's a base blocking scheme that a lot of teams use today, but we used it as more of a change-up play. We didn't use it as a base running play. Considering we hadn't brought out that play during the playoffs, or even the last few weeks of the regular season, we felt we could have success with it since chances were that the Bills hadn't prepared for us to run that in the game.

The Bills had to feel good at halftime with a 13-6 lead. They had beaten us earlier in the year in Texas Stadium, so that helped eased what had happened in the previous Super Bowl. Plus, they hadn't turned the ball over in the game; at least not until the third quarter. Less than a minute into the second half, Leon Lett stripped the ball from Bills' running back Thurman Thomas, and James Washington ran back 46 yards for the game-tying touchdown. That was the turning point of the football game.

The momentum from that turnover helped us come out on the following drive and go down the field for a touchdown, which put us ahead for good. On that opening drive of the second half, Emmitt carried the ball seven-out-of-eight plays. His seventh run, after I caught a pass, was for 15 yards and the touchdown. Emmitt earned the MVP award after running for 132 yards in the game.

Early in the fourth quarter, with a 10-point lead, we had a fourth-and-goal situation from the 1-yard line. A lot of people thought we might kick a field goal and go up 26-13, but that would have kept Buffalo in the football game. Instead, we went for it, and Emmitt again scored. That put us up 27-13. That put the game away. We won 30-13.

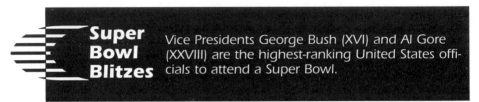

Super Bowl Blitzes Vice Presidents George Bush (XVI) and Al Gore (XXVIII) are the highest-ranking United States officials to attend a Super Bowl.

It was amazing to be part of one championship, but then to be one of a small group of guys who have been able to defend their title was awesome. Especially considering a lot of people counted us out early in the year. Coming out of the gates in 1993, we lost our first two games while Emmitt was in a contract holdout. Then, of course, we heard all the statistics that surround a team with a 0-2 start.

It's very difficult to stay on top of the heap in the NFL once you get there. You get everybody's best effort on a weekly basis. You can't come out flat when you're on top because opponents have had your game circled on their schedule from the time it came out. That is the most difficult part, because it's difficult to maintain that level of intensity for 16 weeks. You don't sneak up on teams when you're a Super Bowl champion.

Winning the Super Bowl was extremely rewarding for us because of our on-the-field struggles up to that point. We went from a record of 1-15 to back-to-back Super Bowl champions within four years. When our record was 1-15, we got absolute no respect, and we shouldn't have. We were in some tight games that year, but we didn't know how to win at that point. A few years later, to be able to beat the New York Giants and the Philadelphia Eagles, and other teams that had roughed us up, made it that much nicer for us. Usually when you're 1-15, it's going to take the team so long to get back on top that you'll be at the tail end of your career when everything good starts to happen. It was special for us to have been able to have a part of back-to-back titles.

The best way for me to describe the feeling of winning a Super Bowl is to say that if you were to reach the pinnacle in your professional life, then you know how we felt. Whether you were a doctor who revolutionized a surgical process, or an actor or actress who performed a role in a movie that was so good that other actors or actresses use that as a measuring stick, or whatever profession you select to be your dream profession, and you achieve the pinnacle in that profession, then you can sense how it feels to win a Super Bowl.

The Super Bowl is the highlight of my career from a point that is the ultimate goal for a professional football player. There are other things from our journey to the Super Bowl that are just as special to me. Being a part of Emmitt Smith's career is one, because I really feel he will break Walter Payton's rushing record. To have been a part of that is going to be very special. To have been a part of the turn around from 1-15, to back-to-back titles, to three Super Bowls in four years is pretty amazing. Obviously the Super Bowl is one way to measure overall success, but when you go back and dissect how you got there, there are some things along the way that may be a little bit more meaningful.

At the same time, I can't really forget our championships, especially the first one. The setting of the first one in the Rose Bowl was unbelievable. Standing in the tunnel just before we were introduced is something I'll never forget. I always remember watching the introductions as a boy growing up and to be a part of that was unbelievable. Everything about Super Bowl Sunday is incredible. It's just difficult to explain to people how you feel at that moment because I don't know anything to compare it to. Nobody who has been associated with the Super Bowl will ever forget it. If you talk to them it will definitely be one of the most important, or most exciting, days of their lives.

Super Bowl XXVIII

Date: January 30, 1994
Place: Georgia Dome, Atlanta, Georgia
Attendance: 72,817

AFC: Buffalo Bills
Head Coach: Marv Levy

NFC: Dallas Cowboys
Head Coach: Jimmy Johnson

Dallas	6	0	14	10	30
Buffalo	3	10	0	0	13

Most Valuable Player: Emmitt Smith (RB, Dallas)

Super Bowl XXIX

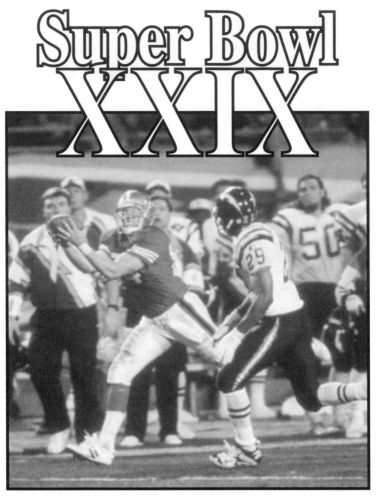

© Jerry Gallegos/NFL Photos

*T*he San Francisco 49ers continued their championship game dominance in
*Super Bowl XXIX against the San Diego Chargers. The two teams had met ear-
lier in the season with the 49ers winning that contest. To their surprise, as tight end
Brent Jones points out in his story, San Diego came out in basically the same
defense as the first game between the teams. Despite their shock, the 49ers took
advantage of the Chargers. In fact, the 49ers took the lead first and for good 1:24
into the game when quarterback Steve Young hooked up with receiver Jerry Rice for
a 44-yard touchdown play.*

*Jones (photo above) made a nice catch against San Diego safety Darren
Carrington. Jones, who admits he always wanted to be a professional baseball
player, probably picked the right profession and landed with the right team. As the
49ers won Super Bowl XXIX, they became the first NFL franchise to win five Super
Bowls. Jones was a part of three of those titles.*

*By the way, in his first and only Super Bowl as the starting quarterback, Young
finished the game with six touchdown passes and 325 yards.*

Brent Jones

It's pretty tough to put the Super Bowl experience into everyday terms. As a child, you watch the game on television and always aspire to reach that level. Once you climb the different playing levels of football and reach the pros, you start to think about the top of that ladder ... the Super Bowl. Going to the Super Bowl is such an unbelievable adrenaline rush. It is so exciting to be introduced and to run out of the tunnel into the stadium, with the fans going crazy and to see yourself on the JumboTron. The experience is so intense because this is the biggest game in professional sports.

When a team is preparing for a Super Bowl, or any game for that matter, you prepare with the knowledge that anything can happen. Going into Super Bowl XXIX against the San Diego Chargers, we had an interesting dilemma because we had played them late in the season and manhandled them in San Diego, 38-15. So, we had to fight the over-confidence associated with already pounding them once. We went back and looked at that game film several times. We reached a fine line between confidence and over-confidence, but we felt good.

One player we had to watch out for with the Chargers on defense was Junior Seau. He can be the most disruptive player whenever he's on the field. Unfortunately, you never know how people are going to react in a game with that much pressure. Turnovers can obviously keep a team in the game. Our defense was good, but we won games in San Francisco with our offense. We wanted to make sure that Junior didn't force us to make any turnovers and get in a hole.

We had to protect our quarterback, Steve Young. We felt like our receivers and tight ends would match up tremendously versus San Diego's defensive backs. Finding Junior was the first thing the offensive line worked on that week in pass protection. We felt if we gave Steve time, it was all over. We didn't think this game was a guaranteed win because it's still the Super Bowl and you still have to respect the other team. But we felt good about our chances.

One of the things that stands out in my mind was the fact we exploited their defense in that regular-season game. We thought they would change it and give us some new looks and disguises for the Super Bowl. We prepared for everything, including the stuff that worked against them the first time. To our surprise (and delight), they came out and played the same exact type of defense. We just gashed them again, 49-26. But, I don't know that anybody could have stopped our offense; it had too many weapons.

Personally, I felt like we had control of San Diego after the third-or-fourth play of the game. You can sometimes see intimidation in the other teams' eyes, when you come out at the beginning of the game and you're so intense and so focused. Even though no coach would admit to that, I felt pretty good about it. There are games when you know it's going to be a battle all the way through, and then there are games when you say to yourself there's no way these guys are going to stop us. We didn't think Denver would stop us in Super Bowl XXIX.

Super Bowl Sunday: The Day America Stops

I think the key for us during that game, and our entire stretch of Super Bowl titles, was the core group of guys, the work ethic and playing together as a team. Being around head coach Bill Walsh, how could we not soak up great football? Those ideas that Bill established and his attention to detail, stuck with us. How could we not soak up how to run a two-minute drill? We ran it all the time. We scored so many points that we got excited about even having the opportunity to get the ball with 40-seconds before halftime. We always went for it. And we had two outstanding quarterbacks who effectively ran the offense, Hall of Famer Joe Montana and then Steve Young.

People often ask me about the differences in Steve and Joe. I don't think it's possible to compare the two. Early on people talked about Young's left-handed spin and all this other stuff, but we played an awful lot in practice with both quarterbacks so it never bothered me. Then, everyone talked about Steve's ability to scramble, but people often don't remember that Joe, in his hey-day, could move out of the pocket and dance around. With either quarterback, we always had to be alert for them to throw the ball out of the pocket. We could never give up on our routes. Both of them were excellent at hitting the third-and-fourth read. I thought they were both very similar quarterbacks.

Our offensive coordinators when I played, Mike Holmgren and Mike Shanahan, are now two of the best head coaches in the league. When Shanahan came in, he didn't bring in his offense; he learned the 49ers' offense. I think that staying power and the knowledge of the people within the system, contributed to a 20-year span that we'll never see again. It was a special place and time. It was Camelot and it just kept going.

It's tremendously special to have been a part of that dominance. At the time things are happening, you can't appreciate them to the fullest. You just take it. Every year we came in and we expected to win a Super Bowl. Our worst record in the 11 years that I played was 10-6, which seemed like a miserable year. That happened three times, one of which turned into a Super Bowl championship season (1988). It's an expectation. It's a goal we set every year that we expected to attain. Sadly, some teams are happy to win five games. That's just the way it is. Getting to the top and staying there is an interesting process. I get excited thinking I was there more than half of one of the greatest runs in professional sports. It was truly a great time. Again, the best way to describe it is calling it Camelot. Things couldn't have come together more perfectly.

Even though I retired after the 1997 season, my adrenaline still gets flowing when I stand out on the field and talk to players on game day. A ton of great memories run through my mind. It seems like we were in championship games every year I played. I played in seven NFC championship games in 11 seasons. It was such a special time. It's about more than the game. It's about the locker room and the guys and the relationships. It's about the inside jokes and all the different things that go along with being a team. Unfortunately, we can never go back and get all the guys together again for another run.

The Super Bowl is still a great game. When you get on the field, it's still the players playing the game. Certainly the championship is a lot more commercialized and people want to make it this or that, but it's still the biggest game between the lines. The Super Bowl is pure football, playing for that unbelievable ring at the end. There are no words to truly describe it.

Super Bowl XXIX

Date: January 29, 1995
Place: Joe Robbie Stadium, Miami, Florida
Attendance: 74,107

AFC: San Diego Chargers
Head Coach: Bobby Ross

NFC: San Francisco 49ers
Head Coach: George Seifert

San Diego	7	3	8	8	26
San Francisco	14	14	14	7	49

Most Valuable Player: Steve Young (QB, San Francisco)

Super Bowl
XXX

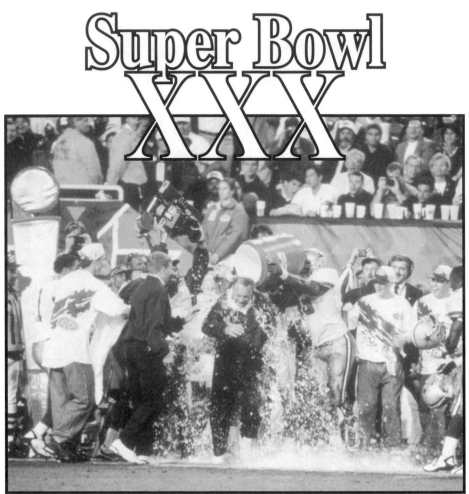

*A*fter more than 15 years, Super Bowl XXX saw the revival of one of the Super Bowl's best and most intense rivalries, the Dallas Cowboys and the Pittsburgh Steelers. After taking a year off from the Super Bowl, the Cowboys were going for their third title in four years.

The game seemed to swing back and forth even though Dallas took a 13-0 lead in the first half and never trailed in the ballgame. As the Steelers tried to mount a late comeback, Dallas cornerback Larry Brown, thwarted those efforts with two interceptions. The Dallas win tied them with the San Francisco 49ers as the only two franchises with five Super Bowl victories. Head coach Barry Switzer was the recipient of the traditional Gatoraide dousing.

Red Cashion was an official in the National Football League for 25 years. Most fans remember him for his creative "first doooowwwwwn" call. Super Bowl XXX was the second NFL championship that Cashion refereed. He also was referee for Super Bowl XX. Cashion refereed one more season in the league. His final game was the AFC divisional playoffs on January 4, 1997, in Denver.

Red Cashion

If I knew how to verbally express the excitement of getting the phone call asking me to work the Super Bowl, I would do it. All I can say is officials work for that game just like the players do. When we found out we were going to the Super Bowl, it was a relief, at the same time it was a sensation of "gee whiz did it really happen?" It was fun to be there with a friend and know that something you worked for all year was going to take place. It was a warm fuzzy feeling.

Being chosen for the Super Bowl means you're the best of the best. It's a measure of accomplishment. I don't think any player ever had any more pride than the officials do. There are no acknowledgments for officials, which is probably the way its supposed to be, but on the other hand when you do get acknowledged as being the best and you get that Super Bowl game, you have to feel a degree of satisfaction.

For officials, the Super Bowl starts with the announcement that you're going to be there. Not only are you going, but also you're going to spend several days there with the other officials. And then there's the commissioner's party and there's always a group of friends that wants to go to the Super Bowl. So now you're trying to find tickets. I think, at one time, I had arranged something like 40 tickets. There's a lot to it.

The hype of the Super Bowl is probably the biggest difference between it and any other game because it is a constant build up. The time leading up to the game is even hectic for the officials. There are a lot of routine things to get ready with the other officials. We get together and sign all kinds of programs so every one can have a copy. We go over all the travel plans, where we're going to meet, when we're going to meet. In the case of the game, we decide on what uniforms we are going to wear. We decide on plans for activities after the game. There are so many more activities that just planning the schedule takes up a great deal of time. Then you start talking about the game itself, and the one thing that that crew wants to do, as much as possible, is have a perfect game. Getting to be with each other and working out some of the details and talking about some of the things that can happen and have happened during the year is a priority.

Officiating, especially a Super Bowl, involves a tough mental process. Your mind has got to be in the right frame. If you're worried about your next pay raise, or the fact that your children are in trouble or sick, or that your wife walked out (and the event doesn't have to be that disastrous), you can't let that interfere with your work or you'll be in trouble. We do a lot during the few days before the Super Bowl to make sure everybody is in the right mental process. The danger is that different people react at different levels. And if you get somebody too high, he can be just as excited as a player and you can have problems. It's a pretty delicate balance of getting everybody together. These are all professional people who have done this before. Even if they haven't worked a Super Bowl, they've all been in big ball games.

◉CBS *SPORTS* Presents

In the Trenches with Phil Simms

What makes broadcasting a Super Bowl exciting for me is that I understand. I know as those guys are in the tunnel about to be introduced, and they don't know whether to throw up or go to the bathroom. Some of them are thinking, "Wow, this is even better than I thought." Knowing all that and how the world views the game is what makes it special. To be able to play in the Super Bowl and then broadcast it, that's pretty cool.

It is not as difficult as it might sound because of the conditioning process of the past, but it is still an important element. Going back to, for example, all the pregame activities. We don't want a canon to go off before the game and surprise somebody. It is just familiarization, talking about basic mechanics, so we work together. We must make sure we are communicating with each other and we are ready. It is very difficult to not get caught up in the hype of the game.

One of the toughest things about being an official in the National Football League is to not watch the great athletes. It's a pretty good bet that officials are big sports fans in the first place. To be out there with the greatest athletes in the world, and not want to watch them is kind of mind-boggling and tough. At the same time, officials are trained to watch the action as it applies to their, what we call, keys. It is absolutely paramount and basic that the first thing that an official does is watch his keys.

Which teams are in the Super Bowl is never much of an issue as far as the game is concerned except as it relates to peculiarities. For instance in Super Bowl XXX, Dallas doesn't use all the movement it used to use, but if it did we would talk about that movement. We talked about Pittsburgh using a lot of different formations and how we were going to cover them. We talked about the movement of the quarterbacks. The main thing is to stay ahead of the teams.

I thought that Super Bowl XXX was an excellent football game. Some of the best athletes that ever played the game were featured in that Super Bowl. It was a game with good illustrations of what momentum could do because Dallas had so much momentum in the first half of the game. Pittsburgh came up with an onside kick to start the second half and just completely flipped the momentum to the other side. For the whole second half, up until Larry Brown's second interception, Pittsburgh had Dallas on its heels. Then Pittsburgh threw that interception, and that put the momentum back in Dallas' hands again. It was a very good illustration of how momentum can affect the game and how quickly it can change. We didn't throw many flags in the game because, without question, those were the two best teams in the NFL.

Super Bowl XXX

The best teams just don't foul much when you get to big and important games. On the same token, the two best teams don't always meet in the Super Bowl. That also made it special. I was convinced almost to the fourth quarter, or to the end of the fourth quarter, we were going to have the first overtime game in the history of the Super Bowl because Pittsburgh had Dallas reeling and it was moving the ball. All the Steelers had to do was go down and kick a field goal, and we would have had a tied game. I was convinced that was the way it was going to end up. In the playoffs, overtime is a little different, because when you go to overtime in the playoffs, you play until somebody wins. During the season, one quarter is all you can have. If it's still tied at the end of a quarter then that's the end of it

Officials have the same type of incredible memories as the players when it comes to the Super Bowl. Well, maybe the guy that made the one-handed, unbelievable catch with two seconds left to score the winning touchdown might have a more vivid memory. That single play experience may not be the same for the officials. As far as the significance of the game and the accomplishment of being there, I don't think it is any different for an official than it is for a player; or any different for a player than it is for an official.

It takes a while for the adrenaline of the Super Bowl to cool down. I think there's a high emotion in officiating just like there is in playing. Super Bowl XXX was of course on Sunday, and I stayed around the Tempe area a couple of days. I expect it was a week later before I came down from that high and got my feet back on the ground.

The experience to have the opportunity to work a Super Bowl is very humbling. It is a huge honor to be able to watch such unbelievable athletes in such a spectacle; the whole thing is a production.

Super Bowl XXX

Date: January 28, 1996
Place: Sun Devil Stadium, Tempe, Arizona
Attendance: 76,347

AFC: Pittsburgh Steelers
Head Coach: Bill Cowher

NFC: Dallas Cowboys
Head Coach: Barry Switzer

Dallas	10	3	7	7	27
Pittsburgh	0	7	0	10	17

Most Valuable Player: Larry Brown (CB, Dallas)

Super Bowl XXXI

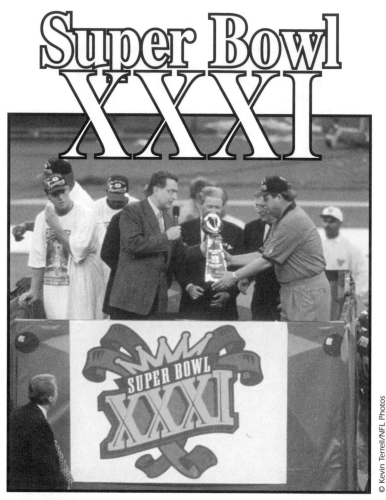

*I*n one of the happiest days of his life, Green Bay Packers' President and CEO,
Bob Harlan (center, behind trophy), accepts the Vince Lombardi trophy along
with head coach Mike Holmgren (baseball cap) and Ron Wolf (next to Holmgren)
after winning Super Bowl XXXI. Presenting the trophy is NFL Commissioner Paul
Tagliabue (to left, with microphone).

After 29 years, one of the most-storied franchises in all of professional sports,
and certainly one of the most successful in the years leading up to the NFL-AFL
merger, made it back to Super Bowl Sunday. Quarterback Brett Favre was involved
in three touchdowns (two throwing and one running) as the Packers downed the
New England Patriots. Harlan, who has worked with the Packers since the 1970s,
had struggled with the team through some lean years. Because of that, it's easy to
understand his excitement. Also, it's easy to see the NFC's excitement after the
Packers' victory ... Super Bowl XXXI marked the 13th-straight victory for NFC
teams in the Super Bowl.

Bob Harlan

Going to the Super Bowl with the Green Bay Packers is something I could never forget. This might sound strange, but for years I had been going to the Super Bowl and I always used to look at how they blow up those big inflatable helmets and roll them out on the field. I used to think how great it would be to see a Green Bay helmet out there. When I walked into the Superdome for Super Bowl XXXI and saw our helmet being inflated, the impression it made on me was monstrous.

Our hotel in New Orleans was only five or six blocks from the dome. The team bus I was riding that day was due to leave at 2 p.m. Finally, around noon, I got so nervous about the game, that I walked over to the dome by myself. The hotel had worn me out. When I got in the Superdome, the only people around were the stadium workers. I walked down by our blown up helmet and thought, "I never dreamed I'd see this helmet on this field." That made a big impression on me, just to think we were there. At times I doubted whether or not I'd see a Super Bowl with this club.

Maybe that's just the fan in me coming out. Even though I've spent almost 30 years working for the Packers' organization, I think of myself as a fan more than as an administrator. Everybody kids me about the number of fourth quarters that I spend walking the hallways, afraid of what's going to happen on the field. I've missed an awful lot of fourth quarters. People at home can change the channels on their televisions if they're nervous about a game; I have resorted to walking the hallways.

I was a fan when I was a student at Marquette in the 1950s. Back then the franchise was struggling. My friends and I could go to Milwaukee's County Stadium (which is where the team played four of its home games), go under the left field fence and into the wooden bleachers in the left-center field area, rather than sit in the normal baseball stands. We could literally walk to where the line of scrimmage was because the place was so empty during games. If the line of scrimmage were the 20-yard line, we'd go stand on the 20 and watch. And if the ball were on the 50, we'd go to the 50. We could do that every Sunday that the Packers played in Milwaukee. I thoroughly enjoyed it.

Interestingly enough, the only time I ever met Mr. Lombardi, I was working for United Press International in Milwaukee when I first got out of college. Lombardi's first game with the Packers was at County Stadium against the Chicago Bears in preseason. I wasn't scheduled to work that night, I was just going to the game with my boss to watch it. As it turned out, the UPI writer who was supposed to be covering the Packer locker room couldn't make it, he was ill. So my boss said to me, "You cover the Packer locker room." At that time, Vince Lombardi really didn't mean anything to me. He had been an assistant coach with the New York Giants before coming to Green Bay. So, Lombardi didn't really strike me as the team's savior at that point.

After the game, I went down to the locker room for his press conference. Three years later I would have been scared to death to do this, but when he finished the press conference, I said, "Coach, could I ask you a couple more questions?" We sat down in the locker room, talked and he answered my questions. Mr. Lombardi didn't have to, but he gave me the time.

I wrote the story and I never met the man again. But I've always remembered how interesting that was and how good he was to me. Again, if that same scenario happened a few years later, I probably never would have asked, "Could I ask you a couple more questions?" He likely would have told me, "No, we're finished," and turned his back. But he did give me the time of day, which I appreciate and will always remember.

The Packers obviously got better under the direction of Mr. Lombardi, but then we struggled through the 1970s and the 1980s. For many years, our organization had gone along with the idea that one person could be both head coach and general manager. Because Mr. Lombardi handled both responsibilities, everybody felt that the men who followed him could handle it. As the game grew and became more difficult, that plan wasn't working. We decided late in the 1991 season that we were going to totally change our football operation and turn it over to one individual as general manager and give him full control of the operation. We selected Ron Wolf.

Ron was a candidate for an administrative position here in 1987. At that point, Judge Robert Parins, who was our president, wanted to split the football operation on a 50-50 basis with two individuals. Ron was interviewed for the job, but quickly withdrew his name. He impressed me enough, at that time, that when I had the chance I wanted to bring him in as the general manager. One of the things that impressed me is he had worked for Al Davis and the Oakland Raiders for 25 years. I felt anybody who did that was knowledgeable and had to be a hard worker, because that's the way Al Davis attacks things. So I went to our executive committee and asked for permission to relieve the gentleman who was in the executive vice president position at that time, Tom Braatz, and offer it to Ron Wolf. They gave me permission to do so and we did it. That was November of 1991.

Timing was probably strange because most people wait until the end of the season to make a move like that. My thought was that I wanted someone to come in here and live with this team, travel with it, see it practice, and watch the coaches work, rather than try to come in, in January or February, and do everything from video tape. As it has turned out, I think it was beneficial to us. The very first thing Ron did when he took over the ballclub was evaluate our quarterback situation and say we had problems. We made the trade with Atlanta for Brett Favre.

Ron also didn't like what was happening on our practice field. He watched practice for one day in November, came back to my office and said, "You've got a country club atmosphere on that practice field. These guys are 4-10, but they're walking around like they're 10-4. We've got to make a change." I kind of knew at that point that Lindy Infante, the head coach, was in trouble. As soon as the season ended a few weeks later, Infante was released with three years to go on his contract. Mike Holmgren was hired and it went from there.

Once Mike and Ron took over the program and we won quickly, our entire organization certainly picked up confidence. Before I became president, when I was down the hall working for Judge Parins, there were two phone calls I used to get all the time from fans. The first call would be, "Who's making your football decisions?" Or, fans would call and say, "You people don't care if you win or lose. You don't care if you're 4-12 or 12-4, you're sold out. You've got a waiting list for tickets.

Winning doesn't make any difference to you."

Once Ron Wolf walked in the door, it immediately became obvious to everybody who was making the football decisions because he made the trade for Favre, then he let Infante go with three years left on his contract. And people said, "By gosh, they do want to win. They're willing to swallow Infante's contract and move on." Ron erased all those previous doubts. Once he got here, those negative calls stopped over night.

The thing that really surprised me was that when free agency was on the horizon in the early 1990s, everybody said the first franchise that's going to have trouble is the Green Bay Packers. Yet, Ron went out and signed the most attractive free agent of all time in Reggie White. We were on the verge of being a big winner. Our organization was optimistic but we just kept our fingers crossed thinking let's hope it comes true for us. It did.

After a dismal 4-12 season in 1991, there was immediately new life in the ballclub when we came back in 1992 and finished 9-7. I think at times you sit back after not going to a Super Bowl for 29 years, and you'd like to have hope but there are various question marks blocking that hope. Are we really good enough to do it? One of my sons told somebody, "I hope my dad wins a ring." I thought, boy that's not going to be easy.

There were even points during the Super Bowl XXXI season when it looked like we weren't going to make it -despite reaching the NFC championship game the previous year. The Packers cruised through the first part of 1996 with only a road loss to the Minnesota Vikings. In November, things seemed to go be going downhill ... fast. One week we lost at Kansas City by a touchdown, then the next we lost at Dallas by 15 points. The following week, the Sunday before Thanksgiving, we went into St. Louis and played a very poor first half. I couldn't help but think, "Here we go again." Early in the second half, Doug Evans intercepted a St. Louis pass and ran it in for a touchdown. That was the exact point during that season when it looked like we were going to turn things around. We went on to beat St. Louis, 24-9.

When the season was over people in the organization agreed that interception was when they really felt like it was going to happen. We finished out the regular season, including that game, with five-straight victories. Everybody felt a sigh of relief to watch Evans run in that touchdown. We had not played overly well at Kansas City or Dallas. And here we were in St. Louis with a bad game going again. Everybody to this day says, "Who can't forget the Doug Evans interception."

We cruised through the NFC playoffs with wins over San Francisco, 35-14, and Carolina, 30-13. The Packers seemed to be hitting on all cylinders when they faced New England in the Super Bowl. In fact, on the first series against the Patriots, Brett Favre hit a 54-yard touchdown pass play to Andre Rison. That gave us great confidence. Frankly, we struck on long plays all day long. By the end of the first half, we led 27-14. I remember wishing at that point that the day were finished. I wished the game were over.

The Patriots started a comeback in the third quarter, but we were always able to answer. Late in the third quarter, New England scored on a touchdown run by Curtis Martin to close the score to 27-21. On the following kickoff, Desmond Howard ran back 99 yards for a touchdown. Once he did that, I had a feeling that no matter what the Patriots do now, we're going to be able to answer. After Desmond's touchdown, neither team scored.

Desmond had a spectacular season. Out of college he was a guy everybody wanted to try to make into a wide receiver. Ron Wolf looked at him as a return guy. And that's where we used him. His contributions were great, and he was the Most Valuable Player of the Super Bowl. To this day it had to be the highlight of his career, at least in the pros.

Brett Favre, on the other hand, was named the NFL's MVP that season. Even though that was the second season for him to earn the honor, I think any doubts of what kind of competitor Favre was, were erased after Super Bowl XXXI. He was just a great individual to have on the team. Another player nobody ever talks about, but a guy who was a factor in the success of Favre and that ballclub was back-up quarterback, Jim McMahon. He was so intelligent with his football knowledge. As care free as the guy was and as much fun as he could be, McMahon knew football. The first guy Favre would talk to when he came off the field was Jim McMahon. I think Favre would admit that McMahon was a great influence.

I felt pretty good about our chances to win Super Bowl XXXI, with about three minutes left in the game, when the security people came to get Ron and myself, and said, "Fellas, it's time to take you down to the field." But again, I just wanted to get on the elevator, get down on the field and just finish it. I just wanted it to end at that point. The guys held on and played well. It was an amazing end to an amazing season. When we won that championship, it felt like the world had been lifted off my shoulders. We, once again, were World Champions!

The funny thing to me about going to the Super Bowl is that people pointed out how we were a young team that possibly could win for a long time. That's not always the case. I had an experience with the St. Louis Cardinals baseball team while I was in their public relations department. When we went to the World Series in 1967 and beat the Boston Red Sox, we looked like a club that could win and win and win. We reached the World Series again in 1968, but lost to the Detroit Tigers. The Cardinals didn't get back to another World Series until 1982. So I said to everybody before Super Bowl XXXI, "We better win it now because you think you're going to go back, but injuries and a lot of other things can change your season." So we won.

As great as it was to win that Super Bowl -and that was the ultimate, there's no doubt about it- it was almost as exciting to win the conference championship at Lambeau Field. The reason I say that is because these fans were so starved for it. They had some doubts, too. But, they always hung by us, evident from the fact we've been sold out every game since 1960. To see the true excitement in this stadium the day we won it was something. It was a sight I will never forget. I was in the north end zone with Ron Wolf the last two minutes of the game because we were ready to go out on the field to accept the championship trophy.

When that game ended and the public address announcer said, "The Green Bay Packers are going to the Super Bowl" it was a little difficult to believe. It was total pandemonium in the stadium. I've never seen such true elation. The players were jumping around on the field like a bunch of kids at a playground. In the stands, everybody was hugging and high-fiving no matter where they sat -end zone sections, club seats, private boxes. Pure excitement. I talked to people who said they'd never been that excited in their lives.

As we were standing there, I said to Ron, "You know, you could almost cry." And he said, "Yes, you could." About an hour later I was meeting with several members of the media in the locker room, and they started asking me what I thought when the game ended. I told them the story about standing in the end zone, and I started to cry. I actually did. I had to pull away from the cameras.

I will never forget that feeling. That was very special. Winning that at home meant an awful lot to me. We won the NFC title the next year, but we were on the road. To win it at home gave us a great, special excitement. It was the greatest thing to see the pure joy in this little town.

We once again saw that elation after we returned from the Super Bowl. We were proud to come home. The parade we had when we arrived back the next day was unbelievable. You just couldn't move through this city. The parade crept through Green Bay for hours. It was a joy. People were just ecstatic. The fan support here is outstanding. Coming to that victory celebration, seeing this little town that euphoric, meant an awful lot to this organization and me.

A couple weeks later, my wife and I were going out for fish on a Friday night. As we drove through town I said, "This is where the World Champions of the NFL live." It's where you would want to live. I feel very fortunate to be a part of it. I felt fortunate to be a part of what went on with the Cardinals in St. Louis because, to me, the two best traditions in all of sports are Cardinals baseball and Packers football. I have a 1967 World Series championship ring and a 1997 Super Bowl championship ring. Those are two of my most prized possessions. Regardless of what happens for the rest of my life, I am very lucky to have been with each of those franchises.

Super Bowl XXXI

Date: January 26, 1997
Place: Louisiana Superdome, New Orleans, LA
Attendance: 72,301

AFC: New England Patriots
Head Coach: Bill Parcells

NFC: Green Bay Packers
Head Coach: Mike Holmgren

New England	14	0	7	0	21
Green Bay	10	17	8	0	35

Most Valuable Player: Desmond Howard (KR, Green Bay)

Super Bowl XXXII

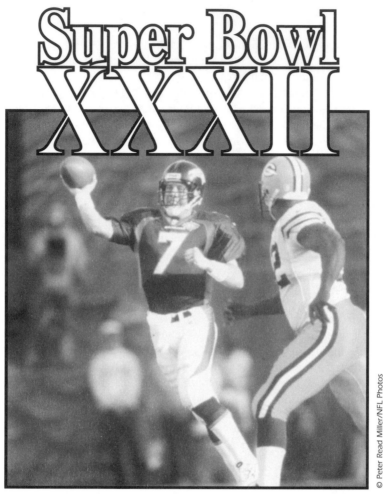

© Peter Read Miller/NFL Photos

*O*n paper, Super Bowl XXXII appeared to simply be a formality before the coro-
nation of the Green Bay Packers for the second-straight year. The Denver
Broncos, hoping to shake the tag of the "team that can't win the big one," came
ready to play behind the arm of John Elway (No. 7) and the legs of Terrell Davis.
As Packers' President and CEO, Bob Harlan, points out, whereas Green Bay
seemed to always answer scoring drives by the Patriots in Super Bowl XXXI, that
wasn't necessarily the case in XXXII. This time the Packers had a difficult time
playing catch-up.

The biggest problem the Packers faced was stopping Davis, who ran for 157
yards and three touchdowns. The game seemed to be close the entire time. The decisive touchdown was a 1-yard run by Davis 1:42 into the fourth quarter. The
Broncos' defense held the Packers for the rest of the game.

Bob Harlan

Coming off our Super Bowl XXXI championship season, we were optimistic in Green Bay heading into the 1997 regular season. However, during the season we lost at Philadelphia by a point after missing a field goal, and lost at Detroit, which is always a nightmare for us. But we played strong at the end of the season. We won the NFC championship game in San Francisco on a miserable day, and were going back to the Super Bowl.

I think we were a very confident group going to San Diego for Super Bowl XXXII to face the Denver Broncos. I know we were. Yet, I can remember telling people again to be careful in their thinking. I kept referring back to when I worked in public relations for the St. Louis baseball Cardinals, "Hey, we beat the Red Sox in 1967 and we were big, big favorites over the Tigers in 1968, but we didn't win it." (That was after being up three games to one, by the way.) Somebody said to me before we left for California, "The coaches think Denver is an awful lot like New England." That gave me confidence because we had defeated New England in Super Bowl XXXI. At the same time, I didn't get the impression from anybody during the week of preparation for Denver that there was over-confidence.

Once the game started, the Packers looked like they were playing with plenty of confidence. We came down and immediately scored on our opening possession. Brett Favre hit Antonio Freeman for a 22-yard touchdown play. I told someone after that score that it was almost too easy. Denver came right back at us and scored. The Broncos eventually took a 17-7 lead in the second quarter. When the Packers came out for the second half, they were just kind of walking; there didn't seem to be any kind of spark in them. That worried me. They just didn't show a lot of spirit. It obviously wasn't supposed to happen twice in a row for us. I started thinking that we could have a problem. Sure enough, in the second half we could start to sense it ... the Broncos might win the game. We didn't have the optimism we had the year before against New England. That day, I felt we were going to answer everything. Because of our Super Bowl XXXI experience, for most of the Denver game, I felt like we could come back. Finally, in the fourth quarter, the Broncos were ahead and they continued to control the clock. I thought, "We're not going to get that play and get it done." It was strange to watch the last couple of drives and kind of have the feeling it wasn't going to happen. We weren't going to beat Denver.

The Denver Broncos did a lot of things to us that day. We just couldn't seem to stop their running game. And, their defense played a very good game. They deserved it. I went into their locker room afterwards and talked to Pat Bowlen, the president and CEO of the Broncos, and said, "I know how you feel right now. It's a huge feeling." To their credit the Broncos came back and won the Super Bowl again the next year, which is very difficult. Every repeat strikes me as difficult. It's definitely tougher to stay on top than it is to get there. Once you get there, everybody wants to hire your people, and a lot of times those offers can be more lucrative to the individual.

◉CBS SPORTS Presents

In the Trenches with Lesley Visser

One of my most memorable Super Bowls was XXXI in New Orleans, 1997, when Green Bay beat the New England Patriots. That was when legendary coach Don Shula was inducted into the Hall of Fame. The day before the Super Bowl, Shula had agreed to give just a couple of exclusive one-on-one interviews. He was nice enough to agree that I could do one of those with him. I was staying in a hotel in the French Quarter and the young man who was supposed to take me, the runner, evidently had a late night in the Quarter and he didn't show up. I was starting to panic, as you might imagine, because here was the great Don Shula, who had agreed to do this interview with me, and now my driver wasn't there. I finally went out into the French Quarter looking for a cab. On the afternoon before the Super Bowl, do you think you can get a cab in New Orleans? I don't think so. I was out there waving at anything that drove by. Finally a cab drove toward me and a guy rolled down his window and he said, "Hey, Leslie, Leslie Visser."

I opened up the cab door and pushed this poor man and his wife over to the other side of the back seat. I started sputtering, "Oh, my goodness, Don Shula is waiting for me ... Agreed to do this interview ... Hall of Fame." The guy finally looked at me and said, "Leslie, it's Steve. Steve Mariucci." He had just been named the head coach of the 49ers. I, of course, totally changed my demeanor.

"Oh, coach, congratulations."

He said, "Yeah, whatever." Then he turned to the driver and said, "Just take her wherever she needs to go."

The Super Bowl is a great celebration; it's a real scene. There are great emotional moments like XXXI when Green Bay finally won its first Super Bowl after 30 years. That meant so much to the franchise.

Following Super Bowl XXXI, the Packers were the darlings of the NFL. There was no doubt about it. NFL Commissioner Paul Tagliabue came through Green Bay during the summer of 1997 to meet with our executive committee. He told them, "The Packers winning the Super Bowl was the best thing that has happened in pro sports in long time, because it's small-town, blue-collar America. The team is owned by the fans. The Packers winning kind of took everybody back to a simpler time." That was a very true statement.

But next year, when Denver beat us, John Elway was the darling. John deserved it because he had a great career. Denver hadn't won a Super Bowl, so the Broncos were

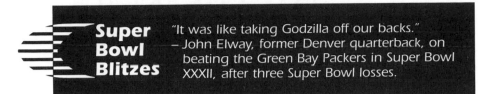

Super Bowl Blitzes

"It was like taking Godzilla off our backs."
— John Elway, former Denver quarterback, on beating the Green Bay Packers in Super Bowl XXXII, after three Super Bowl losses.

the sentimental favorite. However, it kind of bothered me that we weren't the darlings again. There was a feeling of how the Packers won the previous year, so Denver's winning would be a great send-off for John Elway. As it turned out, John had a spectacular day, their running game was devastating and they beat us.

Losing that title game was very disappointing. Losing any championship game is disappointing. I still remember the Cardinals losing to the Tigers in 1968. That loss still bothers me. You just don't have a lot of chances to get a championship. When you get a chance, you've got to take advantage of it. We had a great 1997 season in Green Bay and we were the favorites to beat Denver. I admit, I thought we were going to win that ball game. I can't help but wonder if we will we get the opportunity again of going to the Super Bowl. I can't tell people often enough, "You better win it because it's tough to get back." But the Green Bay Packers have won three Super Bowls and lost a fourth. There are some teams out there that haven't been to a Super Bowl, let alone win one. So we should cherish what we've got. We are the smallest city in the National Football League and we own more world championships, 12, than any other city or team.

I'll continue attending Super Bowls, but obviously I'd love to go back as a participant. It's a great experience.

Super Bowl XXXII

Date: January 25, 1998
Place: Qualcomm Stadium, San Diego, California
Attendance: 68,912

AFC: Denver Broncos
Head Coach: Mike Shanahan

NFC: Green Bay Packers
Head Coach: Mike Holmgren

Green Bay	7	7	3	7	24
Denver	7	10	7	7	31

Most Valuable Player: Terrell Davis (RB, Denver)

Super Bowl XXXIII

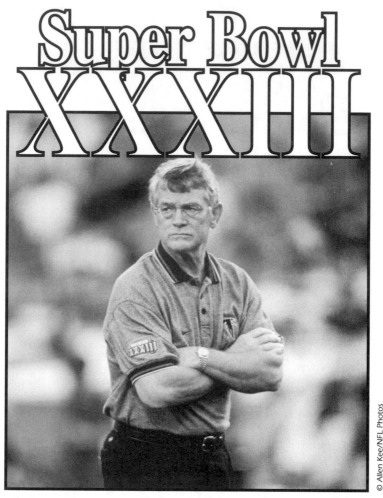

© Allen Kee/NFL Photos

*W*hen Dan Reeves (above) took over as the head coach of the Atlanta Falcons, most fans in the Atlanta area didn't understand the move by the Falcons' front office. After all, the Falcons hadn't enjoyed much success since they joined the league in 1966. However, Reeves quickly turned things around. With some good breaks, exciting playoff games, combined with Reeves' heart surgery, people in Atlanta took notice as the "Dirty Birds" reached the Super Bowl for the first time in franchise history.

Across the field from Reeves was one of his old teams, the Denver Broncos. Not only were the Broncos one of Reeves' former teams, they also happened to be defending Super Bowl champions. Denver quarterback John Elway, who was playing his last NFL game, threw for 336 yards and earned Super Bowl MVP honors.

Dan Reeves

During the early part of my first year in Atlanta, 1997, we struggled a little bit on the field, losing our first five games, but the guys never quit. In the second half of the season, we turned things around and finished the year with a record of 7-9. I knew I had the right kind of people on our football team, but in no way could I have imagined that we'd turn things around in 1998 like we did. We started fast by winning our first five-of-six games. We gained a lot of momentum and a lot of confidence. The chemistry was really good. Quarterback Chris Chandler was able to stay healthy; Jamal Anderson had an outstanding year running the ball; and the defense played great. We were able to reach Super Bowl XXXIII by winning some big games down the stretch.

There was just one problem during that final stretch of games. It came December 13 in New Orleans. The game itself wasn't the problem, we won 27-17 to improve our record to 12-2. What happened after the game was the problem. I was having a burning sensation in my throat. Shortly after the game, I told my doctor what I was experiencing. He said I needed to get checked out. They wouldn't even let me eat anything that night because there was a possibility that I would have surgery the next day. I had an angiogram that next morning at 6:30 in Atlanta; then, sure enough, I had quadruple bypass surgery about 11 a.m.

Having to switch focus from football to my health at that point in the season was tough to swallow. In fact, that was probably the most difficult thing to accept. When the doctors told me there was a possibility that I could be back in four weeks, they gave me a tremendous amount of motivation. My spirits were raised a great deal because here we were in the thick of the playoffs and I thought I was going to miss the most exciting part of the season.

Our team improved my chances of being back for the playoffs by playing well the last couple weeks of the regular season. It won the division and earned a bye week, which let me shoot to return for the first playoff game, two weeks away.

Regardless of the fact that I could come back in time for the playoffs, that was a very scary time in my life. Anytime you go through something that serious, it's frightening. I was helped through this ordeal because I have tremendous faith, and know the Lord has got us in his hands. (I'll admit though, that I was hoping he wasn't ready for me yet.) Because of that, there was a tremendous peace about the surgery and getting through it. The doctors were really good. Certainly, it was a scary situation.

My experience hopefully shows people that heart surgery is not a death sentence. Sometimes a person looks at bypass surgery, I know I did, as life coming to an end. That turned out to be the furthest thing from the truth. Knowing that I could be back in four weeks, in time for the playoffs, quickly lifted my spirits and got me back on the right track. I was able to enjoy all of the thrills that go with the playoffs.

As time passed after the surgery, the doctors assured me that I could do what I

◉ *CBS SPORTS* Presents

In the Trenches with Mike Ditka

Dan Reeves is one of my closest friends. I have tremendous respect for his ability and his talents. The only unfortunate thing for Dan is he hasn't won a Super Bowl. He's been there more than anybody else has, but he hasn't won one. There's an unfair stigma tagged to people that don't win. It's like quarterbacks. There are a lot of great quarterbacks in this league that play at a very high level, but have never won a Super Bowl. They've been there but they haven't won the big dance. People don't look at them in the same light as they do a Joe Montana or a Terry Bradshaw or some of these guys who have won Super Bowls time and time again.

---

felt like doing. During the first week, that was impossible. After about 10 days of doing what I was supposed to do and walking on the treadmill, it was almost like night and day. I started getting stronger and stronger, and was able to stay on the practice field longer without getting tired.

So, I knew I felt good, definitely better than I did before the surgery. The doctors assured me at that point that because I was on a blood thinner, the only real danger of returning to the sidelines was the possibility of somebody inadvertently hitting me. Needless to say, I had plenty of bodyguards around ... although I don't know if they would've taken a blow for me.

Just as the doctors had told me, I was able to come back in time for our first playoff game at home against the San Francisco 49ers. We won 20-18. That's when I was confident that my heart was in good shape. I didn't get that burning sensation when my heart rate accelerated. (That was my indication during the New Orleans game that something was wrong). My heart rate definitely went up during each of our playoff games. That first one with the 49ers and then the next week on the road against the Minnesota Vikings, were two extremely exciting games. The excitement of the playoffs is the fun part of that time of the year. Sometimes people think that postseason is stressful, but it isn't.

Even though we scored first against the Vikings, it was an uphill battle most of the game. In fact, we trailed by 10 points, 27-17, with about 13 minutes left in the game. With 2:07 left in the fourth quarter, and Minnesota leading 27-20, their kicker, Gary Anderson, lined up for a field goal. When he lined up to kick, my thought was that if he makes it, the chances of us to tie the game or take the lead were almost nil.

Anderson hadn't missed all year, so when he lined up with the field goal, the thought kind of went through my mind, "Hey, this has been a great year." He missed it wide left and suddenly a door opened for us, only down by a touchdown.

That's when we really thought we had chance to win the game if we could just get the ball in the end zone. At that point we couldn't think about anything except the next play. We drove down and all of sudden scored a touchdown when Chandler hit Terance Mathis on a 16-yard play. We were headed to overtime.

Super Bowl Blitzes

"Making the trade to get John Elway in 1983 changed the destiny of this organization for a long time. I'm glad that John was able to be vindicated and play as awesome as he did in the two Super Bowls that he won, XXXII and XXXIII. I wish I could have been the kicker on those teams. For a guy playing at his level, with the incredibly high expectations placed on him, it's nice that he got the two championship rings. Winning just one would have been great, but two is even sweeter. John being the MVP in XXXIII was even more special."
— Rich Karlis, kicker, Denver

In OT, our kicker, Morten Andersen, had a shot at a field goal from almost the exact same spot where Gary Anderson missed. Only, our Andersen hit his field goal and we were in the Super Bowl! A lot of people ask me how I could watch Andersen kick it. How could I not? I wanted to enjoy the experience. If he missed it, he missed it. I wanted to see everything that went on. When he nailed it, I started to run out on the field and said to myself, "Ohhh." I started to think about all those people piling on each other. That may not have been real good for my heart or my blood thinners. I kind of pulled back. Next thing I know, Minnesota's head coach, Denny Green, was congratulating me. That was a class act on his part. That field goal by Andersen is something I'll never forget as long as I live.

The Super Bowl has become much more of an event over the years. The game seems secondary after all the build up to "THE GAME." It's almost hard for the game to live up to the two weeks of expectations. Needless to say, there is a ton of hype and hoopla going into the NFL championship. The game has become a two-week event. During that time, the media has to find something to write or talk about. Before our Super Bowl against the Denver Broncos, a lot of emphasis was placed on me going against my former team and the alleged feuds between Mike Shanahan and me. It was just a lot of hoopla. Plus we were playing the defending world champions. They had the experience of being in that position. Because it was the first Super Bowl for the Atlanta organization, it obviously didn't have that experience.

I felt that if we played the way we were capable of playing, then it would be a good game. We had come off a great win against the team that everybody had picked to be in the Super Bowl, Minnesota. We did it on the road and in tough surroundings. So, I felt like we had a chance against Denver. Once the game got going,

Super Bowl Sunday: The Day America Stops

Denver did a good job; and the area we had really been good at all season, the offensive end of the red zone, was really bad for us. A lot of our troubles in that game are to the credit of Denver.

We knew that it could be tough to win if we didn't execute the way we had all year. Unfortunately, we didn't. For instance, on the opening series we drove the ball down to Denver's 8-yard line but had to settle for a field goal. The Broncos came back and scored a touchdown. Late in the second quarter, down 10-3, we had the ball inside the Denver 10-yard line, but couldn't get it in the end zone. Morten Andersen missed the 26-yard field goal attempt. One time we gambled on fourth down and turned the ball over. We threw a couple of interceptions in the red zone, including one at the 2-yard line early in the fourth quarter. If you miss one scoring opportunity in a Super Bowl, usually you're going to lose. We missed four scoring opportunities and Denver did a good job of capitalizing.

The Broncos made some big plays. We gave up a big touchdown play from John Elway to Rod Smith for an 80-yard score. That was a huge turn around because it went from us missing an opportunity to them scoring a touchdown. They made us pay for our mistakes. Elway had a knack for doing that. He had a tremendous game against us. Denver was a team that relied a great deal on the running of Terrell Davis. Sure, if we had to do it over again, we'd probably do some things differently. We felt like the key was to stop Terrell and then we'd make some plays in the passing game, Elway just did a great job.

That Super Bowl loss was tough. They all are disappointing. A loss hurts. I've now been involved in seven Super Bowl losses as a player and a coach. You obviously can't overlook the accomplishments to get there, but when you come up short it's a tremendous let down and disappointment. Going into a Super Bowl, you're on the threshold of achieving something that you worked hard for, but then, boom, it's gone and one team is happy while 29 other teams feel like they're a loser. That's tough. The Super Bowl is a hard game to lose.

I've been involved in the National Football League as a player, player-coach, assistant coach and head coach, and there's no question that when you're a head coach and you lose a Super Bowl, you feel like you let so many people down. It's much more devastating from a head coach's standpoint. All those other losses that I had, hurt but nothing like they have as a head coach. A head coach feels like he has let down his players, his players' family, his family, his owner's family and the fans. Losing a Super Bowl is a tremendous burden that the coach has on his shoulders. It's the responsibility of the head coach to get the team to play as well as it can. When the team loses, the head coach doesn't feel like he did his job. To me, the most difficult loss of all for a head coach is the Super Bowl.

Don't get me wrong, though. I would rather lose in a Super Bowl than not make it to that point. Even though we lost, I can honestly say the first one for me as a head coach at Denver was tremendously exciting because we won the AFC title game on the road against Cleveland. That was a heck of a thrill. And then the Super Bowl with Atlanta will always be special. When your team accomplishes something that nobody thinks is possible, you can hardly beat that.

Super Bowl XXXIII

The 1998 season was capped off for me by being named the NFL's Coach of the Year. That's a great feeling, no question about it. I understand that winning the award is a reflection of our organization and our team's success, being surrounded by good people that believe in the same things that I do. There's no way a head coach can oversee every single detail. He has to have good players, good coaches and a good organization. We certainly have that here in Atlanta. So the award is a reflection of the accomplishments of the entire organization. It was a great thrill to win it.

When I came to Atlanta in 1997, I knew that the Falcons weren't a bad team because they had just been in the playoffs two years before my arrival. However, the Falcons were 3-13 in 1996. So, for me, when I arrived, it was more or less trying to get some people in place.

Quarterback was one area we tried to address first. That's where we came up with the trade to get Chris Chandler, who had always played well in the league but had not managed to stay healthy. Getting him was probably the first big key for our turnaround. We wanted to establish a running game, which is where Jamal Anderson came in the picture. Then I was fortunate enough to get coach Rich Brooks, who put together a good, solid defensive scheme.

There was no doubt that we had some great people in this organization to help us make a run toward Super Bowl XXXIII, and help me win the Coach of the Year award. And now that we've experienced the Super Bowl and all of its hoopla, we're ready to make it back.

Super Bowl XXXIII

Date: January 31, 1999
Place: Pro Player Stadium, Miami, FL
Attendance: 74,803

AFC: Denver Broncos
Head Coach: Mike Shanahan

NFC: Atlanta Falcons
Head Coach: Dan Reeves

Denver	7	10	0	17	34
Atlanta	3	3	0	13	19

Most Valuable Player: John Elway (QB, Denver)

Super Bowl XXXIV

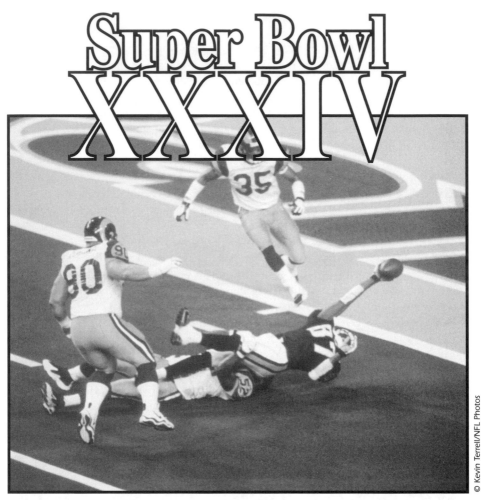

*I*n one of the most exciting Super Bowl finishes, Mike Jones of the St. Louis Rams *(flat on the turf) stopped Tennessee's Kevin Dyson inside the two-yard line as time expired on the Titans' comeback attempt. To some, Super Bowl XXXIV was the most exciting Super Bowl from start to finish. To others, only the final quarter was worth having on a videotape. Either way, what a finish!*

In the third quarter, the Rams opened up a 16-0 lead with a 9-yard touchdown play from Kurt Warner to Torry Holt. As they had done several times in the season, the Titans refused to give up. With 10 points in the fourth quarter, the Titans tied the game to become the first team to come from 16-points down. On the first play on the Rams' possession following the game-tying field goal, Warner connected with Isaac Bruce for a 73-yard scoring play.

K.S. "Bud" Adams, Jr. has been one of the most influential owners in football. Adams was one of the original owners in the American Football League, with the Houston Oilers. In the mid-1990s, Adams orchestrated a move to the Nashville, Tenn. area.

K. S. "Bud" Adams, Jr.

The Tennessee Titans football fans are the greatest in the league. They were voted the top pro football fans last year, and I know they were the loudest! They're great fans. They've really gotten behind the Titans and are very supportive. I couldn't ask for anything more - they have even learned to not do the wave when we've got the ball! They're all wondering why they didn't have pro football sooner. Where has it been all these years?

The late 1990s were tough years, with the move from Houston to Nashville, via Memphis. The relationship with everyone in Tennessee has been great. I knew Tennesseans were great football fans, because each Saturday the highways are clogged with traffic going to Knoxville to see the University of Tennessee play. I've watched Nashville grow over the last 20 years and knew it would be a good place for an NFL team. So when I couldn't get a new stadium built in Houston, I called Nashville Mayor Phil Bredesen and said, "I'll get straight to the point, Mayor. If you'll build me a stadium, I'll move the Oilers there." The reply was fairly shocking at first when he said, "I don't believe who you are; and if you don't mind, I have other business to do. If I find out different about who you say you are, I'll call you."

He called back an hour later. "I apologize, Mr. Adams, but I just thought it was some prank call that got through my secretary," he said. So, we went to work on getting a stadium deal in Nashville that would facilitate a move from Houston. Phil was a very forthright and smart guy, who understood the value of an NFL franchise even though he had seen probably only two pro football games in his life. But he went to work on getting the stadium approved. And it's been a plus for the people of Nashville and certainly for me as the owner of the franchise.

I thought that once fans in Tennessee saw professional football, we'd win them over. But the best way to do it is to win. We did just that in 1999. Someone asked my wife, "What are you going to do when you lose the first game in the new Adelphia stadium?" Luckily, at the time of this writing in early October 2000, we haven't had to face that scenario yet. There were several close games, but that will be the case every season. It's hard to win all of the close ones; however, last year the team just found a way to win.

The season was exhausting, with a great run through the playoffs and into the Super Bowl. Going through the playoffs, this team looked like one of destiny. In fact, talking about close games at Adelphia in 1999, the closest was the final game that we hosted that season, the AFC wild card game with the Buffalo Bills. In that game, Buffalo kicked a field goal with 16 seconds to go in the game to take a 16-15 lead. My wife asked me, "What's going to happen?" I said, "Well, nothing much is going to happen, honey. We can't do a lot in 16 seconds. It would be a miracle if we could do anything. We might get it down to where we can get out of bounds and try to kick a long field goal." It wasn't even in my mind that we could run the kick-off back on that lateral play, which now is called the Music City Miracle. It's so dif-

---

◉CBS SPORTS Presents

In the Trenches with Lesley Visser

The morning of Super Bowl XXXIV, I was on the Rams sideline for ABC. That morning Roland Williams, the tight end from the Rams, had given me a piece of his grandmama's bean pie. He said the pie was the secret of his success, and I would have a great Super Bowl if I had a slice of grandmama's bean pie. Which I can tell you was terrific.

---

ficult to do anything in 16 seconds, but our team found a way to win.

A lot of people have questioned that call on the lateral. Even though I might be biased, it was a good call. Believe me, I looked at the film very carefully. When Frank Wycheck let the ball go, his hand was to the right of that line. The rule doesn't say the ball has to go backwards, the ball just can't go forward. Kevin Dyson planted his right foot back about four inches on the right side of the line. When he caught the ball, the fact that his foot was behind the line tells me that the catch was legal. But it was a close one. The officials said if they thought it was not a lateral, they would have thrown the flag immediately. I'm sure Buffalo head coach Wade Phillips is still questioning that call.

After that game, our team was concerned because every other playoff game was on the road. Knowing our fans, that shouldn't have been a concern. We must have had at least 5,000 people from Tennessee in Indianapolis for the next playoff game. It's funny because the Colts fans were so sure they were going to win. Toward the end of the game, when the Colts had the ball, there was a loud chant in the crowd, "DEFENSE, DEFENSE." I was sitting in the visiting team owner's box, with just a railing separating me from the next box. A lady in the box next to mine asked her husband, "Don't our fans know that we have the ball? Why are they calling for defense, defense?" I finally just couldn't help it. I said, "Lady, let me tell you, those are our people rooting for the Titans." She said, "That can't be, we sold it out here." "Yes, but the Tennessee fans bought the tickets from the Colts ticket buyers who stayed home and watched the game on TV," I replied. That was a great moment for me.

We had a lot of support the next week in the AFC championship game in Jacksonville. By winning that game in Alltel Stadium, we beat the Jaguars for the third time in the 1999 season; it was our second win on their home field in that season. Somebody asked one of our players what he thought about Jacksonville, and his reply was, "That's our home away from home." The Titans especially dominated the Jaguars in the AFC title game, 33-14. The next week we were going to be in Atlanta for Super Bowl XXXIV.

After the game in Jacksonville, a Brink's truck brought the Super Bowl tickets to the Jacksonville airport. Obviously they had planned to give the tickets to the Jaguars or to us. I can happily say they loaded the tickets onto our plane. I just wish there had been a little more time between the AFC championship game and the Super Bowl. We quickly realized that one week just doesn't give teams enough time to finish the championship game on Sunday and head to the Super Bowl site the next day. Our staff went to our office after we got back to Nashville, and worked all night to distribute our allotment of tickets. Our people had to work really hard to get those tickets out, not because the team had to be in Atlanta on Monday but because our fans who were going to the game would be leaving for Atlanta on Thursday. It was a very difficult task for our staff, but they handled it with flying colors. The schedule goes back to two weeks for Super Bowl XXXV.

Super Bowl Blitzes

Ticket prices for Super Bowl I ranged from $6 to $12. Tickets for Super Bowl XXXIV were $325.

You become very popular, I found out, with a team in the Super Bowl. I received calls from people that I hadn't heard from in a long, long time. But it was fun. When someone said to me, "Well, you didn't win," I said, "Listen, I'd rather have been there and lost, than not to have been there at all." I still feel that way.

Going into Super Bowl XXXIV, we knew we were facing an outstanding St. Louis Rams team. We had played a great game against them in Nashville earlier in the season and won, 24-21. In the first half of the Super Bowl in Atlanta, the Rams showed a great passing game but our defense held them to a 9-0 halftime lead. I was really worried. I didn't know what the Titans could do to get back in the game.

Things really picked up in the second half. The biggest motivator for the Titans playing well was head coach Jeff Fisher. He gave the team a halftime talk in the locker room that wasn't very long — it was just basic and straightforward. He told them, "Look, you beat the Rams once this season and you're capable of doing it again. They are already out there celebrating like they have won the game. And you all are playing like you're going to let them win it." On the sidelines just before the third quarter, Jeff again told our team, "Look at them over there. They're celebrating like they already won. Now you get out there and play your butts off and you'll win this game." And our guys really played a hell of a second half. I think Jeff's talk helped the team understand that they were capable of staging a comeback.

At the start of the fourth quarter, I thought we had the momentum going. I had seen that earlier in the year. I felt that if the Rams gave us enough time, we'd get the scores to win the game. I didn't think our guys would leave that field without being the winners. The big thing that really hurt us was that we had to play the last quarter without our two starting safeties, Blaine Bishop and Marcus Robertson. Bishop suffered a concussion during the game so he was out, and Robertson had broken a bone in his ankle in the AFC Championship game.

We tied the game up at 16-16 with 2:12 left to play. I was encouraged by our P/R and security people to go down to the sidelines. I said, "Wait a minute, this game has over two minutes to go." They said, "Once the game is over, if the Titans win, you're going to have to get up on that podium to accept the trophy. The same way with the Rams. We wouldn't have time to bring you down." So I went; and just about the time I entered the tunnel to go out on the field, I heard all this yelling and screaming. I ran out of the tunnel to see what happened. Kurt Warner had thrown a touchdown pass for 73 yards to Isaac Bruce to give St. Louis the lead.

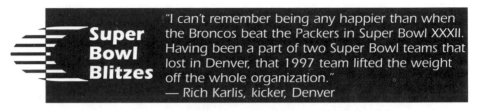

Super Bowl Blitzes

"I can't remember being any happier than when the Broncos beat the Packers in Super Bowl XXXII. Having been a part of two Super Bowl teams that lost in Denver, that 1997 team lifted the weight off the whole organization."
— Rich Karlis, kicker, Denver

With that Warner to Bruce touchdown, the Rams went ahead 23-16. So I told my people, "I'm going back up to my suite." And they said, "No, you can't do that; you have to stay here." At this point, I didn't want to stand on the sidelines and watch the Rams end up winning this game so I headed back inside the tunnel and watched it on the big screen. When we started moving the ball down the field, I got excited and ran out toward the sidelines. When stadium security tried to stop me, I said, "I am the owner of the Titans, and I want to see them win this game." It looked like we were going to pull it out. As time on the clock ran out, Dyson was stopped just one yard short of the goal line. Our guys had played their hearts out. Even though we didn't win the game, we definitely didn't leave as losers. Really, all we needed was one more play.

I never asked Coach Fisher if he would have gone for the two-point conversion if Dyson had scored on that final play, but I have a feeling that he would have and we could have won by one point. What a story that would have been. But it didn't happen. It was wishful thinking.

Hopefully we've got the nucleus for a team that could repeat, but everyone's going to be shooting for us. That could make repeating hard to do. If anyone can get it done, Coach Fisher can. He's not much older than some of his players, and he relates very well to them. Bruce Matthews, our All-Pro LG, and Jeff once played together on the same USC team.

People have wondered what I did during February, after Super Bowl XXXIV. I just relaxed. I wanted to recover. I needed to recover. Ask any owner! Having a team in the Super Bowl is something that you always strive for in the NFL, no matter what your position is in the organization. You don't get to the Super Bowl that often; and when you do, you go there to win. That means putting nearly every ounce of your energy into the team from July through January. The Super Bowl has become "THE GAME" in football.

Super Bowl XXXIV

I first put the Houston Oilers on the field in the American Football League in 1960, and we merged with the National Football League ten years later. Back then, we each put up $25,000 to get our franchise. My player payroll was $350,000 that first year. Things have progressed so fast that 41 incredibly quick years later, our player payroll is $110 million, which includes salaries and bonus money.

The Oilers won the American Football League Championship the first year and again the second year. Then Lamar Hunt's Dallas Texans beat us in a double-overtime game in the third year. Still, the excitement of those games doesn't compare to the Super Bowl.

You always like to brag about some of the investments you make. I have to say that getting into football was probably my best investment, second only to my wife Nancy. I've drilled a lot of oil and gas wells, but those have a way of almost petering out after a certain period of time. This team has just gotten better with age. GO TITANS!

Super Bowl XXXIV

Date: January 30, 2000
Place: Georgia Dome, Atlanta, Georgia
Attendance: 72,625

AFC: Tennessee Titans
Head Coach: Jeff Fisher

NFC: St. Louis Rams
Head Coach: Dick Vermeil

Tennessee	0	0	6	10	16
St. Louis	3	6	7	7	23

Most Valuable Player: Kurt Warner (QB, St. Louis)

Scott Foster

24. Scott Foster
25. Steve Kunkle
26. Wayne Nichols

State Farm Executives Onsite

27. Mike Davidson
28. Jack North
29. Susan Waring
30. Joe Formusa

Others

31. Jack Talley (Enterprise)
32. Greg Williams (Washington Redskins)
33. Charlie Gomez (State Farm)
34. Joe Spicer (State Farm)
35. Andy Mardis (State Farm)

[handwritten notes:]

AnDM THESE 6

ENCLOSED 4B copies of OAK!

Or else WHM of 2 0

PLUS 2 EXTRA

IF YOU NEED THEM

Award Winning Agents

1. Al Clark
2. Arlen Norwood
3. Bob Nowlin
4. Brian Downes
5. Carlos Luis
6. Chris Lo
7. Danny Thomas
8. Darryl Demille
9. Doug Auzat
10. Guy Brinkman
11. J. W. Webb
12. James Brown
13. Jim Russo
14. Jennifer Reynolds
15. Jim Young
16. Joe Vitiello
17. John Nuzzo
18. Mark Marshall
19. Matt Tobben
20. Michelle DeCarlo
21. Phil Nichols

FOR FURTHER STUDY

BOOKS:

IMPARTIAL JUDGMENT
The NFL is the arena; that quality Lombardi called "mental toughness" is the theme. Drawing from 31 years of working with NFL teams and coaches, the "Dean of NFL Referees" discusses leadership and team building. Achievers in all occupations will benefit by the perspective and action in these stories. *Paperback.*

THE WINNING SPIRIT
Dr. Tunney joins Les Brown, Tony Alessandra, Jim Cathcart, Don Hutson and other members of Best of the Masters to discuss techniques for achieving Olympic level performance in business and personal advancements. Endorsed by the United States Olympic Committee.

YOU CAN DO IT!
Jim Tunney, Bob Costas and 116 other prominent achievers give their personal prescriptions for developing the "can do" attitude.

SPEAKING SECRETS OF THE MASTERS
The members of the Speakers Roundtable share what 450 years experience has taught them about giving compelling presentations.

NEWEST BOOK:

CHICKEN SOUP FOR THE SPORTS FAN'S SOUL
Inspiring, funny and true stories from a wide-range of sports. Stories from Bob Costas, Steve Young, Bart Starr, Lesley Vissar and, of course, Jim Tunney. *Paperback.*

VIDEO & AUDIO:

P*R*I*D*E in ACTION
Straight-forward, practical principles for decisions and actions that result in successful performance.
50 minutes — VHS and audio

HERE'S TO THE WINNERS
A classic. Practical advice, sparked with humor, on how to gain personal power and take charge of your life.
60 minutes, LIVE audio.

A PROFESSIONAL WAY TO WINNING
A six-cassette corporate seminar series, taped live, on key techniques to improve productivity, creativity, self-management, leadership and team building. An effective learning tool for all who have career plans.
6 hours, audio, includes workbook.

Make the most of yourself for that is all there is of you.
- Ralph Waldo Emerson ➡ ➡ ➡ ➡

BOOKS:	Price	Number	TOTAL
IMPARTIAL JUDGMENT............................	$20.00	_____	_____
THE WINNING SPIRIT............................	$15.00	_____	_____
YOU CAN DO IT!..................................	$20.00	_____	_____
SPEAKING SECRETS OF THE MASTERS........................	$20.00	_____	_____
CHICKEN SOUP FOR THE SPORTS FAN'S SOUL...	$15.00	_____	_____
VIDEO & AUDIO:			
"P*R*I*D*E in Action" (Audio)...............	$10.00	_____	_____
"P*R*I*D*E in Action" (VHS)...............	$20.00	_____	_____
"Here's to the Winners" (Audio)............	$20.00	_____	_____
"A Professional Way to Winning" (Audio).........	$50.00	_____	_____

TOTAL ENCLOSED: $ _____

(Tax & Shipping Incl.)

Name_____

(Please Print)

Address_____

_____ Zip _____

Please mail order form and check to: JIM TUNNEY ASSOCIATES
P.O. Box 1500
Carmel-by-the-Sea, CA 93921
831-649-3200

SPEAKERS
ROUNDTABLE

MEMBER
NATIONAL SPEAKERS ASSOCIATION

Or order online at www.jimtunney.com/sports